CliffsNotes®

Praxis® Teaching Reading: Elementary Education (5203)

by
Nancy L. Witherell, Ed.D.

Houghton Mifflin Harcourt
Boston • New York

About the Author

Nancy L. Witherell, Ed.D., is a professor at Bridgewater State University in Bridgewater, Massachusetts, where she teaches undergraduate and graduate reading courses. She has presented at numerous state and national conferences, written a number of books on literacy, and is active in teaching children through numerous consultancies.

Editorial

Executive Editor: Greg Tubach

Senior Editor: Christina Stambaugh

Production Editor: Erika West

Copy Editor: Pamela Weber-Leaf

Technical Editor: Mary Beth Allen, Ed.D.

Proofreader: Susan Moritz

CliffsNotes® Praxis® Teaching Reading: Elementary Education (5203)

Copyright © 2017 by Houghton Mifflin Harcourt Publishing Company

All rights reserved.

Cover image © Shutterstock / Mavrick

Library of Congress Control Number: 2017934393
ISBN: 978-0-544-91116-1 (pbk)

Printed in the United States of America
DOO 10 9 8 7 6 5 4 3 2 1

For information about permission to reproduce selections from this book, write to trade.permissions@hmhco.com or to Permissions, Houghton Mifflin Harcourt Publishing Company, 3 Park Avenue, 19th Floor, New York, New York 10016.

www.hmhco.com

Table of Contents

Introduction

Reading is a content area with its own vocabulary, theories, and research—collectively, the knowledge of "what." Yet reading also includes pedagogy, methodology, instruction, and analysis of reading behaviors—in sum, the knowledge of "how." The main avenue into all other academic content areas, reading is one of the most important skills a child can obtain. Therein lies the importance of having expert teachers of reading in our classrooms, and one path to this is taking and passing the Praxis Teaching Reading: Elementary Education (5203) test. So, let's get you ready for it!

How This Book Is Organized

This book is organized into chapters that will help you prepare for the Praxis (5203). The purpose of each chapter is summarized below:

Chapter 1:
This chapter provides an overview of the components of the test, including useful information about test logistics, as well as some study plan recommendations.

Chapters 2–11:
The goal of chapters 2 through 11 is to give you, in concise and clear language, the basic content of reading and reading methodology. These chapters contain the material you need to know and completely understand in order to pass the Praxis (5203).

Chapter 12:
Chapter 12 offers some tips on test-taking and preparing for the day of the test. It also explains how to use this book's two practice tests for best results.

Chapter 13:
This is Practice Test 1, a model practice test that offers 90 selected-response questions and three constructed-response questions. For each selected-response question, the correct answer is provided, along with an answer explanation. Two model answers are given for each constructed-response question.

Chapter 14:
This is Practice Test 2, and it follows the same format as Practice Test 1.

Recalling Information: What Works for You?

Before you begin to study for the test, do a bit of reflection. Think about how you best learn new material. The following questions might help:

- Can you read material and remember it?
- Does highlighting help you to recall information?
- Do note cards help you study?
- Does it help you to record important information and play back the recording, perhaps while you're driving?
- Do game formats, such as matching games, help you to remember definitions?
- Are you tech-savvy and would you, therefore, enjoy an online game study format?
- Can you study better with music or without?
- Do mnemonics help you? (A mnemonic is an abbreviation or a word that helps you remember a larger piece of information, such as ROY G BIV for the colors of the rainbow.)

Your answers to these questions will help pinpoint the best way for you to study and learn the information in this book. At this point in your life, you have been going to school for years. You know how you learn best. Use that knowledge to ensure that you are truly ready the day of the test. When you have studied well, you gain confidence, and that is extremely helpful. Personally, I like to use index cards when I study. This leads to the next topic: the reading and writing connection.

The Reading and Writing Connection

Reading and writing are interdependent processes. What you learn in one process is transferable to the other. When studying, you should take advantage of this interdependence, as it can help you "seal" the information for recall. When reading, you must sometimes remind yourself to focus on what you are reading. When writing, you have to think and interact with the content. During this thinking stage, you categorize, relate one piece of information to another, sequence, clarify, and distinguish important ideas from merely interesting ones. While you may not realize you're doing all these things when you read and write, all of this thinking is a good thing. Take advantage of the reading and writing connection, and make a study notebook or note cards as you review the material in this book.

Organizing Notes in a Notebook

There are two ways of organizing notes in a notebook. (When I am preparing for a lecture and taking notes that I must refer to later, I use option two.)

Option One: Linear Method

With this method, the organization of the writing should begin with the topic label, followed by bulleted information. Start by putting the topic on one line and underlining it. Then, as you read, write the important information underneath. That way, when you study you can cover the bulleted information so that just the topic is visible, and try to recall the information that you have covered. After you attempt to recall each topic's information, you can look to see if you were correct.

Option Two: Two-Column Method

With the two-column method, you organize content by drawing a line down the paper approximately 2 inches from the left side, dividing the paper into two columns. As you read, write the topic and, perhaps, subtopics, in the left column. In the right, wider column, write and bullet important notes. When you study, use another piece of paper to cover the bulleted points in the right column, and look at the topics and subtopics in the left column. Try to recall the bulleted information, then check to see if you have recalled correctly.

Organizing Notes on Index or Note Cards

Index or note cards are more cumbersome to store, but I think they are a bit easier to use than a notebook. To take notes on the material covered in this book, 4"-by-6" index cards would work best. On one side, write the main topic and subtopics. On the other side, write the important information in bulleted form. When you study, look at the topic and subtopic terms on the front of the card, and try to remember the important information that you detailed on the back. Turn the card over to see if you were right. The advantage of using index or note cards is that you can remove the cards that contain information you feel confident about, and study only the ones containing information you are still learning.

Going back to what works for you . . . As I write this, a young man, whom I'll call Adam, a lifetime friend of my 20-something son, sits on our porch with about 400 note cards. Why? Adam has learned what he needs to do to study. His big exam is in the medical field (he analyzes blood samples for various diseases—a very important and life-saving job). Adam failed this test the first time he took it, and at $240 a shot, he really wants to pass this time. Adam knows that the study approach he used last time didn't work. His home is too noisy; so, aware of the solitude at our summer place (when only I am here; otherwise it's anything but quiet), he asked if he could come and stay for a couple of days to prepare for the test. Adam knows he needs quiet to study. He confessed that he had never used note cards before. A coworker who has passed the exam gave Adam about 300 of his prepared note cards to help Adam study. Adam found them extremely helpful, so he has made about 100 more. He is studying the cards, sometimes going back into this 800-page book to clarify what he is studying. He has paced himself. The exam is about a month away, so his study plan is going well. This real-life scenario is why you need to figure out what study approach works for you. You want to pass the test the first time.

How to Prepare for This Book's Practice Tests—Getting Ready for the Real Thing

As mentioned earlier, this book has two practice tests. They each contain 90 selected-response questions (multiple-choice) and three constructed-response questions (essay questions). This setup corresponds to the number of questions on the actual Praxis (5203) you will be taking. The selected-response questions in the practice tests cover all of the test topics. They are set up purposefully, to give you a taste of the real test. The constructed-response section has one question for each of the three broad categories, which are introduced in the next chapter. Chapter 12, "Test-Taking Strategies," explains how to simulate the real testing experience; be sure to review it as part of your study plan.

Formulating a Study Plan

Before you dive in, you need a study plan. Here's a good example:

- First, either register for the test or choose an approximate date that you will take it.
- Open your calendar and plug in study times.
- Reserve 2½ hours of study time for each of the practice tests, perhaps a week before you plan to take the real test. That gives you time to review any weak areas.
- Then, go backward in your calendar and plug in study times that lead up to the practice tests. Be sure to reserve some time to read the "Praxis Study Companion – Teaching Reading: Elementary Education (5203)," found at www.ets.org/s/praxis/pdf/5203.pdf. This study guide contains 24 selected-response practice questions and one sample constructed-response question with three scored sample responses.
- After taking a practice test, allot another hour of study time (1 hour for each practice test) to check your answers and to review the answer explanations.
- The week before test day, continue to study. Retake one of the practice tests if you feel this will be helpful.
- If it is useful to you to study with other people, form a study group, if possible. If you opt to supplement your preparation with a study group, be sure to keep your personal study schedule as well.

Chapter 1

Overview of Praxis Teaching Reading: Elementary Education (5203)

Test Format

The "what" of reading has remained mostly the same over time, with new terms and new literacies supplementing that knowledge. But the "how" of teaching reading to students continually changes with new research, and is often policy-driven. For example, with the passage of the No Child Left Behind Act in 2001, phonics has become a focus area of teaching reading. Therefore, in the Praxis (5203) there is a heavy emphasis on developmental reading. The content of the Praxis (5203) is arranged as follows:

Format of the Test

Content Categories	Subcategories Within the Broad Content	Expected Number of Questions
Assessment and Diagnostic Teaching of Reading	The author's take (not the test developer's): • Informal Assessment • Formal Assessment • Analysis of Assessment	22 selected response (multiple choice) 1 constructed response (essay format)
Reading Development	• Phonemic Awareness and Oral Language Development • Phonics and the Alphabetic Principle • Word-Analysis Skills and Vocabulary Development • Development of Reading Fluency and Reading Comprehension • Reading Comprehension Strategies Across Text Types	45 selected response (multiple choice) 1 constructed response (essay format)
Writing in Support of Reading	• Interdependence of Reading and Writing Development • Reading and Writing as Tools for Inquiry and Research	23 selected response (multiple choice) 1 constructed response (essay format)

Topics Covered

The primary goal of this book is to help you prepare for and pass the Praxis (5203). Studying the material in this book will also help to increase your knowledge of reading and reading instruction so that you can become an effective teacher of the subject. The more you see and study this information on reading and writing, the more you will be able to understand and recall what you have learned.

The following breakdown of the three Praxis (5203) broad content categories is a preview of the information presented in chapters 2–11 of this book.

Note: You'll find vocabulary terms listed throughout chapters 2–11. As you have learned in your studies, children need multiple exposures to vocabulary words before they "own" them. This holds true for adult learners as well. You'll be exposed repeatedly to vocabulary words and material to help your recall.

Assessment and Diagnostic Teaching of Reading

Author's Note: Although the Praxis (5203) objectives begin with "Assessment and Diagnostic Teaching of Reading," I chose to cover assessment at the end of this study guide. That doesn't make assessment any less important. Teachers should initially assess students to find reading levels and needs. In the case of this study guide, many of you reading this may not fully understand the reading terminology referred to in the assessment section. Learning the basics of reading content and terminology prior to reading the section on assessment should allow you to attain a deeper understanding of the material.

The "Assessment and Diagnostic Teaching of Reading" content category is covered in detail in Chapter 11, "Assessment for Optimal Growth." The teaching candidate is expected to:

- **Be familiar with a range of formal and informal assessments.** Formal assessments have standardized procedures that must be followed and are norm-referenced (result in percentiles) or criterion-referenced (pinpoint learning areas), or a hybrid, which includes both measures. Informal assessments may have some standardization, or be part of natural classroom assessment, but tend to be subjective, whereas a formal standardized test is considered an objective measure of student achievement.

- **Know how the different assessment data can be analyzed and used to monitor progress.** Monitoring progress basically means that you are making sure children are progressing with the instruction they are being given. A teacher should continually informally assess, and if progress is not seen, instruction needs to be changed.

- **Be able to analyze the data from assessments in order to differentiate instruction.** Instruction should be differentiated if a child has difficulties or needs a challenge. If informal or formal data show that a group of five children can't identify some letters, and the rest of the class (after two or three assessments) has demonstrated that they can identify all letters, then a teacher decision must be made for those students who are not making progress. The group of five will need to be instructed in letter identification, while the rest of the class moves on to instruction that fits their needs.

- **Know how to use the data to accelerate the development of reading skills.** In other words, "keep students moving forward." If progress monitoring shows that a child has mastered a skill, this signifies that the child is ready to meet new challenges.

- **Understand flexible grouping and its purposes.** Flexible grouping signifies that students are grouped according to their needs and groups change as needs and successes change. For example, a child should not be put into a group, let's say the "low" group, and just remain there. Children learn at different paces, and progress monitoring indicates who is progressing faster, slower, or together. Flexible groups can be structured according to different criteria: skills, reading levels, interests, learning styles, and so forth. For example, a student from the "top" level reading group may need the same skill as a student from the "low" level reading group. In this case, the students would be grouped together to master that particular skill.

- **Be familiar with the Response to Intervention (RTI) process.** This intervention process stems from government policy, ensuring that individual students needing additional support are able to obtain it from the classroom teacher first. If a student with extra teacher support through differentiated instruction is still not progressing, then specialist support is sought.

Reading Development

Phonemic Awareness and Oral Language Development

"Phonemic Awareness" is covered in detail in Chapter 2 and "Oral Language Development" is covered in Chapter 3. In these subcategories, the teaching candidate is expected to:

- **Know a variety of instructional strategies in order to develop students' listening and speaking skills.** The teacher should allow time in the classroom for students to practice speaking and listening skills. Students need to be able to communicate clearly.

- **Know various instructional strategies to expand students' listening and speaking vocabularies.** There are four basic vocabularies: listening, speaking, reading, and writing. You can use different vocabulary words in each. For example, the vocabulary I use in my writing is more formal than what I use in my speech, and the words I use in my writing or my speech tend to be simpler than those in my reading material. It is important for students to develop listening and speaking vocabularies because new words become "known words." When students encounter known words in their reading, they will better understand what they read. They will also be more likely to use these words in their writing.

- **Be familiar with scaffolding methods to help English Language Learners (ELLs) learn Standard American English.** Scaffolding means providing more support, often by dividing up learning (e.g., pre-reading, during reading, and post-reading activities). In working with ELL students, a teacher should use more visuals, and slower, shorter speech.

- **Be familiar with age-appropriate milestones for language development.** The structure of language is usually learned by age 5. However, with ELL students, the language structure may be different, which can make learning English a bit more difficult. For example, in Spanish, the language structure is "ball red," whereas in English we say "red ball."

- **Have the knowledge to create a culturally responsive classroom environment.** This means the teacher shows respect for all students, no matter their differences, and commands that same respect from all students within the classroom. The teacher uses various activities and materials in the classroom to broaden cultural knowledge.

- **Understand the role of phonemic awareness in reading development.** Phonemic awareness refers to the sounds in words—not letters, just sounds. A child has beginning phonemic awareness skills if he can say the beginning sound of "ball." Children do not need to know letters exist to have phonemic awareness.

- **Know a variety of instructional strategies to develop phonemic awareness skills.** This involves playing with letter sounds through segmenting, blending, and manipulating sounds. Again, sounds only, not letters. For example, a teacher may orally model how the word "cat" changes if you take the ending sound of /t/ and change it to the sound of /b/ ("cab").

Phonics and the Alphabetic Principle

"Phonics and the Alphabetic Principle" are covered in detail in Chapter 4. The teaching candidate is expected to:

- **Know methods to promote students' automatic recognition of high-frequency sight words.** Sight words are small words such as *the, were, is,* and *was,* that students needs to know automatically. If students learn to recognize these instantly, it makes the reading much smoother.

- **Know instructional strategies to help students understand the concepts of print.** Concepts of print are the rudiments of reading, such as how to hold a book and the knowledge that text is read from left to right. Teachers may point concepts out explicitly (directly) and have students practice.

- **Know methods to help students identify uppercase (capital) and lowercase letters.** Young children must learn that "B" and "b" are the same letter and have the same sound.

- **Understand the connection between students' inventive spelling and their knowledge of phonetic principles.** Analyzing inventive spelling helps the teacher set goals for students. This way, when children use inventive spelling (i.e., spelling what they think they hear), teachers can analyze what the children write to find out what each child knows and doesn't know about phonics.

- **Understand basic phonetics and phonological principles.** There are generalizations in phonics that teachers are to teach explicitly to students. Phonics generalizations help students identify unknown words, and also help students to spell correctly. This often entails both a base word and its derivatives.

- **Know instructional strategies for reinforcing and developing students' phonetic skills.** Teachers need a toolbox of ideas to teach and reinforce phonics. It is recommended that phonics be taught with explicit and engaging instruction. While teachers want to instill a love of reading in children, they should be careful to not destroy students' motivation to read with excessive repetition of isolated exercises (known as "drill and kill").

Word-Analysis Skills and Vocabulary Development

"Word-Analysis Skills and Vocabulary Development" are covered in detail in Chapter 5. The teaching candidate is expected to:

- **Know how phonics, syntax, and semantics interact as the reader constructs meaning.** Phonics is known as the letter-sound correspondence. Knowing that a letter may correspond to a specific sound helps students sound out letters. Syntax is language structure (e.g., a child would know that a particular word in a sentence should be *ran* and not *run* to match the tense of the sentence). Semantics is meaning, the significance being that a child can figure out a new word if there are hints in the sentence that imply the new word's meaning. Most words are learned through these hints, known as context cues.

- **Know methods to help students apply word-analysis skills independently.** These include strategies that aid in word identification, the use of context cues, and structural analysis.

- **Know how to help students read multisyllabic words by recognizing syllables and using structural analysis.** Syllables allow students to chunk words and help with word identification. For example, students learn that the ending -*ing* makes its own syllable, unless it is a one-syllable word, such as *bring,* which students learn is different from *bringing.* Structural analysis is looking at how the word is built and analyzing the parts. For example, the meaning of the word *multisyllabic* can be discerned from analyzing the parts of the word. It has two parts (or chunks) with meaning. The prefix *multi-* means "more than one," and the root *syllabic* has to do with syllables. Therefore, *multisyllabic* means "having more than one syllable." As students learn more and harder words, they need to be taught Greek and Latin roots and various affixes in order to be effective using structural analysis.

- **Know how to guide students in using context cues to figure out unknown words.** Students need to learn how to identify or pronounce the word, figure out its meaning, and so forth as they read independently.

- **Know instructional strategies for building and extending vocabulary knowledge.** Vocabulary is multifaceted (structural analysis: "has many faces"). Children need to learn how to pronounce words and to understand that some words are spelled differently, but have the same sound. They also need to know that words can have multiple meanings and that words have derivatives. They need to understand what idioms are (sayings with their own meaning outside of the words), and that words have nuances. There are more "faces" of vocabulary than those listed here; all of these aspects of vocabulary contribute to why teachers' need to use a variety of instructional strategies that help children gain word knowledge.

- **Know ways to help children use word reference materials.** Being able to use word reference materials (e.g., a dictionary, thesaurus, or glossary) is important to word knowledge. With electronics, reference materials also include links that students can access by clicking on a word to get the pronunciation and meaning. For ELLs, a reference material may be a visual of the word being used.

Development of Reading Fluency and Reading Comprehension

"Development of Reading Fluency" and "Development of Reading Comprehension" are covered in detail in chapters 6 and 7. The teaching candidate is expected to:

- **Know instructional strategies to increase fluency.** Fluency has four main components: automatic word recognition, rate of reading, accuracy, and pragmatics. Teachers need to know how to foster these areas and assess them in order to monitor student progress.

- **Know how linguistic, sociological, cultural, cognitive, and psychological aspects influence the reading and reading development processes.** Students come from a variety of backgrounds, languages, socioeconomic status, learning abilities and disabilities, and attitudes. All of this affects teaching in general, and must be taken into consideration for each student to have an optimal learning experience.

- **Be familiar with how linguistic, sociological, cultural, cognitive, and psychological aspects influence reading comprehension.** The more background a student has about an event or topic or the more informational facts he has when reading, the more accurately and fully he will understand the text. Various backgrounds and living situations can enhance or hinder comprehension. If a class is reading a book on a homeless child, a child who is or has been homeless will construct a much deeper meaning of this text than the child with the backyard pool or summer home.

- **Understand the different types of comprehension: literal, inferential, and evaluative.** Literal means facts that are directly stated in the text. Inferential comprehension is understanding implications that the author has included in the text. Evaluative is being able to make a reasonable judgment, such as whether a character deserved a particular outcome or not.

- **Know how to teach strategies to increase reading comprehension.** This includes taking into consideration the linguistic, sociological, cultural, cognitive, and psychological aspects that affect reading achievement. When teachers detect a problem with reading comprehension in students during progress monitoring, they must be able to use a variety of strategies to help these students.

- **Understand the role of independent reading and its effect on reading comprehension and fluency.** The more students read, the better readers they will become. Students need both guided practice and independent practice. Students' progress needs to be monitored so that their reading is always challenging enough to help them improve.

- **Know ways to increase reading in and out of the classroom.** I want to say "Offer them candy," but . . . bad idea. There are many effective strategies for getting children to read more, such as motivation through choice and modeling by the teacher. The more a teacher is able to motivate students to read during free time and outside of school, the more progress students will make.

- **Know ways to promote family and community involvement in literacy activities.** Getting families and the community involved in students' literacy activities is a win-win. The results are more student motivation to read and write and more opportunities for them to read and write, and, therefore, increased literacy skills.

Reading Comprehension Strategies Across Text Types

"Reading Comprehension Strategies Across Text Types" is covered in detail in Chapter 8. The teaching candidate is expected to:

- **Know ways to promote students' comprehension, enjoyment, and appreciation of various genres.** A genre is a type of text, such as historical fiction, mystery, biography, or poetry. Teachers should offer students a smorgasbord of genres so students can gain familiarity with a wide range of text structures.

- **Know how to select literature and informational text at appropriate reading levels.** In some ways, teachers are matchmakers. They need to match students with the correct reading level and interest in a variety of genres. This requires that teachers be familiar with a tremendous number of books in order to make appropriate recommendations.

- **Know various reading strategies to help students comprehend fiction.** Reading fiction is different from reading informational text. Strategies may include analysis of plot and of characters and their motives. Teachers need to be able to model and help students analyze fiction.

- **Know reading strategies for different genres and types of literature to improve comprehension.** Various comprehension strategies, such a close reading, visualization, and summarizing, need to be modeled and practiced. For example, students need to know that sometimes they must reread for understanding and, in the case of informational text, slow down their reading.

- **Know how to help students recognize different genres and types of literature.** Genres have criteria that need to be taught to students. For example, a fairytale often begins with "Once upon a time," ends with "They lived happily ever after," and may include magic. Further, a biography is about a person's life, an autobiography is about a person's life and is written by the person, and a mystery has clues and diversions. Various genres need to be read in the classroom, and their components taught to students.

- **Know ways to develop students' literary response and analysis skills to improve their comprehension.** Literary usually refers to the bigger picture in the story, such as theme or mood.

- **Be able to select and use a variety of informational, descriptive, and persuasive texts at appropriate reading levels and topics to increase students' comprehension when reading this material.** This relates to selecting material whose concepts and content are at the appropriate grade level. Each type of material needs to be approached differently and analyzed carefully.

- **Know how to help students build on their prior knowledge and connect this to new knowledge while reading informational text.** Teachers often do a KWL with informational text. The "K" stands for activating prior knowledge, asking students to say what they already know. This gets the brain ready to make mental connections. The "W" represents what students want to learn, and their motivation for reading the text. The "L" stands for what they have learned. A semantic web can also be used to activate prior knowledge. Teachers put a word in a circle, such as *cities,* and students add information they know about cities.

- **Know how to help students use metacognitive strategies before, during, and after reading.** Metacognitive means thinking about thinking. An example of a pre-reading strategy is having students think about what they know. A during-reading strategy may be to ask as they read, "Does this make sense?" A post-reading strategy may be to think about the message or theme the author is sending and the student continues to ask if the information makes sense.

- **Know instructional strategies to help students identify the author's purpose.** If a student knows that an author is writing to inform them what makes the seasons change, the student will read with a different perspective than if he were reading general information about the four seasons. Knowing the author's purpose can help with understanding the main points and important concepts.

- **Know strategies to help students recognize the difference between main ideas and supporting details in informational text.** Students need to learn how to select what is important in a text. For instance, it may be interesting to find out a town near them was destroyed by a tornado, but if the text has been written to explain why tornados exist, the students will miss the key concepts because of the interesting trivia.

- **Know how to help students recognize text features and organizational patterns to increase comprehension of informational text.** Students need to know that text features such as subtitles, bold, graphs, graphics, glossaries, and so forth are used in nonfiction writing to support what is being said in the primary text. Informational text is based on a variety of text structures, such as compare and contrast or cause and effect. Students need to know that authors choose a particular text structure to emphasize what is important in the text, and students should be familiar with the text structure.

- **Be familiar with how digital media impacts comprehension.** Reading on a tablet or computer is different from reading a hard copy. Digital reading may be interactive; it may include text features that differ from print. Teachers need to help students navigate these differences.

- **Understand how to help students locate and use evidence from the text to support predictions, opinions, and conclusions.** The students' comments or answers to questions should be text-based. If a chapter ends with a young boy about to fall into a river, a teacher may ask for a prediction. The students' predictions should be something about the boy either falling into the river or being able to catch himself. Some students who do not comprehend the story may offer predictions that are not text-based, such as forecasting that the boy will play with his toys. Students should be able to go back into the text and locate what they read that made them think their prediction would happen.

Writing in Support of Reading

The Interdependence of Reading and Writing Development

"The Interdependence of Reading and Writing Development" is covered in detail in Chapter 9. The teaching candidate is expected to:

- **Understand the interdependence of reading and writing development.** When a child grows in the area of reading, that child also grows in the area of writing. When we teach a child to decode the letter "d" to the sound of /d/, by reversing that learning, the child can encode the letter by saying the sound of /d/ in a word and then writing the letter.

- **Know that writing is a developmental process.** Writing and speaking are expressive. We have all witnessed toddlers as they begin speaking, but many do not realize that this process is paralleled by the growth of writing. A child begins with scribbles and drawings, but with teachers' guidance, a student can develop to write essays or even books.

- **Understand that spelling is developmental.** Just like reading, spelling has stages. Students may begin with the first letter or the first and last letter of a word to spell the word, such as *fn* for *fun* in initial writings. Students are learning to encode; through instruction, they will learn that all words must contain at least one vowel.

- **Be familiar with instructional strategies to improve spelling.** Students begin to write with inventive spelling, but must be required to use conventional spelling, at least for final drafts, by third grade. We begin teaching spelling through word work with orthographic patterns (onsets and rimes) in which children can change the beginning letter to make a new word. For example, a beginning spelling/phonics lesson may include the following word family: *bat, cat, fat, hat, mat, pat, rat,* and *sat.* The "at" is an orthographic pattern.

- **Know how to promote reading comprehension through writing activities.** Such activities would include written responses to reading. When writing, the writer must think about the writing subject; so in essence, when writing a response, the student must review his comprehension of the text.

- **Know instructional strategies to teach writing mechanics.** Writing mechanics are sometimes called writing conventions. Students need to be taught, through modeling, the use of capital letters, end marks, and so forth.

- **Know strategies for promoting writing development.** Teaching writing with mini-lessons on skill work is beneficial to writing development. Writing for a variety of purposes and genres is also important for increasing writing skills.

- **Be familiar with the teacher's role in the recursive writing process.** The term *recursive* means happening again, a repetition. Writers go through stages, such as pre-writing (brainstorming) and drafts. A teacher needs to model good writing, conference about the student's writing, give feedback, and conduct mini-lessons to help students improve their writing.

- **Know various ways to provide feedback throughout the writing process to help students improve their writing.** Feedback methods include conferencing, checklists, rubrics, and peer editing.

- **Know the traits of high-quality writing.** Good writing has distinct characteristics, or traits. Most schools emphasize the following traits: ideas, organization, voice, word choice, sentence fluency, and conventions.

- **Know how to teach students to write in different forms for a variety of audiences.** An author needs to know his audience. Students are young authors and should adhere to the same rule. They need to be taught to think about whom they are writing for, and the form and purpose of that writing. If students were going to write to the school principal to request an extra recess, it would be a formal letter, and much different from having fifth graders writing directions for third graders to follow. Teachers need to know how to model and guide students through the different forms and purposes.

Reading and Writing as Tools for Inquiry and Research

"Reading and Writing as Tools for Inquiry and Research" is covered in detail in Chapter 10. The teaching candidate is expected to:

- **Be able to teach students to use a variety of research sources.** Most students are not familiar with the research process. They need to know how to obtain important information from a range of resources, including print, electronic, interview, and observation. If students are doing interviews for a project, they need interviewing skills. There are various protocols and procedures to be followed during interviews, investigations, and resource inquiries.

- **Know ways to teach students research skills.** Research may start with "the big question" and then narrow it to a manageable scope. Students need guidance in how to obtain information; they need the research technique or process modeled for them.

- **Know strategies to help students make effective use of reference materials and resources.** Students need to know not only how to obtain important information but also how to organize the information in their writing and stay on topic. Students need to understand that the purpose of their writing guides what they include.

- **Know a variety of ways to help students "publish" their research through technology.** The results of research can be published in a variety of ways. The end result could be a poster board made with printed materials. It could be a PowerPoint presentation, an online presentation program, or a blog. Students need to be taught how to publish in a variety of formats and contexts, and what is expected in a published work.

- **Know how to evaluate and select reference materials and electronic resources.** In order to do quality research, students must be introduced to quality material. Being able to evaluate whether a website is most likely to have accurate and fact-checked material is important. Teachers need to teach students criteria for selecting reputable sites.

Answers to Frequently Asked Questions

Q: How do I register for the test?

A: You can register for the test online. Go to www.ets.org/praxis/register to see the test sites, test dates, and to register. You must create "My Praxis" account in order to get your admission ticket and, ultimately, your scores.

Q: What can I expect on test day?

A: At the test center, you will need to show your admission ticket and a photo ID. Once inside, you will be given the opportunity to see how the test works via a tutorial. There is also a "What to Expect on the Day of Your Test" video at www.ets.org/praxis, which may be helpful.

Q: Will I take the test on paper or on a computer?

A: The test is given on a computer; it is not a paper-and-pencil test.

Q: How long is the test?

A: Plan to spend 3 hours at the testing center. You will have 2½ hours to take the test, plus an additional 30 minutes up front to complete a tutorial. The test is composed of 90 selected-response (multiple-choice) questions and three constructed-response (essay) questions. (*Note:* The test may contain questions that won't count toward your score. This is because the test developers are "testing" some new questions to see if they are valid or reliable.)

Q: Should I guess?

A: If you don't know an answer to a question, give it your best guess and move on.

Question Types

There are two question types on the Praxis (5203): selected response and constructed response. These are described in detail below.

Selected-Response Questions

There are 90 selected-response (multiple choice) questions on the Praxis (5203). Each selected-response question has four answer choices. Questions may ask you to identify a term, analyze classroom instruction built into a classroom scenario, state a concern about one child or a group, or set a goal for students. Select the best answer. Expect to see an "attractive distracter"—one that will be *almost* right—among the answer choices. That is why you need to know the terminology and content in this book!

Constructed-Response Questions

There are three constructed-response (essay) questions on the Praxis (5203). There is one question on a topic from each of the three broad content categories: "Assessment and Diagnostic Teaching of Reading," "Reading Development," and "Writing in Support of Reading." A constructed-response question may require the addition of some comments that connect the other two broad categories to your explanation. For example, analyzing a running record would necessitate comments on word identification from "Reading Development," even if it is an assessment question.

Each constructed-response question has a high score of 3. A score of 3 requires that the response meets the following criteria:

- Answers *all parts* of the question offered clearly and with details
- Shows strong knowledge of the reading content
- Provides an explanation that strongly supports the response

A good approach to earning a score of 3 on a constructed-response question is to answer the question clearly and specifically. Be sure to show that you understand the teaching of reading. Give a strong explanation, and support it. Proficient writing is expected.

Chapter 2

Phonemic Awareness

Phonemic awareness is the ability to hear, isolate, and manipulate individual speech sounds. It is important to remember that phonemic awareness refers only to sound; it is an auditory process. In phonics, children learn that there is a sound-letter correspondence. *Children do not need to know that letters exist to have phonemic awareness.* Since a phoneme is defined as a single unit of sound, we ask children to manipulate or count sounds; this activity does not involve the actual letter or letters. For instance, the word *bat* has three letters and three sounds: /b/, /a/, and /t/. (*Note:* Sounds in reading are designated by the / / symbols.) In comparison, the word *back* has four letters, but it still only has three sounds: /b/, /a/, and /k/. A child who is phonemically aware should be able to understand that both of these words have three sounds. This same child does not need to know anything about letters, but he must be able to hear and identify separate sounds. If a question on the Praxis (5203) refers to letters, then the topic is most likely phonics. If the question or scenario does not involve letters, but instead talks about beginning, ending, or middle sounds, the topic is most likely phonemic awareness. It may be helpful to remember that a child can show you that he is phonemically aware even if his eyes are closed. Pictures may be used in a phonemic awareness activity, but no letters are involved.

Technically, phonemic awareness also includes being able to separate and count syllables, and to recognize rhyming sounds. Usually phonemic awareness activities are designed for very young children, up to second grade, and focus on speech sounds.

The Role of Phonemic Awareness in Learning to Read and Write

Phonemic awareness has become more important, as research has shown that students who have it are more ready to learn to read than those who do not. Being phonemically aware supports a student in "breaking the code." If a young child understands the concept of sounds, he will use that knowledge when he is taught decoding skills. So, when a teacher says "d" sounds like /d/, the child recognizes that /d/ is a sound and will be able to learn more easily that the sound corresponds to the letter being taught.

Vocabulary Worth Knowing and Understanding

Elkonin boxes: Boxes drawn on a piece of paper, so that children can place a token in an individual box for each sound they hear in a word. This activity helps to build and assess phonemic awareness.

grapheme: A visual representation for a single sound, usually a letter or group of letters. For example, "t" says one sound, /t/; "gh" says one sound, /f/. Another example is the "igh" in *high*.

morpheme: The smallest unit of sound that has meaning. For example, the word *rebook* contains two morphemes: the prefix *re-* and the root *book*. The meaning of the word *rebook,* therefore, is a combination of the meanings of its two morphemes.

phoneme: A single unit of sound.

phonemic awareness: The ability to identify, isolate, and manipulate sounds in a language.

phonological awareness: Encompasses letter sounds as well as syllables, rhymes, onsets, and rimes. Some experts also include phonics under the phonological awareness umbrella.

syllable: The part of a word that contains one vowel sound. For example, in the word *eating* there are two syllables, even though there are three vowels (*eat/ing*).

Check Your Understanding

Read each of the following scenarios and determine whether each one involves phonemic awareness. Explain your answers.

1. A teacher is showing Sarah a group of pictures and asking her to pick out the pictures that begin with /h/.
2. A teacher is showing Jerome the letter "b" and asking him what picture begins with this letter.
3. Mrs. Welter says the word *cat* and asks her students to put a token in the Elkonin boxes for each sound they hear.

Answers:

1. Yes, there are no letters involved—just pictures and sound.
2. No, this is not phonemic awareness; it is phonics. This is teaching letter-sound correspondence.
3. Yes, this is checking phoneme segmentation; no letters are involved.

Instructional Strategies to Develop Phonemic Awareness Skills

Continuum of Phonemic Awareness

Levels of phonemic awareness overlap one another, and understanding this structure aids teachers in planning a student's next steps. Although it is difficult to distinguish precise degrees of difficulty, the easiest level is considered to be phoneme segmentation—separating sounds; the most difficult level is phoneme substitution—more specifically, being able to substitute the medial phoneme (middle vowel sound). The point to remember is that as a phonemic awareness activity becomes more difficult, the child participating in the activity is considered to be more phonemically aware, and therefore is getting ready or is ready for phonics instruction. (Often in kindergarten and first-grade classrooms, this happens simultaneously, as the teacher provides instruction on letter identification and sound, but the child needs to know the concept of sound and sound blending.)

Levels of Phonemic Awareness

Note: The terminology used below can also be found in the booklet "Put Reading First," a publication developed by The Center for the Improvement of Early Reading Achievement (https://lincs.ed.gov/publications/pdf/PRFbooklet.pdf).

Level of Phonemic Awareness	Description
phoneme isolation	Recognizing an individual sound in a word. For example, a child can tell the teacher the first sound in the word *luck*. This is considered the easiest skill in phonemic awareness.
phoneme identity	Identifying a spoken sound in different words. For example, a child can recognize that /d/ is the same sound in *duck, dark,* and *dot*.
phoneme categorization	Identifying an odd sound. For example, a child can identify that the /f/ sound in *fun* is different from the /b/ sound in *bug* and *bike*.
phoneme blending	Being able to hear individual sounds and blend them together to make a word. A child can listen to a group of phonemes (sounds) and combine the phonemes—blend them together—to say the word. For example, if a child is given the sounds /h/, /i/, and /t/ separately and in order, the child will say the word *hit*.
phoneme segmentation	Being able to hear a word and distinguish the individual sounds within the word. For example, a child is told the word *bug,* and can say /b/, /u/, and /g/, and also state that there are three sounds.

(continued)

Level of Phonemic Awareness	Description
phoneme deletion	Recognizing a smaller word within a word when a sound is taken away. For example, when told the word *stall* and asked what word is left when the /s/ is taken away, the child would answer *tall*.
phoneme substitution	Substituting one phoneme for another. A child is told the word *cat* and asked to change the /a/ to /u/, and the child says *cut*. This is considered the most difficult skill in phonemic awareness.

Strategies for Teaching Phonemic Awareness

In general, any letter sound activity or listening game involving letter sounds would aid in children becoming phonemically aware. The following are samples of activities that can be used to teach and at the same time assess children's phonemic awareness.

- The teacher says a word and asks the student to say the first, middle, or ending sound. The teacher might say the word *hat* and ask the student to isolate and say just the beginning sound.
- Students are asked to tell which sounds are the same or different. The teacher might ask a question like "Which words begin with the same sound when I say, *bike, can, boat, and mouse*?" or "I am going to say three words. Tell me what word ends differently from the other two: *tall, bat, fall*".
- The teacher puts up a chart of different pictures and asks students to point to a picture that start with the /h/ sound. The students would be expected to point to, perhaps, a house, hat, or hammer.
- The teacher uses Elkonin boxes and gives students tokens. When the teacher says a word, the students put a token in a box for each sound they hear. For the word *pen,* three boxes would each have a token. For the word *make,* the answer would be the same.
- The teacher says the sounds /p/, /i/, and /g/, and stretches them out as she speaks. She has the students point to different spots on their other arm in order to put the sounds together. Beginning at the top, the /p/ is said at the upper arm, they glide down to the elbow and say /i/, and then say the /g/ sound at the hand level. The teacher asks the students to do this again, faster, and then has them identify the word as *pig.*
- The teacher is working with a series of words, and wants students to isolate and substitute the middle sound. The teacher says, "Listen carefully to the word *cup,*" and she stretches out the word. She then asks, "What does the word become when we put in the /a/ (short "a" sound) in place of the /u/?"

Check Your Understanding

Read the following scenarios and identify whether each is considered a phonemic awareness activity. Explain your answers.

1. A teacher is showing a student a chart of pictures that all begin with the /b/ sound. She has the student name what the picture is, such as a bag, and then say what letter the picture begins with.
2. A student is listening to the teacher as she says the word *dog*. The student is to tell the teacher what sound he hears in the middle of the word.
3. A teacher stretches out the sounds /n/, /o/, and /t/, and students have to identify what word is being said.

Answers:

1. No. Because the teacher asks for a letter name, the activity is phonics; it involves letter-sound correspondence.
2. Yes. This is sound isolation.
3. Yes. This is sound blending.

Chapter 3

Oral Language Development

When we use words to send a message in either speech or writing, we show our understanding of new words through **expressive language.** We learn new words through **receptive language**—when words bring us information through listening or reading. In this chapter, you will learn about oral language development and the importance of teaching active listening skills.

Stages of Oral Language Development (Milestones in Language Development)

In the 1950s, linguistics expert Noam Chomsky discovered that all the world's languages had a common developmental structure. Chomsky theorized that language abilities are innate, and the human brain is predisposed to learn language. Studies show that all children go through developmental stages in their language acquisition. Today, Chomsky's doctrine that language is acquired in six sequential stages is widely accepted. Other theorists have suggested developmental stages similar to Chomsky's. Some theorists focus on the function of the language, meaning the child's use of language—whether it is to demand, question, socialize, and so forth. A linear progression exists in language growth as a child matures, and there are age-appropriate milestones in language development. Study the chart below, and become familiar with how this linear growth occurs.

Chomsky's Six Universal Stages of Oral Language Development Adapted

Stage of Language Development	Description of Language Behaviors
Prelinguistic Stage (Cooing and Babbling)	In the first 12 months, a baby makes noises and gestures as pre-speech is used to communicate. Sounds might be interpreted as "I'm hungry, tired, wet," and so forth.
Holophrastic Stage (One Word)	Starting around 10–12 months, a child begins to use one-word communication to express what he wants. (Examples: *mama, dada, baba*)
Two-Word Stage	Around 20 months, a child begins to use two-word phrases to communicate, saying things like "me drink," "daddy out," "no shoe," "no eat." These words can be understood in the context of their use and have a function—in these cases stating a want.
Telegraphic Stage	Around 2½ to 3 years old (sometimes earlier), children begin to express themselves with shortened speech, as in a telegraph, saying things like, "me go now," "me get down," "daddy me go car." These words send a message in short form.
Intermediate Development Stage	The beginning of this stage is marked by simple sentences. Language structure is usually in place by age 5. For example, a child says "I" instead of "me." Children start school knowing approximately 5,000 words. As children age, their sentences are increasingly complex, and they are learning acceptable pragmatics (expression) in social situations.
Adult Stage	In this stage, speech is refined, strong vocabulary is present, and pragmatics (the way in which the speech is expressed) is as expected.

Strategies for Developing and Expanding Students' Listening Skills

Hearing begins in the auditory cortex, located in both hemispheres of the brain. The auditory cortex receives signals from the ears and transmits those signals to other parts of the cerebral cortex, which decode the sounds into meaningful words.

Hearing is not necessarily the same as listening. Students need to be active listeners by being cognitively aware, meaning they need to understand what is being said both verbally and nonverbally.

A good listener:

- Focuses on the speaker and does not interrupt the flow of language.
- Looks at the person speaking and gives nonverbal signals that he is listening.
- Shows interest in what is being said.
- Is respectful of the speaker's enthusiasm, concerns, and so forth.

In the classroom, children need to be taught to:

- Know that they listen for different reasons—e.g., to get directions, to learn something new, or to hear an opinion—so being a good listener is important.
- Be attentive and mindful of what is being said. They should ask themselves if they understand what they are hearing.
- Look at the speaker.
- Give encouraging nonverbal responses.
- Pay attention to nonverbal cues and gestures from the speaker.
- Listen for understanding, and ask questions when appropriate.

To help students learn to be active listeners, teachers should:

- Model good listening behaviors for the class.
- Let students know from the beginning that you will say most things only once, and they need to listen.
- Hold students accountable for listening—get their feedback in some way.
- Have students paraphrase what has been said.
- Make time for questions, as it allows you to know what was heard and understood, and if something needs to be clarified.
- Build in activities that allow students to practice their listening skills with each other (e.g., standing back-to-back and following oral directions or playing Simon says).

Strategies for Developing and Expanding Students' Listening and Speaking Skills

Oracy, the ability to express oneself fluently and correctly, is important in the classroom and in life. Students should learn to be good conversationalists.

To help students become good conversationalists and speakers, teachers should:

- Model behaviors of a good conversationalist.
- Build in less teacher talk; foster more student talk.
- Make students expand on what they are saying; don't accept one- or two-word answers to a question. Teachers often say to young children, "Use your words."

- Tell students to look at people when they are talking (and listening).
- Tell students to speak clearly and loudly enough for the listeners to hear.
- Tell students to watch for nonverbal cues from their listeners. These nonverbal cues might be able to help them determine if they have spoken the right length of time, or if someone is confused.
- Instruct students to take turns talking.
- Ask open-ended questions such as "Do you have experience in this?" "Can you tell me what you are thinking?" "Can you add something more?" Questions like these can get reluctant speakers to join the conversation.
- Consider using strategies, such as a talking stick or ball (an object that can be passed around), that will encourage student participation. When the speaker holds the stick or ball, it means no one else should be talking. The object is passed to a new speaker at the appropriate time.
- Communicate time expectations for oral presentations. If students are giving a class presentation, tell them the amount of time they are allotted, and that you will be using a timer. Advise them to practice and time themselves at home.

Increasing Vocabulary Through Listening and Speaking

Listening is one way in which we receive language and new vocabulary (reading is the other). Speaking involves an expressive vocabulary (as does writing) and allows children to use and apply new language. The listening and speaking vocabularies of your students are directly linked to their reading comprehension and their all-around academic development. The more vocabulary a student knows in the oral realm, the greater his understanding when reading. In addition, having an extensive vocabulary allows students to be precise and accurate in their communication.

The use of high-level vocabulary in the classroom is a fundamental method to get students to use and apply new vocabulary in their own speaking. Not only should the teacher model excellent speech and frequently use high-level vocabulary, but students need to be given the opportunity to use this vocabulary in the classroom. Oral vocabulary can be increased through teacher-led activities or via collaborative activities, in which students do most of the talking. (*Note:* Teaching vocabulary for reading and writing is covered in Chapter 4, "Phonics and the Alphabetic Principle.") The listed activities that follow will help engage students in using new speaking vocabulary learned through listening to the teacher and others.

Teacher-led vocabulary activities:

- Instruction of new vocabulary words through discussion and actions.
- Read alouds using books one or two years above students' reading levels. When new or interesting vocabulary words are used, these words should be discussed and expanded upon.
- Vocabulary words of the week, in which students get rewarded for using the new words. Unless words are used multiple times, students may not remember them.
- Turn and Talk: After listening to directions or information containing new vocabulary or concepts, students turn to a partner and talk about what they have just learned.
- Open-ended follow-up questions to foster discussion.
- The Language Experience Approach: The class or group does an activity, such as a baking soda/vinegar volcano explosion. The teacher leads the students in a discussion about what they experienced. Then, the teacher writes, on large chart paper or an interactive whiteboard, what students say about the experience, making sure to include the new vocabulary.

Collaborative activities:

- Prior to reading, have partners look at pictures in the book and discuss with each other what they think is going to happen. Teachers can use the vocabulary to guide students through the pictures, as a way to implant new words prior to reading.

- Have small groups create a puppet show to foster language use. This can be a retelling of a book students have read, thereby encouraging students to use new vocabulary from the book.

- Using pictures that represent students' various cultures, have the students tell each other stories inspired by the pictures.

- Have students play games that allow for ample discussion. For example, divide students into teams and have the teams discuss each answer among themselves prior to announcing the answer to the class. (Use the talking stick so that more students have a chance to give the answer to the class.)

Scaffolding Learning for English Language Learners

The teaching ideas given thus far in this chapter will be appropriate for more proficient English Language Learners (ELLs), but most ELLs will need repeated oral exposure to new words. ELL students have a double learning challenge when it comes to oral language development: They are learning to read and also learning to speak a language that is most likely not spoken at home. The following ideas work better with students who are relatively new to the English language:

- Speak slowly (not loudly), so students can clearly hear your pronunciation.

- If a child is completely new to the English language, initially use telegraphic speech, or what is more commonly called the Total Physical Response (TPR) technique. Telegraphic speech is followed by a sentence using actions, and then the telegraphic speech is repeated. Let's take a scenario where the ELL student must hang up his coat. The teacher says, "Hang coat." The teacher then walks the child toward the classroom coat hooks and says, "You [pointing to child] need to hang your coat [pointing to coat] on the hook [pointing to hook]." Then the teacher repeats "hang coat" as she hangs the coat up for the child or helps the child hang the coat.

- Constantly use visuals. If students can't understand the language, they will most certainly not be able to understand a definition of a word.

- Ask questions that can be answered with one or two words, or even by pointing.

- Use rebuses (pictures or symbols substituted for words in text) as hints, e.g., thumbs-up/thumbs-down pictures for "agree/disagree."

- Use audio- or computer-assisted reading. Have students listen to talking books or listen to stories on CDs or the computer. Send these resources home, if possible (parents will most likely use these, too).

- Read repetitive books to students (repetitive books repeat the same language or line several times). Have students repeat the lines with you. Then, using puppets from the story if possible, have children act out the story using words from the book.

- Choose one or two target words and use them multiple times when speaking to the ELL students.

- Do shared reading, a read aloud often done with a big book. During this experience, point out new words and discuss them; point to pictures in the book that explain the word, using actions when needed.

- Create 30-second action videos or slide shows. For example, when teaching the word *different,* you would show a video or a slide show with four or five slides, each with an item unique to that slide, and the speaker would say what is different.

Cultural Responsiveness

Cultural responsiveness is the ability to be open to, learn from, and relate respectfully to people of all cultures, including your own. To communicate effectively with children and parents of different cultures, a teacher cannot let any type of stereotyping, discrimination, or prejudices interfere with her communication.

A teacher must be sensitive to a child's home culture. Teachers need to be culturally responsive to children's belief systems, cultural traditions, and any language patterns that may interfere with communication. Both verbal and nonverbal communication are essential in connecting with other cultures. When possible, learn about each of your students' cultures; cultural differences may cause difficulties in meeting academic expectations. For example, in some cultures, children are taught to look down when speaking to adults; therefore, intergenerational eye contact is considered disrespectful.

To aid in cultural responsiveness in the classroom:

- Teach students that respectfulness of other cultures is an expectation in the classroom.
- Nurture a classroom with a safe environment where students feel comfortable and accepted, so ELLs will use their new language without fear of making mistakes.
- Teach students that learning a second language can be difficult and their help and courtesy in helping an ELL student learn is appreciated. ELLs can reciprocate and teach native English speakers some of their words.
- Teach students that cultural differences and similarities exist and make the world more interesting.
- Invite all students to be learners, and show them that their participation is valued.
- Let students see their respective cultures reflected in classroom visuals, activities, and books (such as in the classroom library, or for read alouds).
- Encourage students to express themselves, and explain cultural expectations when acceptable.
- Encourage students to analyze and discuss the multiple perspectives of various cultures.
- Communicate high expectations to all students.
- Build collaborative activities into your classroom instruction.

To show cultural responsiveness to parents:

- Always respond with respect and understanding.
- Be understanding to language difficulties that might cause unnecessary confusion.
- Stay sensitive if a parent seems frustrated or upset; try to figure out the bigger picture of what is happening to cause the frustration.
- When possible, send notices home in the parent's language.
- Ask parents questions that will aid in their child's learning.

Chapter 4

Phonics and the Alphabetic Principle

Phonological awareness is considered the crux of beginning reading. Recognizing sounds in words, then eventually being able to correspond a letter or letters to that sound are beginning steps in "breaking the code." How to teach phonics is most likely one of the most controversial issues in reading instruction. Research points to explicit instruction, which can be reinforced in a variety of ways. Beginning readers must understand the concepts of print—knowing how a text works—as well as the alphabetic principle. Teachers use a variety of techniques to help students gain this knowledge.

Concepts of Print

You have probably seen a small child "read" a book upside down, but what you might not know is that this scene is actually informative about early developing reading skills. Concepts of print are the basic understandings of how printed text—books—work. An informal literacy assessment of the concepts of print was first introduced by Marie Clay; it includes a list of expected reading skills for very young children. Teachers use a checklist with the expected behaviors to assess a child's reading development. This allows teachers to examine exactly what a child knows about print—even basic book-handling skills, such as holding the book right-side up and turning pages in the correct direction.

The concepts of print assessment is an informal literacy assessment used with primary grade students and preschoolers. When checking students' knowledge of concepts of print, teachers will ask a student if he can show her the following:

- the front and back of the book
- the title of the book
- where the story begins
- a letter, word, and sentence
- where a sentence ends, and the end marks, such as a period
- a space between letters or sentences
- a word, or how many words are in a selected sentence
- directionality (English print is read from left to right)
- the top and bottom of the page
- upper- and lowercase letters (recognizing them and matching them)
- a picture versus printed text

This informal assessment gives important information on a child's reading development. A teacher will ask leading questions, such as "Can you use two fingers to frame one word?" When children "pretend read," they may say fifteen words while "reading" a seven-word sentence because, although they may follow the print with their fingers, they do not understand the concept of what defines a word. Teachers use the concepts of print checklist to show student growth.

Teaching Concepts of Print

The following are examples of ways in which concepts of print can be taught. Direct instruction is the recommended procedure. Teachers tell students what they need to know, model as they explain, and then have students identify.

The teacher shows a book and, pointing to the cover, directly states that this is the front of the book and asks students to notice how the pictures are right-side up. The teacher then moves to the title of the book, the beginning pages, and the back of the book, explaining each section.

Using a student's name, the teacher will explain that words are made up of letters. For example, the name "Sam" has three letters; together with the class, the teacher counts the number of letters. This is repeated with other names and simple words.

As the teacher reads a book, she moves her finger or pointer along the words to show directionality. She also mentions other concepts of print, such as the top and bottom of the page, where a sentence begins and ends, punctuation marks, and so forth.

A teacher takes a simple sentence from a book she is reading to the class, such as "The cat has a hat." Putting each word on an index card, the teacher shows the students the sequenced sentence. She then tells students that there is one word on each card. They count the five words together. She explains that in sentences, you leave a space between words so you can tell where a word begins and ends. Volunteers in the class point to where each word begins and ends.

Teaching Recognition of Uppercase and Lowercase Letters

The best predictor of reading success corresponds to a student's ability to recognize uppercase (capital) and lowercase letters. If the student can recognize the letter "t," then when a teacher states that "t" says /t/, the child is well on his way to learning letter sounds. He already knows the name of the letter, as compared to a child that is learning the name of "t" and the sound at the same time. Some educators feel that lowercase letters should be taught first, as there are more of these than uppercase letters in reading.

Strategies to Teach Letter Recognition

Teaching letter recognition should be fun and engaging. Here are a few strategies you can try:

- **Direct instruction:** Write the letter "B" on a card, and state that this is the uppercase letter "B" and the lowercase letter "b." The name *Ben,* written out for children to see, starts with the uppercase letter "B." The word *box,* written, begins with the lowercase letter "b."
- **Find the letters:** Tell students that Freddie Fox came into the classroom last night and hid big and small letter "f's." Show students what the upper- and lowercase (big and small) letter "f" looks like, and have them find the letters hidden in the room.
- **Letter tracing:** When working on a letter, teach students both the upper- and lowercase letter, and have letters for students to trace. You could also use letters cut from sandpaper and have students do a "rubbing" as they say the letter name.
- **Cut and paste:** After explicitly teaching a letter, have students cut out the letter from magazines and glue it to a paper labeled with the letter.

The Alphabetic Principle

The alphabetic principle is the concept that specific letters and sounds correspond to one another. This principle is known by a variety of names: phonics, breaking the code, sound-symbol correspondence, and letter-sound correspondence. If you see any of these terms on the exam, they are all referring to phonics. In the classroom, the alphabetic principle is spoken about in terms of a child's decoding skills.

Vocabulary Worth Knowing and Understanding

alphabetic principle: States that there is a predictable correspondence between a letter and a sound.

consonant blend: When two or more consonants appear together and each consonant can be heard in sequence, there is a consonant blend. When there are three consonants together, it is called a consonant cluster. Examples: _blow, stream, bust_.

digraph: Two letters that represent one sound. For example, the "ai" in *pail* is a digraph, making an /a/ sound; so is the "ph" in *digraph,* making an /f/ sound (a nice way to remember the definition).

diphthong: Two vowels that, when spoken together, make a glided sound (e.g., "oi" in *oil,* "ou" in *ouch*).

grapheme: Written text that represents one phoneme. For example, "b," "oa," and "t" are the three graphemes in the word *boat.*

morpheme: The smallest unit of sound that contains meaning. For example, the word *bag* is a morpheme. Adding an "s" to the end of it makes it plural and, therefore, gives it another meaning; *bags* is called a bonded morpheme.

onset: The initial consonant of a syllable (e.g., the "b" in *big*).

phoneme: The smallest unit of sound (e.g., /b/ or /o/).

phonics generalizations: A rule that governs letter sounds under specific conditions. For example, a silent "e" makes the preceding vowel long; when a "c" is followed by an "i" or "e," it makes the soft sound, as in *city;* when a "c" is followed by an "a," "o," or "u," it makes the hard sound, as in *cake.*

phonological awareness: Encompasses letter sounds as well as syllables, rhymes, onsets, and rimes. Some experts also include phonics under the phonological awareness umbrella.

rime: The part of the syllable that comes after the initial consonant and begins with a vowel (e.g., the "ig" in *big*).

systematic phonics: Teaching phonics in a systematic manner from part to whole, letter sound to word.

word family: A group of words with the same spelling pattern: *tug, bug, hug, chug,* and *shrug.* The words in a word family don't just rhyme—they have the same spelling pattern, too. In contrast, *through, shoe,* and *boo* rhyme, but they are not a word family.

Common Phonics Generalizations

There are numerous phonics rules that can be taught. The following table contains some very basic rules that are apparent in elementary teaching. There are exceptions to many of these rules, but the ones listed here are fairly predictable.

Before learning the general phonics rules, students should have an understanding of long vowel sounds and short vowel sounds. In a long vowel sound, the vowel says its name (for example, "a" in *cake,* "e" in *be,* "i" in *bike,* "o" in *tow,* "u" in *unit*). In a short vowel sound, the vowel does not say its name (for example, "a" in *cap,* "e" in *bet,* "i" in *lip,* "o" in *hot,* "u" in *cut*).

In addition to these general phonics rules, students should be aware of silent consonants and the schwa sound. Students need to be taught that some words include silent letters. These letters are in the word when they are written, but do not say a sound when the word is read. Some common patterns for silent letters besides the silent "e" discussed in the VCe rule are the "k" in *know,* the "w" in "wr" in *write,* the "gh" in *night,* the "b" in *climb,* and the "t" in *listen.*

The schwa sound is a reduced vowel sound that sounds like "uh." Any vowel can make the schwa sound. The schwa is represented by an upside-down "e" (ə). Examples of words with the schwa sound include *amazing, item, pencil, money, syrup,* and *syringe.*

Some General Phonics Rules

Sound	Rule	Examples
CVC	When a single vowel comes between two consonants, that vowel is usually short.	*mud, bat, stuck*
CVCe	When "e" is the final vowel in a word, the preceding vowel is usually long and the "e" is silent.	*home, make, like*
Closed syllable—VC	When a single vowel is at the beginning of a word, it is usually short.	*am, is, up*
Open syllable—CV	When a syllable ends with a vowel, the vowel sound is usually long.	*ba/by, ta/ble*
CVVC	When two vowels are together, usually the first vowel says its name and the second vowel is silent. (***Remember:*** When two vowels do the walking, the first one does the talking.)	*goat, pail, beat*
"y" as a vowel	When "y" is acting as a vowel at the end of a one-syllable word, it usually has the sound of a long "i." When "y" is acting as a vowel at the end of a two-syllable word, it usually has the sound of a long "e."	*fly, try* *candy, silly, happy*
"r"-controlled	When "r" follows a vowel, it controls and changes the sound of the vowel.	*car, fir, murky*
Hard and soft "g" and "c"	When "g" is followed by an "a," "o," or "u," or is the last letter of a word, it has the hard sound. When "c" is followed by an "a," "o," or "u," or is the last letter of a word, it also has the hard sound. When "g" is followed by an "e," "i," or "y," it has a soft sound, /j/. When "c" is followed by an "e," "i," or "y," it has a soft sound, /s/.	hard: *garage, gate, good, got, guilty, gum, frog, leg; cat, cake, coat, cold, cut, cuddly, sac* soft: *general, angel, giraffe, engine, gym; cell, space, citrus, rice, cyclops, icy*

Strategies to Promote Letter-Sound Correspondence

Research has determined that phonics should be taught explicitly through direct instruction. In explicit instruction, information is clearly communicated using a process of explaining, showing, and then having the students try it. A teacher teaching the letter "m" would show the letter, say that the letter is "m" and that it says /m/, and inform students that words like *man, map,* and *money* start with /m/ because they start with the letter "m." In contrast, implicit instruction is indirect. In this case, the teacher reverses the instruction. The teacher would say and show the words *man, map,* and *money,* and then ask students what sound the words begin with. After the students responded that the words start with the /m/ sound, the teacher would ask what letter the words start with, and finally ask, "So what sound does the letter 'm' make?" Explicit instruction states what needs to be known, whereas implicit is a bit more exploratory for students. The following table shows activities that can be used to reinforce letter sounds once they have been taught.

Letter-Sound Correspondence Activities

Activity	Description
Find the letter	Direct students to find something in the room that begins with the sound of the letter "f" and put a cut-out letter "f" on the item.
Beanbag toss	A student throws a beanbag onto a mat containing the letters of the alphabet. If it lands on the letter "p," for example, the child says /p/.
Make a word (short vowel sounds)	Use word cards with the letters to be taught or reinforced to make words. In the case of short "a," the letters "a," "n," "f," "m," "c," and "p" can be used to make a four-word word family. Explain that short "a" says /a/. Give students a card with "an" and say the sound. Then have students put the "f" in front of the "an" and ask what that says. Continue through *man, can,* and *pan.* (This can be adapted to any sound.)
Make a word (long vowel sounds)	Explain to students that when words have a vowel, consonant, and then an "e" pattern (VCe), the "e" is silent and the vowel says its name. Then explicitly show some VCe-patterned words, and say some examples. Take a short vowel word and change it to a long vowel word by adding an "e" to the end. Word pairs such as *can/cane, fat/fate,* and *con/cone* can be used to explicitly teach the difference. Eventually, students are encouraged to read the word pairs and tell you why the vowel makes the long sound.
Bossy "r" ("r"-controlled sounds)	Explain to students that when a vowel is followed by the letter "r," the "r" becomes the "boss" and changes the sound of the vowel. Use the "make a word" lesson format and add the letter "r" to reinforce how the "r" becomes boss and changes the sound. For example the following word pairs can be used: *cat/cart, fist/first, hut/hurt,* and *pot/port.*

Inventive Spelling

In inventive spelling, young children attempt to write words as they hear the sounds of each word. For example, a young child might write *bg* for *big* as he identifies the beginning and ending sounds of the word. Inventive spelling is considered acceptable until about third grade, when children should know the skills needed for traditional spelling. The idea behind inventive spelling is to allow children to concentrate on the content of what they want to say, and not the mechanics of the writing.

Inventive spelling is also used as a tool to assess a child's phonics skills. In encoding, you think of the letter sound (phoneme) and write the corresponding letter or letters (grapheme). In decoding, you read the written letter (grapheme) and say the sound (phoneme). If a child consistently writes a letter or letter pattern incorrectly, it should become a focus for a phonics lesson. For example, suppose a child writes, *I lik mi new bik. It maks me happe.* The spelling errors can be analyzed and the teacher can set goals for the child. In this example, the child might need to learn the VCe rule and that "y" says the sound of /e/ at the end of a two-syllable word.

Look carefully at the following sample written with inventive spelling. Search for any patterns in the spelling or phonics generalizations the child may have used.

I wnt to the star wth Mom to gt bred.

Analysis: When analyzing this sample, you can see that the child knows the following: sentences begin with a capital and end with a period; consonant sounds; and *Mom* and *to* as sight words. On the other hand, the child does not yet know that all words should have a vowel, the "r"-controlled rule, or the proper spelling of *store* using the VCe rule.

Let's try this one:

> *me lik yu vere muh yu gd techr*

Analysis: This child has some understanding that vowels belong in words and has a strong control of consonant sounds. On the other hand, the child does not yet know the VCe rule (*lik* to *like*), the "r"-controlled rule (as in *teacher*), or that the /e/ sound at the end of a word is usually spelled with "y" (*very,* not *vere*).

This next practice analysis is from a young child at the end of second grade. Look for what the child knows and still needs to learn.

> *Wher going to camp at my house With the hole cub Scouts because We have the bigest yard.*

Analysis: This child has a good understanding of common spelling patterns, that a sentence begins with a capital letter, that "wh" sounds like /w/, that sentences end with a period, and the correct use of tenses. On the other hand, the child overuses capital letters (as in *With* and *We*), but this could be because both words start with "w," like the word at the beginning of the sentence or because the upper- and lowercase "w" look so similar. He does not understand contractions (*Wher* should be *We're*) or homophones (*hole* should be *whole*). He has some understanding that *Cub Scouts* is a proper noun and should utilize capitalization.

Promoting Automatic Word Recognition and High-Frequency Sight Words

Sight words are words that readers know instantly, automatically. High-frequency words are the most commonly used words in print in English. Why is it important for a reader to be able to recognize high-frequency words by sight? A child with a large bank of sight words that he automatically recognizes is able to concentrate on comprehension while reading. The focus of the reading can be on meaning instead of decoding words. On the other hand, if a child has to decode several words in each sentence, this detracts from his focus on comprehension. In addition, knowing words by sight aids in reading speed.

Vocabulary Worth Knowing and Understanding

automatic word recognition: The ability to recognize words quickly, effortlessly, and automatically.

high-frequency words: Words that are frequently used in reading and writing. Examples include *a, the, she, he, they, as,* and *it*.

sight words: Words that readers recognize automatically, and therefore can be read immediately with no decoding necessary; sight words cannot easily be decoded.

word wall: A board or wall that features isolated words students are learning, usually in alphabetical order. These words can be practiced on a regular basis, with whole group and small group activities.

Techniques for Teaching Automatic Word Recognition

The best method for aiding children in automatic word recognition is repeated exposure to the words being learned. Repetition and reinforcement are important. There are multiple ways to employ repetition and reinforcement to aid in automatic word recognition:

- Use predictable and decodable books that offer repeated phrases.
- When reading with the child, point out the targeted sight words that are to be learned.
- Identify, model, and reinforce sight words during paired and assisted reading.
- Utilize repeated reading with sentences and phrases that include the targeted words.
- Create a word wall to ask game-like questions so that students select targeted sight words. For example, "I am thinking of a word that rhymes with *Jim*." (*him*).
- Try game formats such as bingo, in which children "cover" the words they are learning.

Instructional Strategies for Developing and Reinforcing Students' Phonics Skills

A developing skill is one that has not been mastered. Most likely, the child needs more explicit instruction, followed by reinforcement. Reinforcement is not direct instruction, but guided practice in which instruction can continue as the learner begins to "own" the skill. Previously, a number of ideas were given to reinforce students' knowledge of letter sounds and phonics generalizations, most in isolation of reading text. Reinforcing developing readers and writers while they read is also effective methodology. When talking about reinforcing children's skills in using phonics, the focus is on how a child uses phonics to both read and write.

As a child begins developing literacy skills, the teacher encourages the child to sound out words when reading and writing. For example, a child is trying to read the sentence "The dog barked at the cat in the tree." He comes to the word *barked,* stops, and looks up to the teacher to say the word. But the teacher knows that effective phonics teaching methods dictate her to not say the word, but instead to guide the child to decode the word. This approach will aid in reinforcing what the child knows about sounding out words and using phonics or context to help figure out a new word. So, when the child looks up, there are a number of guiding questions the teacher can ask: "What sound does the word begin with?" "What sound does the word end with?" "Can you tell me the sound in the middle?" "What vowel do you see?" "What do you see after the vowel?" "Do you remember what happens when an 'r' follows the vowel?" Can you chunk the word and read a part of it?" Or, using context to aid in figuring out the word, the teacher may ask, "What does a dog usually do when it sees a cat?" Then, "Yes, how can you tell that is the word *barked*?" These types of guided questions allow the teacher to reinforce phonics skills. The point being that when a student begins to use phonics, the teacher needs to respond to the developmental need of the student to help him progress independently, yet give the student a vehicle to eventually be able to decode unknown words independently. For example, a student is reading a book about football and comes to the word *tackle* and stops. Instead of saying the word for the student, the teacher may tell the student to cover the "le" and say the word. Once the student says "tack," the teacher may ask what word is used in football that begins with "tack." In this way, the teacher is showing the student how to chunk words for pronunciation and to use context to aid in decoding and recognizing words.

Activities aiding in the development of phonics skills:

- **Letter manipulation:** Have students use a group of letters, such as "p," "r," "t," "a." Guide the students to form the following words: *pat, tap, at, part, art, tar, par.* Emphasize how the vowel sound changes when it is followed by "r."

- **Chunking:** Have students practice chunking words to see if they can read parts of each word. For example, give students the word *worker,* have them cover up the *-er,* and ask if they can read the first sound of the word. Practice this with numerous words.

- **Analogy strategy:** Have students compare one word to another or others. When using onset and rimes, similarities can be found. Once students know the consonant sounds, they can use the analogy strategy to identify unknown words. For example, working with the rime "ike" from the word *bike,* students can use the analogy strategy to decode *hike* and *like.*

Some techniques for reinforcing phonics skills:

- Ask for the beginning and ending sounds of the targeted word.

- Ask what vowel is in the word, and what sound the vowel makes in the word.

- Bring up any phonics generalizations that may help, such as, "I see the word ends with an 'e.' What sound does that make the vowel say?" Or "Two vowels are together; what does that mean?" Be sure to explicitly explain any generalization the child cannot remember.

- Chunk the word and ask if the child can recognize a part of the word.

- Use word family comparisons or the analogy strategy, such as stating to the child "I have seen you read this word [writing down *butter*], but the new word begins with 'sh,' so it would be what?"

Chapter 5
Word-Analysis Skills and Vocabulary Development

As an adult, when you read this sentence it appears that your understanding is automatic. Now, read the following sentence:

> *The guitarist's fado was enjoyable as we finished our dinner.*

The word *fado* probably brought you to a stop. But, because you automatically use your cueing systems, you have an idea of what the word may mean. Using phonics skills, you most likely came up with some kind of pronunciation of the word. Next, using syntax, you determined that the word is a noun. Finally, using the context information in the sentence, the semantics, you may have decided that *fado* is some type of a song, since substituting "The guitarist's song" for "The guitarist's fado" makes sense in the sentence.

You now have a good idea of the meaning of the complete sentence because you have utilized the three main cueing systems: phonics, syntax, and semantics. With respect to pragmatics, the tone of the sentence is as gentle as the background music it references. All of these cueing systems have aided you in constructing meaning. (In case you are curious, a *fado* is a Portuguese folk song.) Children use cueing systems in the same way. As a teacher, you must model strategies and ask guiding questions to help your students use these systems.

The Cueing Systems: Phonics, Syntax, and Semantics

Cueing systems are cues that readers use to aid in figuring out unknown words. There are three main cueing systems: phonics, syntax, and semantics. Some teaching includes a fourth: pragmatics.

- **Phonics:** A correspondence between letters and sounds.
- **Syntax:** The structure of the language.
- **Semantics:** Meaning; how words relate to form meaning.
- **Pragmatics:** The way in which expression can provide meaning to language.

Word-Analysis Skills

A word-analysis skill refers to any of a number of ways in which readers analyze unknown words. Word analysis is often used simultaneously with structural analysis, which will be described in more detail later in this section (see page 29). Word analysis includes using phonics to decode words, being able to chunk words into parts (syllables), and being able to recognize meanings of these parts. However, word analysis is broader than structural analysis, as students also analyze at the letter level. In word analysis, students are to focus on the structure of the word and recognize known word parts. This may be by prefix, suffix, base word, or letter patterns. Of course, letter patterns can be found in prefixes, suffixes, and base words, but analyzing words by common letter patterns aids students in phonics, spelling, meaning, and word retention. What is important to recognize is that students analyze unknown words in some way.

Methods of Teaching Word-Analysis Skills

There are several methods for teaching students word-analysis skills. A few of them are described here:

Making word families: Teaching word analysis at the letter level. The teacher gives students a group of letters, such as "c," "f," "l," "m," "p," "v," "a," "s," and "t" in order to work with the spelling pattern "ast." Working with the students, the teacher models and then has the students apply their learning. To start, the "ast" may be on one card, with the other letters separate. The teacher begins by making the word *cast* and saying a sentence like "When I broke my arm, I had to wear a cast." Next, the teacher makes the word *fast* and recites a sentence, "Did you see how fast Aiden was riding his bike?" Then, the teacher gets students to analyze the words by asking, "What sound did both of these words end with?" After helping students determine the sound of "ast," the teacher has the students make the following words: *last, mast, past,* and *vast,* and form a sentence with each. As the students make the word, the teacher supports the word analysis by asking what three letters make the "ast" sound. Teaching students to analyze words when making or building word families will lead them to be more successful in the following activity.

Word sorts: Students are given a group of words to sort into various categories. A word sort can be a "free" or "guided" sort.

- **Free sort:** The teacher tells the students to sort the words any way they wish and to note how they sorted them. Students may sort words by beginning sounds, ending sounds, rhymes, parts of speech, and so forth.
- **Guided sort:** The teacher directs students to sort into particular phonetic categories, such as the "at," "ing," and "ake" rimes. Then, the category is changed and the teacher may direct students to group words that begin with the same consonant blend, such as *brat, bring,* and *brake.*

Take apart: Students build a word, take it apart, and build it again as they study the word formation.

Blending wheel or T-scope: Different onsets can be matched to the same or different rimes to make a new word. A rime, such as "ab," is written on a cardstock paper. A slider with beginning consonants is pulled through two slots to show one word. The rime "ab" can have a slider with the consonants "c," "d," "f," "g," "l," "n," and "t." As the student pulls on the slider, he says each newly made word (*cab, dab, fab, gab, lab, nab,* and *tab*).

Word walls: Word walls can be used to build categories of words, such as various word families, number of syllables, or beginning/ending consonant blends.

Vocabulary Worth Knowing and Understanding

Meta-language is defined as language about language. Words such as *nouns, verbs,* and *adjectives* are considered meta-language because they label types of words. In reading, there are a number of words that label specific types of words, such as the following:

acronym: An abbreviation that is used as a word. Examples: *ASAP* (as soon as possible), *laser* (light amplification by stimulated emission of radiation), and *sonar* (sound navigation and ranging).

affix: A letter or group of letters added to a root word to change its meaning. Prefixes and suffixes are affixes. Prefix examples: *re-* ("to do again"), *un-* ("opposite of"), and *pre-* ("before"). Suffix examples: *-less* ("without"), *-er* ("one who does"), and *-acy* ("state or quality").

anagram: A word or phrase that can be made by rearranging the letters of another word. Examples: *era/are, ocean/canoe,* and *south/shout.*

antonyms: Words that mean the opposite. Examples: *hot/cold, guilty/innocent,* and *exciting/dull.*

base word: A base word is a word that stands alone, but affixes can be added. Examples: *test, retest, pretest, testing, tester.*

compound words: Two words that are joined together to form one word. Examples: *upstairs, hairdresser,* and *shoelace. Note:* Not all compound words must be written as one word. Examples: *high school* and *ice cream.*

contraction: One word that abbreviates a two-word combination and uses an apostrophe to substitute for the subtracted letter or letters. Examples: *can't, don't, wouldn't,* and *could've.*

etymology: The study of the history of words or phrases. Examples: *pizza* (Italian, meaning *pie* or *tart*), *bagel* (most likely from the Yiddish word *beygl,* which is likely from the German dialect word *beugel,* meaning "ring" or "bracelet"), and *T-bone* (taken from the shape of the steak bone).

euphemism: An expression or word that is substituted for something that is considered too harsh or vulgar. Examples: *in the family way* for *pregnant; darn* for *damn; let go* for *fired*.

homographs: Words that are spelled the same, but have multiple meanings and may not be pronounced the same. Examples: *fair, bow, desert,* and *minute*.

homophones (or homonyms): Words that sound the same, but are spelled differently and have different meanings. Examples: *bare, bear; pail, pale;* and *surf, serf*.

idiom: A group of words that have a different meaning than what is expected. Examples: *go jump in the lake, at the drop of a hat,* and *the ball is in your court*.

palindrome: A word or phrase that is spelled the same forward and backward. Examples: *mom, madam,* and *racecar*.

prefix: A morpheme that is attached to the beginning of a word. Examples: *re-* ("to do again"), *un-* ("opposite of"), and *pre-* ("before").

suffix: A morpheme that is attached to the ending of a word. Examples: *-less* ("without"), *-er* ("one who does"), and *-acy* ("state or quality").

synonyms: Words that mean the same thing or nearly the same thing. Examples: *nice/polite, cold/chilly,* and *sleepy/drowsy*.

Structural Analysis: Multisyllabic Words and Syllabication

Structural analysis is part of the continuum of learning to read that begins with phonemic awareness and moves into phonics (or the alphabetic principle) until third or fourth grade, where this analysis should become part of the word study curriculum. Structural analysis focuses on teaching children to look at words through word parts and their meanings (i.e., root words, syllables, and affixes), which aid in identifying and understanding unknown words. In the next section, "Instructional Strategies for Building and Extending Vocabulary," you will learn how structural analysis can aid readers throughout their lives in understanding and pronouncing unknown words. This section focuses on multisyllabic words and syllabication rules to assist in identifying the root word.

Vocabulary Worth Knowing and Understanding

closed syllable: A syllable that ends with a consonant (CVC pattern) and usually has a short vowel sound. Examples: *can/ter* and *but/ler*.

multisyllabic words: Words with more than one syllable; these can often be challenging to readers.

open syllable: A syllable that ends with a vowel (CV or V pattern) that usually has a long vowel sound. Examples: *ba/by* and *a/way*.

structural analysis: The ability to look at words and analyze them through word parts and their meanings.

syllabication: The act of dividing words into syllables.

Basic Syllabication Rules

Reminder: A syllable contains one vowel sound, an affix is a prefix or suffix, and a root word contains meaning.

Knowing where to break words into syllables can help with identifying different parts of a word, and in discerning the word's pronunciation through accented and unaccented syllables. There is a syllable for every vowel sound.

The following are the basic syllabication rules—but remember, language rules often have exceptions. The following rules stem from the six basic syllable types: open, closed, "r"-controlled, VCe, vowel teams (digraphs and diphthongs), and consonant-le.

- When two consonants are consecutive, with a vowel before and afterward, the word is divided between the two consonants. Examples: *but/ton, muf/fin, mar/ket, bas/ket.* The first syllable is usually accented.

- If there is only one consonant between two vowels, divide the word after the first vowel. Examples: *ta/ken, bi/son, de/clare, fu/tile.* The first syllable is usually accented.

- When dividing words into syllables, keep consonant blends and digraphs together. Examples: *to/geth/er, ful/crum, mi/grate, friend/ship.*

- Vowel digraphs and diphthongs are never separated. Examples: *beat/er, oil/er, joy/ous.*

- The consonant-le portion at the end of a word has its own syllable. Examples: *ba/gle, man/tle, fid/dle.* The consonant-le syllable is unaccented.

- VCe makes its own syllable, usually at the end of the word. Examples: *com/plete, graph/ite.*

- Affixes have their own syllable or syllables. Examples: *re/make, cook/ing, in/ter/lock, pre/tend/ing.* The root word is usually accented.

- Do not separate part of a compound word into syllables unless the part contains more than one syllable. Examples: *grass/hop/per, fin/ger/nails, house/keep/er.*

Checking Your Understanding

Divide the following into syllables per the basic syllabication rules. Note that some of these words follow more than one rule.

1. graphite
2. tablespoon
3. pealing
4. transatlantic

5. pattern
6. subtle
7. cashew
8. casino

Answers:
1. *graph/ite* (digraph *ph* together or *ite* VCe)
2. *ta/ble/spoon* (open syllable, *ble*)
3. *peal/ing* (one vowel sound)
4. *trans/at/lan/tic* (VC pattern, separate between two consonants)
5. *pat/tern* (separate between two consonants)
6. *sub/tle* (consonant-le)
7. *cash/ew* (blend)
8. *ca/si/no* (CV pattern; one vowel sound)

Instructional Strategies for Building and Extending Vocabulary

Vocabulary is the crux of comprehension. (If you don't know what *crux* means, you may not understand this statement's full meaning. Crux means "the root of.") Readers need to know words to understand what they read, but more importantly, readers need to know how to figure out the meaning of words in text.

In teaching vocabulary, the teacher's role is to: (1) teach targeted vocabulary words explicitly, (2) teach students dictionary skills to look up words, (3) teach structural analysis, and (4) teach students strategies to figure out unknown words in text.

Selecting Vocabulary to Be Taught

Words that will be taught need to be selected using the following criteria:

- Be central to concepts within the text.
- Not be defined within the text. (Informational texts are an exception, as the concepts need to be discussed.)
- Occur in the text in a way in which the meaning cannot be discerned from the context.
- Will most likely be seen in other texts, and are not isolated, oddly used words.

Education authors Isabel Beck, Margaret McKeown, and Linda Kucan developed a relatively easy path for selecting targeted vocabulary. Their three-tier method of selection is recommended by the Common Core State Standards. This method is described in the following table. *Note:* Beck, McKeown, and Kucan recommend that only tiers two and three be taught.

Selecting Words to Teach: Three Tiers of Vocabulary

Tier	Description	Examples
Tier 1: Do Not Teach	Basic words—words that children are familiar with	*table, crayon, coat, jump, goat, room*
Tier 2: Teach	High-frequency words that are more difficult than basic words	*logical, basically, intertwine, absurd, relevant, significance*
Tier 3: Teach	Domain-specific vocabulary (content area words with content area definitions)	*peninsula, photosynthesis, isosceles, the Great Depression* (of the 1930s)

EXCEPTIONS: Basic words need to be taught to beginning readers for word identification so that the young readers can recognize them in print, but a teacher does not need to elaborate on the definitions. There is an exception for English Language Learners (ELLs). For example, although ELLs may know the word *table* in their own language (in Spanish, *mesa*), the word *table* would be new to them as an English word, so the word meaning would have to be introduced to the ELL student.

Explicit Teaching of Targeted Vocabulary Words

There are numerous variations on how to explicitly teach vocabulary. The commonalities are as follows:

- The word must be visible (i.e., on a word card, chart, or whiteboard).
- Either the students can try to pronounce the word or the teacher can say the word, but the correct pronunciation must be given.
- The word must be used in context so that readers can learn to use context. The context in which the word is used should provide the same meaning as in the text. For instance, when teaching the word *bank,* as in the *bank of a creek,* the teacher should use a sentence like, "He slid down the bank of the creek into the water." (not "He took money out of the bank.").
- Students should be exposed to new words multiple times so that they will "own" the word.
- Reinforcement—students should practice using the word in context through writing, speaking, and games.

Structural Analysis: Using Root Words or Base Words

Although the terms *root word* and *base word* are often used interchangeably, they are technically different. A base word is a standalone word that can have affixes added (*bike* → *biker*). A root word carries meaning; it can be a standalone word, but it also may be dependent on affixes for clear meaning, such as *aqua* and *aquarium*. Root words contain meaning. According to *The Literacy Dictionary: The Vocabulary of Reading and Writing* (Harris, 1995), root words can be base words like *alter* in *altercation,* or they can be word pieces that must be connected (bound) to another word, such as *liter* in *literature*. Some resources will identify the word *alter* as a base word, and *liter* (when in *literature*) as a root word. Knowing the meanings of root and base words enables readers to recognize small parts in a larger word, which can help them identify and understand unknown words.

Etymology, the history of words, plays an important part in structural analysis. Students learn that words come from Greek or Latin beginnings, and contain meanings similar to their original use. Etymology is interesting and useful in the elementary and early childhood classrooms. It is a great tool for word study, helping students to remember new words and to expand their vocabulary.

Students must be able to figure out some very general etymologies of Greek and Latin roots. In addition, it would be helpful to discern whether a word has a root. For example, the Latin root *cent* means "one hundred," and helps in understanding such words as *centipede* and *century*. Yet, this would not help in understanding the word *scent,* because in this case the word *scent* is a base word itself and has no history with the Latin root *cent,* although it does contain *cent*. Additionally, compound words are usually composed of two base words, such as *snowman, baseball,* and *keyboard,* and can be analyzed by structure.

There are numerous sites online that list Latin and Greek words, their meanings, and their word derivatives. The following chart is a very small sample of common roots.

Examples of Latin and Greek Root Words

Latin Root Words		
Root	**Meaning**	**Derivatives**
aqua	water	*aquarium, aquamarine, aquatic*
fract	to break	*fracture, fraction*
port	to carry	*portable, airport*
multi	many	*multitude, multiply, multiuse*
rupt	to break	*rupture, corrupt, bankrupt*
Greek Root Words		
Root	**Meaning**	**Derivatives**
morph	form, shape	*morpheme, metamorphosis, amorphous*
phon	sound	*homophone, phonics, telephone, phonograph*
graph	writing	*graphics, photograph*
dia	across, through	*diagonal, diameter, diagnosis*
logy	study of	*biology, psychology*

Structural Analysis: Using Affixes

Affixes have their own meaning, and also can come from Greek or Latin roots, such as the Latin *inter,* which means "between," or the Greek *hemi,* which means "half." The chart below lists common affixes used at the elementary level and their meanings. (Numerous lists of affixes and their meanings can be found online.)

Common Affixes

Common Prefixes		
Prefix	**Meaning**	**Examples**
re-	to do again	*remake, redo, rewrite*
pre-	before	*prefix, preview, prewriting*
un-	not	*unlike, unnecessary, unkind*
in-, im-	not	*impossible, improbable, inconsistent*
Common Suffixes		
Suffix	**Meaning**	**Examples**
-able	to be done	*comfortable, manageable, accomplishable*
-er	one who	*baker, worker, writer*
-less	without	*guiltless, fruitless, fearless*
-ness	state or condition of	*happiness, fondness, likeness*

Teaching Structural Analysis

Structural analysis is taught by using word parts and by teaching similarities in meanings between words using the same base word, root, or affix. Students need to know that base words, roots, suffixes, and prefixes have meaning, and that affixes can change the meaning of an original root or base word. Structural analysis instruction can be directed in a variety of ways:

- Teach the meaning of the base words, roots, and affixes.
- When reading a book aloud or working with a group, discuss words with roots and affixes.
- Explicitly show how affixes can change word meanings (e.g., *like, unlike, dislike, likeable*).
- In a game format, build words using different roots and affixes.
- Make a "word tree" by building onto the root word. Cite derivatives, how they may change from the original spelling, and how word parts can change the meaning. For example, the root *port,* which means "to carry," has these derivatives: *deport, import, portable, portage, deportation, importation, important,* etc.

Strategies for Using Context Cues

Wide reading means reading a great number of books on a variety of topics. Children learn most of their vocabulary words through wide reading. How can that be? Using the cueing systems, children are able to figure out unknown words. They use phonics to try to sound the words out. Then they are asked to see if they can figure out the words through context—by what the sentence (or pictures) tells them. Finally, they use syntax; for example, they will read "a house" instead of "a houses" because they understand the structure of our language. Consider the following scenarios:

A first-grade student does not recognize the word *bus,* and sees the following sentence in a book: "The children rode a bus to school." First, the student tries to sound out *bus,* but gives it the long /u/ sound, and the sentence doesn't make sense. Rereading the sentence, the student realizes that it is something the children rode to school, so then he pronounces it correctly. Although the word ends in "s," the student knows the word is not *buses* because it is preceded by the word *a,* indicating that the next word is singular.

A fifth-grade student does not recognize the word *originals* in the following sentence in a book about Van Gogh: "Although there are thousands of copies of Van Gogh's art, the majority of originals are now in museums." First, the student tries to sound it out. Using phonics, the student gets the *or,* but says "gin" with a long /i/ sound, and leaves off the "s." Realizing what he read does not make sense, the student goes back to the beginning of the sentence. Once he rereads "thousands of copies," he realizes, through semantics, that the author must be using the word *original.* Finally, as he rereads the rest of the sentence, he also sees that *originals* is plural and corrects his miscue.

Strategic readers use context cues continually, and, therefore, increase their vocabulary through wide reading.

The teacher's role is teaching students, through modeling and thinking out loud, how to use context to figure out unknown words. Questioning can also assist students in learning these words. The following are questions that students can ask themselves, or that teachers can ask to guide students to decipher unknown words.

Guided questions for developing readers: (The unknown word is indicated in italics.)

- Can you make out the beginning sound? The ending sound? The middle sound?
  Example: The hat *blew* in the wind and went on the grass. (/bl-oo/)

- Read past the word you don't know, and see if you can figure out what it is.
  Example: The dog *jumped* up and barked loudly. (the word *up* should help the student figure out *jumped*)

- Chunk the word to see if you can figure it out.
  Example: He went *upstairs* to get his new truck. (cover *up* to read *stairs;* cover *stairs* to read *up*)

- Are there any pictures on the page that could help you think of what the word is?
  Example: The sentence says, "There are cookies on the *table.*" The picture shows a plate of cookies on a table; therefore, the child can look at the picture and see the cookies and the table.

- Are there words in the sentence that can help you figure out the unknown word?
  Example: The sentence says, "The *monkey* ate the banana." The sentence talks about a living thing eating a banana; through semantics, the child would realize it must be a monkey.

- Does the unknown word have a particular function?
  Example: The sentence says, "The *alarm* buzzed and woke up the girl." The reader does not know the word *alarm,* but as he reads the context of something that buzzed and woke up the girl, he realizes through meaning that the word must be *alarm.*

Questions for intermediate readers: (The unknown word is indicated in italics.)

- Are there any parts of the word that you recognize?
  Example: The guide pointed to the northern *hemisphere.* (*hemi* = half; *sphere* = ball)

- Do any words in the sentence give you a hint of what the word may mean? (If not, go to a dictionary.)
  Example: The buttons on the *remote* won't change the channels. (*change channels→remote*)

- Can you categorize or group the word with other things or animals?
  Example: I need pencils, paper, and *crayons* for school. (school supplies→*pencil, paper→crayons*)

- Does the sentence contain a problem and/or solution?
  Example: The young boy needed *glue* to fix his broken plane. (*fix broken plane→glue*)

- Is there a definition in the sentence? (often given as an appositive)
  Example: My *cosmetologist,* a hairdresser, is the nicest person. (*hairdresser* is a type of *cosmetologist*)

- Can you identify something that directs you toward something opposite?

  Example: That island is so small to have such a *gigantic* mountain. (*small→gigantic*)

- Can you tell what the unknown word does?

  Example: The *telephone* kept ringing and ringing. (the *telephone* rings)

- Are there familiar cues that can help you figure out the new word?

  Example: The huge dog, a German *shepherd,* tried to jump onto my lap! (*dog, German*→leads to *shepherd*)

Working with Homographs and Their Pronunciation

As stated earlier in this chapter, homographs are words that are spelled the same, but have multiple meanings and may not be pronounced the same (Examples: *fair, bow, desert, minute*). Students need to be taught about homographs and that, although they are spelled the same, they may not sound the same or have the same meaning. Teachers often talk about words with multiple meanings. In the case of homographs, the focus is on words that are spelled the same, may sound differently, and have different meanings. Some common homographs found at the elementary school level include *lead, wind, wound,* and *desert.*

It is best to teach homographs in context, when a more common meaning is expected. However, the following mini-lesson may also prove helpful:

1. Give the definition of *homograph,* and tell students you will work with some examples.
2. Introduce the words one at a time. (Example: *wind* means fast-blowing air.)
3. Use the word in a sentence. (Example: The *wind* blew my hat off my head.)
4. Introduce the second word. (Example: *wind* means to make tighter, or twist)
5. Use the second word in a sentence. (Example: The man had to *wind* the clock.)
6. Discuss how the two words are spelled the same, but sound differently. Explain that when a student is reading, he may have to reread and use the context to make sure he has the correct pronunciation to correspond with the meaning in the sentence.
7. Share other examples, such as *lead, minute,* and *wound.*

Teaching the Use of Word Reference Materials

Many people believe that hard-copy dictionaries and thesauruses will go the way of the slide rule. (For those of you that have never heard of a slide rule, it is a manual calculator-like device that can perform multiplication, division, etc.) But, for young children, dictionaries are still in use, as are glossaries in textbooks. Therefore, it is important that students can still look up words alphabetically, and have knowledge of what word reference materials offer.

Using a Dictionary

Students should look up words in a dictionary when they have exhausted their word strategies and cannot figure out the meaning of an unknown word. Students need to be taught that a dictionary does more than give definitions. Teach the following dictionary functions:

- Guide words can be used to locate words alphabetically.
- The pronunciation key, located at the bottom of each page or at the beginning of the dictionary, can assist in determining the pronunciation of unknown words.
- There are multiple definitions for some words, and a student needs to figure out which one is being used in the text.
- Along with giving a word's meaning, the dictionary also provides the part or parts of speech, depending on how the word is being used.
- The dictionary offers derivatives, such as past tense, plurals, and other word forms.

For students to get the full benefits of a dictionary, they need to explore it. Teachers should point out each feature and explain its use. Students need to be guided through practice. For example, they may use the guide words to look up a word, and state the page the word is on; identify the meaning in a sentence you give them; and identify the part of speech, and so forth. (*Note:* For very young students, "dictionaries" are picture dictionaries.)

Using a Glossary

A glossary, a short dictionary-like feature at the end of a content textbook or trade book, is much easier to use than a dictionary. (*Note:* The term trade book is used for regular library-type books, to differentiate these books from textbooks.) The definition given in a glossary coincides with the word's use in the book. The pronunciation is usually done in a "readable" fashion, not with a pronunciation key. A glossary is shorter, and does not usually give the part of speech.

When teaching students how to use a glossary, focus on the one meaning given, as the meaning will be domain-specific and, therefore, very important to the content being taught. As an example, the word *shuttle,* in its most common use, is to take someone or something back and forth (Example: We will take the hotel *shuttle* from the airport.). But in science, the term *space shuttle* refers to a rocket-launched type of spaceship. And, in industry, the word *shuttle* means a device that is pointed on both ends and used in weaving cloth.

Using a Thesaurus

A thesaurus is a book that gives a list of words that are similar in meaning.

Teachers use thesauruses in the classroom to expand vocabulary. Students often use a thesaurus to find a new, longer word that would be the best fit and, perhaps, impress the teacher. This doesn't always work. One child, choosing from an online word synonym list, once mistakenly used the word *delicacy* to describe an expensive pair of soccer shoes. It is important to model the proper use of the thesaurus to students and explain that words come with "environments" and are often used in particular situations. The word *delicacy* does mean "the best," but usually in relation to food or luxury items.

Using Online Resources to Build Word Knowledge

Most of you reading this book will be very familiar with online resources. But knowing how to use online resources effectively to teach children is different.

- Children can disregard alphabetical order when using an online dictionary. Be specific in recommending the dictionary source. Some "children's dictionaries" online do not offer definitions that are simple enough for young children to read independently and understand.

- Some apps will pronounce the word orally along with giving the definition. Be aware that apps from England or Australia will contain a different accent, so pick carefully.

- There are some excellent children's thesauruses online. Some state the word, such as *exciting,* and give pictures depicting similar words, like *inspiring, fascinating,* and *thrilling.* These pictures place the similar-meaning words in a context that aids students in gaining a better idea of the correct usage.

- Use online sources to make your own resource to build word knowledge. There are many short videos online showing actions. It could take less classroom time to show a 30-second action video than it might take to describe a difficult word's meaning. In addition, the visuals are extremely effective, especially for ELLs.

Chapter 6

Development of Reading Fluency

Fluency is more than just reading accurately and quickly, although that is the basic definition. A thorough definition of fluency also includes reading with expression, to show understanding.

Understanding Fluency

Think of the word *no* and how it can be expressed in numerous ways to give a different meaning. How does *no* sound when a parent is frustrated? When someone is surprised? When someone is joking? When someone says, "No, not happening." Although it's the same word, each of these scenarios has a tone and an expression that tell the listener more than just the word. In these cases, the expression used leads to understanding of the word's contextual meaning. A similar process happens during reading. If you can hear a child read with the right expression (surprise, joy, sadness, irritation), along with the expected grade-level reading rate and accuracy, you can designate him a fluent reader.

Vocabulary Worth Knowing and Understanding

accuracy: The percentage of words correct.

error: Although not a part of fluency per se, error indicates a misread word, and fluency is sometimes judged on words read correctly per minute instead of words read per minute.

prosody: The expression and intonation used in oral reading.

rate: The speed of reading, counted as words per minute (WPM) or words correct per minute (WCPM).

Reading Rate

Reading rate is the number of words read per minute and, in some assessments, the number of words read correctly per minute. Although being able to read fast is not a direct route to becoming an effective reader, reading at a good speed can aid in comprehension. If a child has to stop and decode frequently, the child is focusing less on comprehension because of the effort he must put into decoding. Knowing a huge bank of sight words and being able to decode with ease aids children in both fluency and comprehension. Having an idea of a child's reading rate helps a teacher monitor progress.

You do not need to memorize reading rates, but you should understand the basics:

- Silent reading rates are usually faster than oral reading rates. The exception is first grade, where many students subvocalize (so they are basically reading aloud).
- The average silent reading rate for first grade is around 60 WPM by the end of the year.
- The average silent reading rate for sixth grade is around 190 WPM.
- The average increase is 25 to 30 WPM each year.
- Fluent readers can concentrate on comprehending the text and not have to concentrate on decoding.

Fluency Activities

Fluency can be taught in a lot of fun and creative ways. Fluency activities should include repetition. Teachers build into instruction reasons for students to reread text in order to reinforce word recognition. In this way, students increase their sight word knowledge.

Fluency Activities

Activity	Description
Word sorts	Using word cards with selected words, students do a guided sort. Students may sort in ways that bring up the word meaning as they consistently reread words to select the correct ones. For example, students may sort the words *bacon, baby, beef,* and *butterfly* as words that begin with the letter "b." Then, the teacher may say to sort the words into food and living things, so the sort would now show the words *bacon* and *beef* in one pile and *baby* and *butterfly* in another. Changing the purpose of the sort forces students to reread the words as the categories are changed. For example, with just a single pile of words, students may be guided to sort as follows: • select the words that are nouns • select the words that show action (verbs) • select the words that are past tense (certain verbs) • select the words that describe (adjectives and adverbs) Students are rereading the words, reorganizing the pile, and thinking about the word's meaning each time they do a new sort.
Echo reading	Using a text that students can see, the teacher reads a line and has the students repeat. In this activity, the teacher models reading speed and expression. The students then "echo" the teacher's modeling.
Readers' Theater	This activity is typically a classroom favorite. Students are given characters in a story and parts they are to read, much like a "read like a character" activity. Since Readers' Theater is eventually "performed" in front of others, students must reread in order to practice saying their lines correctly and with the correct expression.
Choral reading	Choral reading can also be done for a performance. Children are grouped to practice a poem or short piece of text. They reread and work together, reading in unison and with expression. When the teacher deems them ready, the group chorally reads in front of the class. In addition, small groups of beginning or transitional readers can read short pieces of text together in reading groups and then discuss. This ensures that all students participate in the reading.
Wide reading and rereading	Frequent reading aids children in developing fluency. Wide reading has students reading a large number of books in a variety of genres. For beginning readers this would include predictable and repetitive books.
Taped reading	Students tape themselves reading, listen to the tape, and then try again to improve.
Timed readings	This works well with older students. A student times himself as he reads a selected piece, and then graphs the amount of time it took for him to read. Then the student times the reading as he rereads, and graphs the second reading and then a third. The student can tell by the graph that his time is improving with each reread.
Computer-assisted reading	A computer can be used to increase fluency in a variety of ways: • A student can read along orally as the computer reads. • In some computer programs, the student can click on unknown words and hear the pronunciation. • Some programs will move the text at a set speed, so a student is forced to read faster in order to read all the text.

Assessment of Accuracy: Running Records

Running records are informal assessments that allow teachers to assess children's reading level, accuracy, and rate (if wanted) in a natural setting. A teacher will sit next to a child who is reading his book. As the child reads orally, the teacher looks at the words and codes what the child says as he reads (see "Coding a Running Record," below). After the child reads, the teacher analyzes the miscues to set future goals for him. In some cases, the term running record is used when a child reads a passage or story, and the teacher has a copy of the story and writes the coding over the words. If the Praxis (5203) offers you a running record, you should be able to analyze it in order to determine what the child's further instruction should entail. A running record may give a hint of a child's understanding, but it is an evaluation of word and letter-sound accuracy, not comprehension. So the instructional level given indicates word recognition.

Coding a Running Record

Familiarize yourself with coding marks by reviewing the chart below. Coding is standardized to enable teachers to read and analyze any child's running record. The chart lists the main codes that are used for miscues. If a child repeats a word, called a repetition, it is not counted as an error. If a child makes an error and then corrects himself while reading, this is called a self-correction and also is <u>not</u> counted as an error.

Items to Be Coded	Coding (What the Teacher Writes)
Correct word	Makes a checkmark

Substitutes another word for a word in the text	Writes incorrect word over the correct word.
	
	    Reader says: **dram**
	    Text states: dream

Omits a word	Draws a line
	
	    Reader says: ———
	    Text states: horse

Inserts a word	Uses a caret (^) and writes word inserted
	
	                red
	    Reader says: ^
	    Text states: jump into the car

Is told a word	The child tries to pronounce the word, but gives up. The teacher may say the word, or tell the child to read on.
	
	    Reader says: **mo-mo**
	    Text states: The lion headed up the mountain.

Self-correction	SC (not counted as an error)
	    Reader says: **shine SC**
	    Text says: The sun shone brightly.

Repetition	R (not counted as an error)
	    Reader says: **crashed R**
	    Text says: The waves crashed against the rocks.

Analyzing the Running Record

Teachers need to be able to identify what the coding means in order to analyze the running record. In this analysis, the three cueing systems become very important for pinpointing a child's strengths and weaknesses. In addition, when analyzing a running record, it is extremely important to look for patterns in what the child gets correct, and in what the child gets incorrect, as well as what cues the reader used when making the miscue. These patterns enable the teacher to recognize strengths and weaknesses. If a child gets a particular item incorrect once, it is not necessarily a weakness.

Phonology (Visual) Errors

Phonology errors focus on errors made with letter-sound correspondence and accurate pronunciation of words. Things to think about include the following: Are the child's mistakes due to errors in how the word is said? Is there a pattern to the errors? Some common phonology error patterns that may be found in running records are:

- **phonemes:** Letter sounds—initial, medial, and/or final.
- **affixes:** Prefixes or suffixes. Examples: *re- return, rewrite, redo; -ing bending, licking, ducking.*
- **diphthongs:** Blending vowel sounds for words with "oy," "oi," "ou,"and so forth. Examples: *ouch, boy, oil.*
- **digraphs:** Two vowels or consonants together that make one sound. Examples: <u>*bea*</u>*t*, *p*<u>*ai*</u>*l* (vowels); *tou*<u>*gh*</u>, <u>*graph*</u> (consonants).
- **compound words:** Two words combined to form a new word. Examples: *lighthouse, shoebox.*
- **homophones:** Words that have the same sound and might confuse meaning. Examples: *hear, here; byte, bite.*
- **multisyllabic words:** Words with more than one syllable. Examples: *mountainous, important.*
- **chunking:** In chunking, the reader can read smaller sections or pieces of the word, then blend them together to read the word correctly. Example: *im-por-tant.*
- **sight words:** Frequently used words that readers should memorize. Examples: *was, the, in, they, saw.*

Semantics (Meaning) Errors

Semantic errors occur when a reader incorrectly reads a word and replaces it with a word that does not make sense in the sentence. Things to think about include the following: Are the child's mistakes due to not knowing a word's meaning? Does the child make errors that do not make sense? For example, a child might read the sentence "The bird flew into its nest" as "The bird found into its nest." This makes no sense, and thereby it is a semantic error.

- **Context cues:** Using the known words within the text to identify unknown words. There are two types of context cue errors:
    - Error from not using context cues: The child makes an error that makes absolutely no sense with respect to the sentence or paragraph.

      Example: The child reads, "He rode the blue *bunk,*" but the text states, "He rode the blue *bike.*"

      In this case, the child is not using metacognition; he is not aware of whether or not he is understanding. Metacognition is defined as thinking about thinking. He does pick up the visual cue of "b" and says that phonically, but just replaces it with a word that begins with that sound.
    - Error from using context cues but not phonics: The child makes a miscue, but it still makes sense in the sentence or paragraph. In this case, the error is not terribly bad, but if it happens too often it could confuse the child.

      Example: The child reads, "The little girl held the *bunny* in her lap," but the text states, "The little girl held the *rabbit* in her lap."

      In this case, the teacher recognizes that although there is a phonological error, the child is using semantic (meaning) cues and metacognition.
- **Synonyms:** Words that mean the same.

    Examples: The child reads *home* for *house, feeling sad* for *feeling blue, sloppy* for *messy.*
- **Omission:** The child omits words from the text. There are two types of omission errors:
    - Omission with meaning change: A word is left out, and the meaning is changed.

      Example: The child reads, "The mosquito itched, and I stopped to scratch it," but the text states, "The mosquito *bite* itched, and I stopped to scratch it."
    - Omission without meaning change: A word is left out, but what is read basically retains the same meaning as in the text.

Example: The child reads, "The skirt went down past the girl's ankles," but the book states, "The *long* skirt went down past the girl's ankles."

- **Self-monitoring:** The child recognizes that he has made an error in either phonics, semantics, or syntax—all of which are tied to meaning. If the child does a lot of self-correcting, then he is self-monitoring, because he realizes that what he just read doesn't make sense (once again using metacognition). This pattern could be considered a strength.

  Example: The child reads, "We had fried cherries for supper." Then he corrects *cherries* to *chicken,* as that makes more sense in the context. If the child does not make this change, he is not self-monitoring (checking his understanding.)

Syntax (Structure) Errors

Syntax involves using the structure of language to aid in identifying unknown words. The structure of language is usually well known to a child by age 5. So, when reading, unless there is a local or cultural dialect, children should be able to recognize when a syntactic error has been made.

Example: The child reads, "The bird *fly* to its nest," but the text states, "The bird *flew* to its nest."

Running Record and Analysis

This section will give a short running record example and an analysis. The words that have miscues are in italics to help you for this practice. In the following running record, the dash between the student-read words means a second syllable. The text is the plain print, with the words missed in italics. The student miscues, as the child read the words, are in bold.

Running Record Example

walk-ed   **tap-ed**

Matt and Emma had *walked* to the park with their mother. Matt *tapped* Emma on the shoulder and

turn-ed

said, "Look," as he *turned* his head to face behind them. To Emma's surprise, there was a puppy

following them.

yell-ed

"Here, puppy, here," *yelled* Emma as she stopped to let the puppy catch up. When Emma bent down,

lick-ed

the little puppy *licked* her hand.

holler-ed

All of a sudden, a little boy came running from around the bush and *hollered* with delight, "I found

clip-ed

him! I found him!" He *clipped* a leash on the puppy's collar, thanked Emma for finding his puppy,

and headed back the way he came.

grin-ed   **sh-sh d**

Matt and Emma *grinned* at each other and *shrugged* their shoulders.   (117 words)

Analysis

Note: This analysis has been written as an essay question response.

The code marks on this running record show both a strength and a weakness for this child.

This child has strong word-identification skills in the area of phonology. The child did not make any errors in identifying individual or cluster letter sounds, even in the words that received miscues. The child was able to pronounce without trouble the majority of the words in the passage, including the following multisyllabic words: *shoulder, surprise, following, sudden, running,* and *around.* Words with errors, such as *walked* and *tapped,* had their base words pronounced correctly.

This child shows a weakness in the pronunciation of the suffix "-ed." This passage had nine errors, and in eight of them, the child pronounced the "-ed" as a second syllable. The child was able to read *thanked* correctly, possibly due to the frequent use of the word *thanked.* The child also correctly read the word *headed,* as the "-ed" is correct as a second syllable in this particular word. The child needs instruction on the pronunciations of the suffix "-ed." The child needs to learn that "-ed" has three pronunciations: (1) as a /d/ as in *played,* (2) as a /t/ as in *kicked,* and (3) as an "id" sound, as in *headed,* which he read correctly in this passage. The child did not correctly read the words *walked, tapped, turned, yelled, licked, hollered, clipped, grinned,* and *shrugged.* All of these words, with the exception of *shrugged,* showed a miscue with "-ed" pronunciations.

Reading Level

Running records can also be used to tell whether a text is too easy, too hard, or "just right" for a child. This is determined by the percentage of words read correctly. The expected reading level percentages are defined as follows:

Independent: 95–100% correct (This text is too easy for the child.)

Instructional: 90–94% correct (This text is considered the "just right" level for learning to read.)

Frustration: 89% or below correct (This text is too hard, and is not the optimal learning level for the child.)

In the running record on page 41, there are 117 words and nine errors. That means the student read 108 out of 117 words correctly, or $\frac{108}{117} = 0.92$ or 92%. Therefore, the percentage correct in this running record was 92%, which means this text is in the child's instructional or "just right" level.

Reading Speed

A running record can also be used to time readers. Reading speed can be assessed by timing the reader for 1 minute. When 1 minute is up, put a mark on the word the reader was on. Then count the number of words the reader read in that 1-minute time period to get his word-per-minute rate.

Checking Your Understanding

For practice, try analyzing the running record below. The idea at this point is not to write an essay-style response, but to analyze. Look for a strength and a weakness, and be able to state what the child needs to work on (set a goal). Again, the words with the miscues are in italics to help you with this practice; what the child said is in bold. See if your analysis matches the suggested analysis.

> cooting
> Mia and her friends were playing hide and seek in Mia's backyard. Sarah was *counting* down from
>
> ran   enug
> ten as everyone *scattered* to hide. Mia ran past a small tree, not wide *enough* to hide her. She looked
>
> barl SC   ———
> behind the trash *barrel*, but Julia was *already* there. Another friend was behind the car. Mia was
>
> nervous   ——   numb SC   foond
> getting a bit *worried*. Sarah had *just* said the *number* three and Mia still hadn't *found* the place she
>
> carton
> wanted to hide. Then Mia saw the *container* that hid the hose. She ran quickly and hid behind it,
>
> as Sarah ran over to look behind the car. Mia knew she was safe!   (104 words)

Suggested Analysis:

There is often not one right analysis of a running record, even if you are asked to name just one strength or one weakness. What is important is what you determine to be the child's goals and how you support that finding.

A strength could be any of the following, as long as your answer is supported.

- Sight words: Child was able to read fluently because sight words such as *the, was, there,* and *then* were correct. This enables the child to focus on meaning.
- Reading for meaning: Although the child made errors, there were two self-corrections. The miscues (*ran* for *scattered, nervous* for *worried,* and *carton* for *container*) adhered to the sentence meaning. Finally, although two words were omitted (*already* and *just*), the sentences made sense without them.

A weakness could be one of the following, as long as your answer is supported.

- Vowel pairs: Three out of eight miscues were made with words that contain the "ou" vowel pair: *counting, enough,* and *found.* In *counting* and *found,* the "ou" is a diphthong, and a digraph in *enough.* The child needs to know that "ou" has more than one sound, and words need to be corrected if they don't make sense in the reading.
- Multisyllabic words: Of the eight miscues and two self-corrections, eight of the words had more than one syllable. The child needs to learn how to chunk a word into parts and to read the complete word.

What level (independent, instructional, or frustration) is this text for the child's reading?

There were eight miscues out of 104 words, meaning the student read 96 words correctly, or $\frac{96}{104} = 0.92$; therefore,

the child read with 92% accuracy. This means that this text was on the instructional, or "just right," level for the child according to word accuracy.

Chapter 7

Development of Reading Comprehension

Comprehension is the goal of reading and refers to the reader's ability to make meaning from text. A reader's comprehension can be deeply influenced by outside factors. When you view literacy from a linguistic, sociological, cultural, cognitive, and psychological perspective, you come to understand the reader as a "whole child," not just the body sitting before you trying to read. How a child is brought up; where a child is brought up; the child's experiences, economic status, cognitive abilities, and attitude—all of these contribute to whether the child is a struggling, grade-level, or advanced reader. Each of these aspects influences the child's growth as a reader in different ways.

Understanding Literacy Through Linguistic, Sociological, Cultural, Cognitive, and Psychological Influences

The five literary influences are described in detail below.

Linguistic Influences

In the broad sense, linguistics is the study of language. There are four different types of vocabulary: speaking, listening, reading, and writing. How many times have you gone to write a word and changed it because you were not sure of its spelling? That would be because your speaking vocabulary is larger than your writing vocabulary. Children enter school with different levels of vocabulary. Some students are stronger in oral language (or reading, writing, or listening) than others. Students with a strong oral language encounter fewer unknown vocabulary words in their reading than do students with a weak oral language.

Students' language experiences can affect their reading and writing in a variety of ways. With an English Language Learner (ELL), the repercussions are easily understood, as the language itself is new. With a native English speaker, the child's language experiences have less impact, and the child's need might be less noticeable. Some native English speakers come from homes where the parents do not speak English. In some states, that child is still given ELL status. Some students come from homes where the vocabulary used is not broad or repeatable; television consumes family time, and not many activities are offered that encourage language. On the other hand, there are students whose parents use and explain new vocabulary whenever possible, discuss daily news and events to broaden language and concepts, and focus on experiences that will immerse their child in vocabulary. When my 6-year-old son was asked what a square was, he described the carpenter's tool because at the time we were building our home and he was frequently handing his daddy "the square." Further expanding the range of language abilities in the classroom are children born with a language processing disorder, delaying their language development; such a disorder can also affect their growth in reading and writing. All of this is crucial because, as discussed in Chapter 3, "Oral Language Development," when children are exposed to and know a great deal of oral language, it highly impacts their reading.

Sociological Influences

Sociological influences include the child's economic status and his school district's economic status and culture. Both are described here.

- **Economic status:** Money buys food and healthcare, enriching experiences, and a lot more. When students are well fed and healthy, they can learn more easily. If a child comes from a home that can afford books, family field trips, and other luxuries, the child comes to school with a more than adequate background knowledge of both book-handling skills and vocabulary gained from those experiences. In addition, being dressed to a "peer norm" can boost his confidence, which can aid his academic performance.

- **School district:** Inequality between school districts exists. The economic status of the district and the culture within the district or classroom affects learning. School districts with strong pre-school intervention programs aid in setting up disadvantaged children to be more successful in school. The system's ability to supply the optimal in the following will enhance learning: supplies, traditional and technological learning materials, the learning environment, various school opportunities, teacher-pupil ratio, teacher professional development, etc. A well-run economically advantaged school district can make a difference in a child's learning.

Cultural Influences

Cultural influences can also impact literacy growth in children. The following have significant impact:

- **Class and race:** Class and race can either confer or limit privilege. Cultural beliefs strongly influence family culture and children's attitudes toward learning.
- **Language and dialect:** The educational concerns for ELL students have been discussed, but parents who speak another language may not be aware of what school districts offer; important advantages, such as early intervention, can be missed. Culturally influenced dialect can impact reading and writing. Standardized tests do not take dialect into consideration. Students will often write as they speak, and certain dialects do not follow traditional English.
- **Customs and traditions:** Being familiar with our culture aids in background knowledge and often deeper understanding when reading a story. A child from China will most likely construct deeper meaning of a story set in China than someone who has never been there. A goal of reading should be to let children "see themselves" in stories.
- **Family culture:** Family and peers have a culture that influences learning. Family culture encompasses family habits, rules, beliefs, roles, activities, and other areas of family life. Examples include reading to children, bed time, and family rules. A tired child does not learn well, and a child who is allowed to misbehave at home may be more likely to misbehave at school, affecting his learning and that of others.
- **Values:** If a family does not value education, they will be less likely to support a child's learning and habits that encourage learning.

Cognitive Influences

The pace of children's development is widely divergent. Cognitive influences include areas of thinking, ability to reason, and ability to understand. Cognitive processing matures with growth. A very young child thinks he can hide behind a thin pole, while a 6-year-old understands this is not possible. Cognitive development in each of the following areas affects learning:

- **Information processing:** The ability of a child to understand and categorize information.
- **Perceptual skills:** The ability to develop a mental image, or to see similarities and differences in objects.
- **Language processing:** The ability to receive information with correct understanding and then express it verbally.
- **Visual information processing:** The ability to make sense of images taken in by the eye.
- **Auditory processing:** How the brain interprets and understands information that is heard.
- **Working memory:** The ability to store and decipher information temporarily.
- **Attention span:** The amount of time a person can concentrate on the task at hand; this usually lengthens with age.

Psychological Influences

The mind-set of the learner and the perspectives the learner has on a wide range of areas vary with each individual and have a significant effect on learning. Some of these psychological areas, or influences, that can impact learning are:

- **Biases:** Having a bias against an idea or value can impact learning.
- **Motivation:** The goals, interests, and needs of a student can motivate him to try harder to achieve success in a particular task or can deter that success.

- **Attitude:** A student's position or feeling about learning. A "bad" attitude toward learning can negatively affect student growth, whereas a positive attitude toward learning enhances the learning experience and growth.

- **Self-esteem:** How a child feels about himself can affect his ability to learn.

- **Self-efficacy:** How a person views himself. A child who believes he is a good reader is more apt to become one. A child who views himself as a nonreader may have more difficulty learning to read.

- **Emotional conditions:** At some point in their lives, students may undergo trauma that makes conditions not conducive to learning. There are myriad reasons for a child to be upset, such as divorce, misunderstandings, punishment at home, violence in the house, death in the family, loss of a pet, or simply a bad morning because mom was having a bad hair day or couldn't find her car keys. At the opposite end of the spectrum, an impending trip to Disney World and the excitement it brings can also impede learning.

- **Level of learning activity and scaffolding:** If a child is frustrated and not well supported, he may develop attitudes and feelings that can impede learning.

- **Reaction to teachers:** Sometimes a child's emotional reaction to particular teachers can interfere with learning.

- **Environmental factors:** External noise or commotion can cause stress and disturb the learning process.

The Interactive Model of Reading

Readers bring different pieces of knowledge to what they read. As they read, they absorb the author's words and construct meaning from prior knowledge and experiences. The linguistic, sociological, cultural, cognitive, and psychological influences discussed in the previous section all impact what the reader brings to the text. In a scenario where a 6-year-old in Guam is reading *Snowy Day* by Ezra Keats, much more background building would be needed than for a 6-year-old in Alaska reading this book. On the other hand, if this 6-year-old moved to Alaska and then read a story about sea cucumbers, the Alaskan students' comprehension would be impacted, while the Guamanian could be perfectly comfortable with the story. If background building was not done, the Alaskan children would be wondering why a green cucumber grows in the sea, and if it could be eaten. On the other hand, the young Guamanian, now in Alaska, would remember fondly dodging these elongated, blackish sea creatures when swimming in the shallow waters in Guam. As you can see from this scenario, prior knowledge gleaned from experiences can impact reading comprehension.

Scaffolding reading experiences should be done with a three-tiered reading lesson: before reading, during reading, and post-reading. The lesson before reading may include activating prior knowledge, building background, teaching selected vocabulary, and predicting. This scaffolding allows students to begin the reading with enough preparation to fully comprehend the text. Students should be taught to activate their prior knowledge before reading any book, as thinking about the topic prior to reading has been shown to increase comprehension.

During reading lessons include purpose setting and the mode of reading. Purpose setting gives students a focus for reading, such as telling students to read to see if their predictions come true. Mode of reading defines how the students will read (partner, silently, and so forth).

Post-reading usually includes discussion questions and reader response. Discussion questions should be text dependent and help students get deeper meaning from the text. Reader response is an activity that reinforces what students have learned in the text.

Vocabulary Worth Knowing and Understanding

building background: When a teacher directly teaches, or has students work with materials that will increase their relevant knowledge, before reading a particular text. For example, if students were to read a text on the art of weaving, the teacher might share some artistic samples or have students weave from a shoe box loom.

interactive model of reading: This model posits that a reader comes to the text with prior knowledge and concepts that allow him to construct meaning while reading.

metacognition: Thinking about thinking. (Is the reader thinking about his understanding of the text as he reads?)

prior knowledge: The knowledge and beliefs that a reader brings to the text.

schema: A mental concept or generalization. This includes the concept of prior knowledge, but is much broader. Try this experiment: Think of your favorite chair. Where is it? What does it look like? Everyone has a mental concept of a chair. You may have thought of a rocking chair, a recliner, perhaps a couch—but because of schema, you did think of something that we sit on. Our schema allows us to think in general categories.

transactional theory of reading: This theory is the basis for the interactive model of reading. Louise Rosenblatt, who proposed the theory, found that a transaction occurs between reader and text, and that the reader constructs meaning through background knowledge and personal notions, making each reader's understanding unique.

Literal, Inferential, and Evaluative (Critical) Comprehension

Literal, inferential, and evaluative comprehension refer to the type of thinking that is needed to read and understand a text. The following passage will be used to explain these three terms.

> Kayla and Sarah were going to the beach. Kayla was a really good swimmer. Sarah was afraid of the water, but she wanted to be with her friend so she did not tell Kayla that she could not swim. When they got to the beach, Kayla ran into the water and yelled for Sarah to follow. Sarah put her feet in the water, but said she didn't want to get her whole body wet. Kayla yelled again, "Come on in!" Sarah said she wasn't feeling well, and sat down on the towel while Kayla went swimming. When Kayla got out of the water, Sarah said that now she felt fine, and the girls went for a walk down the beach.

Literal Comprehension

Literal comprehension means understanding what is explicitly stated in the text. This is sometimes called "reading by the line," and is text-dependent because the reader must read the text to state the fact. For example, the passage explicitly states that Kayla and Sarah were going to the beach. So, if the question is asked, "Where are Sarah and Kayla going?" the answer is literal and can be found directly stated in the text: "the beach." Literal questions are considered the easiest to answer, as they require minimal thinking. Consider the question "Who went swimming?" Again, this is a literal question with a "right there" answer; the text states, "Kayla went swimming." Literal questions are text-dependent.

Inferential Comprehension

Inferential comprehension means understanding what is inferred or implied in the text. This is sometimes called "reading between the lines," because the idea or statement is not right there. Inference questions are considered text-dependent because information from the text must be used to answer questions. To answer an inference question, the reader must take what the author states and what he, the reader, already knows, in order to make the proper inference. When answering inference questions, a reader must use prior knowledge and schema along with text information to get the correct answer. Using the above passage, one inference question might be "How did Sarah feel about going to the beach?" The answer depends on the reader's interpretation of the text—what the text says and what the reader, through prior experiences, thinks is happening. The answer could be "Sarah is excited because she will be with her friend." Or "Sarah is uncomfortable because Kayla probably thinks she likes to swim." Another inference question could be "Did Sarah really not feel well? Explain your answer." Again, answers could vary, depending on the reader's background and cognitive abilities. Someone with a literal interpretation may say, "Yes, because she went and sat on the towel." Others who are reading between the lines may say, "No, she was hiding the fact that she is afraid of the water," or "No, she didn't want Sarah to know that she couldn't swim, and she felt fine when Sarah came out of the water." Inference questions are also text-dependent.

Evaluative Comprehension

Evaluative comprehension is making a judgment about what is said in the text or about the text, such as when the reader has an opinion, a favorite, or a dislike. In some way, the reader is placing a value on what is being said. The reader needs to both know the facts and have some sense of opinion, value, or background on the experience being evaluated. Using the above passage, one evaluative question might be "Was it fair of Sarah not to tell Kayla that she was afraid of the water?" Some might answer yes, as Sarah wanted to be with her friend. Others might say it was not fair because Kayla should have been able to play in the water with the friend she brought to the beach. Another evaluative question might be "In your opinion, was it right of Sarah to lie to her friend?" Some might say, "No, she should have been honest and said she was afraid of the water." Others might say, "Yes, being afraid of the water is embarrassing." Evaluative questions may not be text-dependent; being able to answer these questions takes critical comprehension.

Author's Note: Although the Praxis (5203) objectives do not refer directly to the evaluative comprehension question type, since it is not always text-dependent, you should be able to recognize it if you come across one. There is one type of question referred to as *scriptal* in the *No Child Left Behind* booklet. This is a "beyond the line" question, which means a child can answer the question without having read the text. Two examples of a scriptal question using the above passage are "What do you like to do at the beach?" and "Tell me about a time you have been at the beach." These questions help children make a connection to the passage, but a teacher cannot use them to evaluate the child's comprehension of the reading material. Scriptal questions are not text-dependent.

Checking Your Understanding

Read the passage below and the six questions that follow. Identify each question as asking for literal, inferential, or evaluative thinking.

> Noah rushed into the classroom, promising himself he would never be so stupid again. He had just walked by Ava, and had wanted to ask her to hang out after school. She was standing there talking to her friends. So, he snuck up and playfully pinched her arm. She turned around and stuck her tongue out at him, and her friends laughed. He just foolishly grinned, and then took off fast. Man, did he feel like an idiot.

1. Why did Noah pinch Ava's arm?
2. Was it right of Noah to pinch Ava?
3. Why did Ava stick out her tongue at Noah?
4. How did Noah feel?
5. Do you think it was a good idea for Ava to stick out her tongue? Explain.
6. What did Ava's friends do when she stuck her tongue out at Noah?

Answers:
1. Inferential
2. Evaluative
3. Inferential
4. Literal
5. Evaluative
6. Literal

Independent Reading

Independent reading is when students are reading apart from the teacher, in or outside of school. Many primary classrooms have color-coded baskets so that students can choose their "just right" books for independent reading. Fostering independent reading is important because:

- wide reading builds vocabulary, fluency, and comprehension.
- it develops interest in reading, and reinforces reading as a habit.
- it allows students more time to practice their reading skills.
- it allows students to be exposed to a variety of topics.
- reading more books helps build the background for more complicated books.

Promoting Independent Reading in the Classroom

When teachers foster independent reading, they get students to read more. Research has shown that this, in turn, improves reading achievement.

Ways independent reading can be promoted in the classroom:
- Create a literacy-rich classroom environment. Supply plenty of books in pleasant displays.
- Read aloud daily, if possible, to the class, and encourage students to read the book on their own.
- Do book talks that get your students excited about reading books you have available.
- Lay books out so that students can see their covers; this draws the students' interest, making them more likely to pick up the books and read.
- Let your students see you reading.
- Set aside classroom time for free reading.
- Get students interested in series books, so that they will want to read the next one. (The Harry Potter books are an example of a series; students will read the first book, get to know the characters, and become hooked to read the next one.)
- When a student discusses a book he liked, recommend another one like it.
- Have students work on small projects such as video teasers to promote books to each other.
- Share a variety of genres with the class; this encourages students to read different types of books.

Family and Community Involvement

Independent reading outside of school also improves reading achievement. The more teachers, parents, and the community can work together to encourage children to read, the better readers the children will become.

Encouraging family involvement:
- Create child and parent book clubs.
- Encourage parents to give books as gifts.
- Recommend that an allotted reading time become a routine in family life.
- Encourage parents to read with their children and to ask questions as they read.
- Hold "literacy nights" at your school (pajama party, author visits, and so forth).
- Hold a Dr. Seuss (or other author) celebration and invite parent readers.
- Invite parents into your classroom as "mystery readers."
- Encourage families to visit the library.

Encouraging community involvement:

- Form a partnership with the town library.
- Use community resources as incentives to get children to read.
- Invite guest readers from the community.
- Search for resources that can provide free books to the school and children.
- Use organizational motivators such as "Get Caught Reading" and "Read Across America."

Chapter 8
Reading Comprehension Strategies Across Text Types

Understanding and Promoting Reading a Variety of Genres

A genre is a category of literary work, characterized by similarities in form, content, and writing technique or formulas. Genres are further identified through specific literary devices, such as a mystery having clues leading up to the solution or a fairy tale beginning with "Once upon a time" and ending with "They lived happily ever after." Genres can be defined very broadly, transcending book types. A letter, a poster, or even a website may be considered a genre because each is a specific writing/reading product. New genres emerge, such as nonfiction mixed with fiction and, thanks to advances in technology, graphic media mixed with printed text.

Things to consider when teaching genre:

- There are different genres written for different purposes.
- Students need to be exposed to a variety of genres, each of them multiple times.
- Teachers use "mentor texts" (texts that model good genre writing) to teach genres and writing.
- Teachers need to identify and discuss the uniqueness of each genre.
- Genre knowledge helps readers predict and navigate the text for needed information.
- Different genres can require different styles and speed in reading.
- Knowing characteristics from a particular genre will aid in writing in the genre.
- Authors choose the genre that will best fulfill their writing purpose.
- Authors can use genre to influence the reader, such as the persuasive genre or deciding what to include or not include in a person's biography.
- Reading one genre can influence the comprehension of another. For example, pairing a historical fiction with an informational text about the same time period enables students to have a much deeper understanding of both texts.

Students can be taught genre in two different ways: explicit teaching or inquiry learning. In explicit teaching, the teacher names and explains the genre, such as a biography, a story of someone's life. The teacher reads or assigns biographies to be read, discusses the characteristics for these biographies, and has students apply that knowledge. With inquiry learning, the whole class reads books from the same genre, such as memoir. With teacher guidance, students discuss what characteristics are similar about memoirs (all really happened; it's a written memory of an event or series of events). Students apply this new knowledge in some way.

Common genres and their characteristics are detailed in the table that follows. Not all genres are listed, but popular text genres used in classrooms are included.

> **HINT: You don't need to memorize the following table for the Praxis (5203), but do familiarize yourself with these genres, know that authors use different genres for different purposes, and understand that genre study is important in teaching both reading and writing.**

Common Genres and Characteristics

Genre	Characteristics
Realistic fiction	Stories that could actually take place. Examples include romance, satire, drama, action and adventure, horror, thriller, tragedy, and so forth.
Historical fiction	Fictional characters and a true historical setting. Examples includes historical pieces.
Mystery	Involves some sort of wrongdoing. The genre ordinarily has clues that can lead the reader to the solution.
Fantasy	Involves occurrences and/or creatures that do not exist. The genre ordinarily includes strange and imaginary characters.
Fairy tale	Begins with "Once upon a time…" and ends with "They lived happily ever after." The genre frequently includes magic.
Myth	Story told as if it were fact, and explains a natural phenomenon and teaches a lesson.
Fable	An imaginary short story that has a moral. The genre ordinarily has two to three animals as the main characters.
Legend	Story that may be based on fact. When the genre alludes to a historical truth, it includes imaginary events as well as heroes whose great deeds are exaggerated.
Tall tale	Story that is exaggerated with humor. Examples include heroes that can perform the impossible.
Poetry	Verse that comes in a multitude of subgenres within this genre. Examples include couplets, free verse, haiku, concrete, diamante, and so forth.
Graphic novel	Written with pictures and dialogue.
Expository (nonfiction)	True information, usually focused on a topic or theme.
Narrative	A story that may or may not be fact-based.
Personal narrative (nonfiction)	Fact-based written memoir. This is ordinarily an essay-like piece on an incident that occurred in the writer's life.
Persuasive	Contains convincing and believable statements that are meant to persuade the reader to agree with the author's viewpoint.
How-to	Practical advice. The genre ordinarily consists of directions on how to create or assemble a product or an explanation about how to perform a task.
Biography/autobiography	Writings about a person's life, events, important incidents, inventions, and so forth. In the case of an autobiography, the author is writing about herself.
Descriptive text within genres	A structure within genres. No matter the content, the genre includes very detailed text that carefully describes a person, place, thing, or event. The text ordinarily contains specifically chosen adjectives and uses attributes such as qualities, characteristics, and parts.

Selecting Literature to Promote Reading Growth

To promote reading growth, there are a number of areas teachers should consider. Four factors are discussed here. First, teachers should consider each student's instructional or "just right" reading level. The "just right" level is defined as when the student can read 90% to 94% of the text correctly (89% and below is too difficult; 95% and above is too easy). These percentages are guidelines to help teachers keep students on a reading level that is best for their optimal reading growth. Students need to be challenged, an area for growth that Vygotsky explains in his zone of proximal development theory. In this theory, Vygotsky states that the learner needs to be at a place where he has more to learn with guidance from an expert. So, if a student reads a beginning grade 2 level book at 92%, this shows that he has a bit more to learn at that level. When the percentage increases to over 95%, the student needs a higher level book to keep growing as a reader. Second, when selecting texts teachers need to consider the developmental needs of the student. Some students have higher word recognition than comprehension, so although they can score at a higher reading level through word recognition, they may not understand what is being read. Third, the reader's fluency needs to be taken into consideration. If a student reads too slowly and without expression, repetitive books at that student's reading level might be the best fit for this reader. Finally, reader interest is also important when selecting texts. The more a student is interested in a text, the more likely his attitude toward reading it will be positive.

Reading Stances

Louise Rosenblatt, the creator of the transactional theory in reading, stated that the stance (purpose/position) of reading can be characterized in two different ways: aesthetic and efferent. In the aesthetic stance, the reader is reading for pleasure, be it a fiction or nonfiction book, and there is no outside pressure to perform. In the efferent stance, the reader is reading for information, most likely to apply in some situation after the reading, such as when a teacher assigns a text to be read along with follow-up questions to be answered. In reality, most reading has some of each.

Selecting Texts for Multiple Levels of Reading

Classrooms should contain an abundance of books in different genres. Selecting texts for students can be challenging, especially with the variety of reading levels that may be present in the classroom. This section provides some guidelines in selecting texts, as well as some important vocabulary terms.

Vocabulary Worth Knowing and Understanding

author studies: A unit lesson that gives students the opportunity to delve deeply into an author's life and body of work. When a class does an author study, the students are inspired to read as many books written by the author as they can.

leveled text sets: Texts that are at a particular grade level. In primary classrooms, these are often placed in different colored baskets, and students are directed to the basket that contains their "just right" reading level.

series books: Books that have the same characters and often the same setting in time, but vary the problem and solution.

text sets: Can be books on the same content, written by the same author, or from the same genre, but may represent different reading levels.

Books for Emergent Readers or Early Readers (Usually Grades K–1)

For emergent and developing readers, predictable books are utilized in the classroom. Predictable books, which encompass a number of different genres, ordinarily follow some predictable pattern. Books can be predictable because they rhyme, they follow a known sequence, they repeat certain phrases, they have a particular text structure, they are songs children have heard, and so forth. Books in this category make it easier for emergent and developing readers to predict what their text is about to say, aiding in their understanding of the book and making the experience enjoyable. Readers also begin to memorize the repetitive materials, thereby increasing their vocabulary.

When teachers work with these books, they are modeling for young children various book handling and text skills, as discussed in Chapter 4 (see "Concepts of Print" on page 20). These concepts include the following:

- Books communicate meaning through pictures and the printed word.
- Pictures can tell what is happening in the story and have meaning, give hints (inferences), and so forth.
- Words in the book are used to tell stories or to present facts about topics.

Types of predictable books used in classrooms:

- **Cumulative sequence:** The story builds on a pattern. It starts with one person, place, thing, or event. Each time a new person, place, thing, or event is introduced, all the previous ones are repeated.
- **Chain or circular story:** The story's ending leads back to the beginning.
- **Familiar or known sequence:** A common, recognizable concept, such as the alphabet, days of the week, months of the year, and so forth.
- **Pattern stories:** The scenes, events, or episodes are repeated, often with some variation.
- **Question and answer:** A question is repeated throughout the story, such as "Mama, do you love me?"
- **Repetitive sentence or phrase:** Text, such as "The sky is falling," is repeated throughout the story.
- **Repetitive rhyme:** A rhyme, rhythm, or a refrain, such as "It was too [big, or hot, or difficult]," is repeated throughout the story.
- **Songs:** Familiar songs that repeat sentences and phrases, such as "The wheels on the bus go 'round and 'round."

Books for Early Readers (Usually Grades 1–2)

Early readers need less repetition and more practice with using the cueing systems. Very simple books, such as those with picture cues, are best. The books can be fiction or nonfiction, but they should contain vocabulary that can be decoded using semantics and the context of the reading.

Transitional or Developing Readers (Usually Grades 2–3)

Transitional readers can read "just right" books fairly easily and are practicing their word attack strategies as they read. Transitional readers are beginning to not rely as heavily on picture cues, if they have done so in the past. They do well with simple series book sets, reading-level author studies, and simple chapter books.

Fluent Readers

Fluent readers are ready for challenges. Their reading pace is solid and at grade level or above. They understand how text works, how to apply word attack skills and strategies, have a large bank of sight words, and read independently with minimal guidance. Fluent readers can read longer passages of texts and utilize strategies that enable them to understand more complex text.

Author's Note: No matter what grade or reading stage a child is in, the "just right" or instructional level of the child must be considered. Instructional level means the child can read the text with 90%–94% accuracy, and this is the best context for teaching students new strategies or processes for making meaning of text.

Types of Reading

Children's comprehension can be impacted by *how* the reading is accomplished (see the list that follows). The following list details different types of reading. It begins with a type that is fairly dependent on the teacher; as you go down the list, the reading types are less dependent on the teacher.

- **Shared reading:** The teacher has a book and points to the words while reading. The story is reread, and children begin to chime in and read along.
- **Computer-assisted reading:** Students listen to a story on a tablet or computer. In some cases, the student can click on words for meaning to aid in their comprehension.
- **Echo reading:** The teacher reads a line, the children read the same line as if echoing her, the teacher reads the next line, the children read that line, and so forth.

- **Choral reading:** Children read aloud together. A teacher can use choral reading with a small group and a simple text to ensure that all children in the class are engaged in the reading; groups of children can also practice reading together, independent of the teacher.
- **Partner reading:** Children are paired and each child takes a turn reading a predetermined section to his peer. The children help each other out and discuss the reading.
- **Sustained silent reading:** Children read independently and will most likely discuss the reading at group time.

Reading Comprehension Strategies for Fiction Texts

Reading comprehension strategies are tools that readers use to help them understand the text. These strategies can be employed before, during, and after reading; many use metacognition, in which the reader self-monitors as he constructs meaning. Metacognition, you may remember, is thinking about thinking. When using metacognition, students think about what they are reading and understanding. By being taught metacognitive strategies students will ask themselves questions like:

- Am I reading the word right? If not, what can I try?
- Does this make sense? If not, do I need to reread? Is there something on the page that will help me understand?
- Am I reading too fast? Too slow?

Students should use metacognition when reading both fiction and nonfiction, as it allows them to self-monitor their understanding of the text. Metacognition strategies lead to students using "fix-up" strategies. Fix-up strategies are what a reader uses during rereading when he realizes he is not understanding; strategies may involve asking for clarification, looking back, reading ahead, and so forth. Many comprehension strategies that focus on fiction can also be used with nonfiction. A few of these are included here:

- **Setting a purpose:** When a student sets a purpose for reading, whether for pleasure or to acquire specific information from the text, he can focus on the task.
- **Activating prior knowledge:** Students need to be taught to think of what they know about the content of a text prior to their reading, in order to assimilate and accommodate the new knowledge. If students are going to read about someone who is at a city park, they should think about what they know about parks. This allows them to approach the reading in the correct mind-set for understanding. Semantic webs are often used for group brainstorming. (A semantic web is a diagram with a word in a middle bubble and lines branching out from it on which to write brainstorming ideas.) As students add their knowledge to a semantic web, the teacher can use this as an informal assessment by gauging how much prior knowledge students have on a topic. Let's say a student reads the sentence "The car slid off the icy road into the snow bank." If the student has no concept of a "snow bank," then he might conceptualize a car having crashed into a financial institution that is covered with snow. As you can see, it is advantageous to find out if students have erroneous or inadequate prior knowledge prior to reading.
- **Building background:** There is some controversy among reading experts about building background, but the important thing is to build background only on necessary topics without telling students what is happening in the text. The controversy focuses on time spent on building background and teachers giving so much background that students don't need to read the text. Although teachers shouldn't overdo, adequate and correct background knowledge aids in reading comprehension. When a teacher builds background or has students do a research-type activity to look up needed background knowledge, the stage is being set for deeper comprehension. This is especially important for English Language Learners (ELLs), who may be confused because of cultural differences.
- **Teaching vocabulary:** Explicit teaching of confusing vocabulary prior to the students' reading aids them in comprehending the text. (Vocabulary is covered in detail in Chapter 5.)
- **Making predictions:** When students make predictions about what is going to happen in a particular text, it allows students to infer and motivates their reading. Predictions must be based on evidence from the text and not off-the-wall guesses. Students' predictions rely on inferential comprehension of the text. Well-made predictions force students to use information from the text along with their prior knowledge about the situation in the text to infer what might happen. Predictions can be made before the book is started by looking

at the cover or reading the book jacket. Teachers may have students stop and predict at specific pages in the book, using text clues to help confirm or adjust those predictions and perhaps make new predictions.

- **Visualizing:** Often referred to as "making a movie in your mind," visualizing is a great strategy in which students create mental images of the events in a text to help themselves "see" what is happening. When there is a lot of action in a book or a detailed description of a scene has been given, if students create a picture in their minds, it helps them "see" and understand what the author is saying. In addition, visualizing can aid in recall of text information. *Tip:* When taking the Praxis (5203), you will be reading classroom scenarios. Use the visualization strategy to "see" what is happening in the classroom. This will help you select the correct answer.

- **Questioning:** When students ask questions as they read, it helps them to interact with the text and gain a deeper meaning. For example, a question could focus on a character's motive, such as "Why is the stepmother so mean to Cinderella?" When a student asks questions like this, it makes him think about the text—the stepmother was jealous, Cinderella was more beautiful than her stepsisters, the stepmother wanted to ensure that she retained control over the family inheritance, and so forth. Questioning the text, or the author's purpose, often leads students to predictions and inferences that help to deepen their understanding.

- **Clarifying:** Clarifying is used to monitor understanding. Using clarifying, students learn to recognize when something in the text does not make sense to them. If they don't understand a part of the reading, then they stop and use other comprehension strategies.

- **Summarizing:** When students are asked to summarize a book, they must determine what information is important and then recall that information. In order to do this well, students need to learn to concisely restate ideas as they recall information. Graphic organizers can help students learn how to summarize. Students can summarize sections of text and/or the whole text.

- **Synthesizing:** Students must synthesize information, connecting new information to information they already have. Doing so can make them think more deeply about what is happening in a text. This thinking process allows students to re-evaluate what they think is happening to see if new information alters that perception.

- **Making connections:** When students make personal connections to a text, it deepens understanding and aids in recall. Making such connections entails the use of background knowledge and schema. These connections are categorized into three types.

  - **Text to self:** Connections made between the student and the student's personal background and experiences. (Example: My mom cleans ashes out of our fireplace just like Cinderella.)

  - **Text to text:** Connections made between the text currently being read and a text the student had read previously. (Example: Snow White was kind to animals just like Cinderella.)

  - **Text to world:** Connections made between the text being read and something that has occurred or is occurring in the world. (Example: There is a prince in the story, and England currently has a few princes.)

- **Inferring:** When students infer from their reading, they form the best guess about what is happening in the story by using evidence from the text and their background knowledge. That evidence can be from context cues or pictures, but in some way the students draw conclusions about what is happening or, in the case of a prediction, what is about to happen. Sometimes it can be as simple as "The mother of the three girls was yelling for them to come over to her." The student can actually infer from this sentence that the girls are sisters, as the evidence from the text says "the mother of," and his background knowledge should tell him that this makes the girls sisters. So, when the next sentence states "The sisters ran to see what their mother wanted," it is clear that *sisters* refers to the three girls. This is probably one of the most important comprehension strategies a student reader can use.

- **Picture walk:** For young students who are having problems with comprehension, or just learning comprehension strategies, a picture walk is often used. Before reading the text, the students and the teacher will "walk" through the text, discussing pictures and the information they convey about what is happening in the book. The picture walk provides students a preview and a mental map of where the story is going.

Reading Comprehension Strategies for Nonfiction Texts

Reading fiction and nonfiction text requires two different skill sets, although many of the same comprehension strategies can be used to foster understanding. Young children grow up to be much more familiar with fictitious stories, but they do not have as much exposure to informational text. Because of this, around fourth grade, when children begin to read more nonfiction texts, it is often much harder for them to understand the structure. The Common Core requires that students in earlier grades be exposed to much more informational text than they have in the past. The following are recommended strategies to use with nonfiction texts:

- **Use a KWL chart:** A KWL chart is recommended in order to activate prior knowledge when reading informational text. The chart is divided into three sections, and can be addressed by individual students, by a small group, or by a whole class. The K and W sections of the chart are completed during pre-reading. The K stands for "What I Know," and the W stands for "What I want to Learn." The K column involves brainstorming and using prior knowledge on the topic to be read. The elements of the W column build anticipation and motivation for the reading, as students list things they are hoping to learn about the topic. (*Note:* The L column, "What I Learned," is completed during post-reading and is a great vehicle for summarizing and recalling information learned.)

- **Preview material:** Prior to reading a nonfiction text, students should look at the bolded headings, italicized words, and bolded words or phrases; analyze pictures; and glean pertinent information from graphs and diagrams. Taking these steps before they read the text provides students the gist of what the text is about to tell them and aids in their comprehension and their recall of the material in the text.

- **Determine the author's purpose:** The motive or reason why an author writes a fiction or nonfiction text is called the "author's purpose." Texts can be written to entertain, inform, teach, persuade, or convince. Nonfiction texts are written to inform. Signal words and phrases may hint at the author's purpose for that particular section (e.g., *let me explain, to illustrate my point, comparing this to*).

- **Identify the text type:** There are three major nonfiction text types: informational, descriptive, and persuasive. If students know and can recognize the text type, this will help them in identifying the author's purpose.

  - **Informational text:** Written to inform readers about a particular topic. This text might include numerous facts, pros and cons, how-to books, definitions, conclusions, and summaries.

  - **Descriptive text:** Written to give a picture of what is being talked about. This text could include locations and descriptive details such as movement and background information.

  - **Persuasive text:** Written to convince the reader to agree with the author's opinion about a topic. The text is meant to portray that the author's opinion or view is the best about that topic. This text could include qualities, activities, advertisement-like statements, and repetition of strong points.

- **Identify the text structure:** Text structure, described in detail in the next section, is the organizational structure of a text. This can refer to the overall structure of a book, sections within books, or paragraphs within sections. Often, one text structure is embedded in another. The author chooses the particular text structure that fits her purpose and that conveys what she wants the reader to learn. For example, an author writes a book on alligators to inform the readers about alligators. But an author writes a book on alligators and crocodiles in order to compare and contrast the two animals. The reader's understanding is aided when knowing that text structures underlie what is important to learn from the text.

- **Learn content area vocabulary:** Words in the particular content areas have definitions that correspond to that content. When students are discussing hiking, the word *compass* refers to the device that directs the user to go north, south, east, or west. But, in social studies, a *compass rose* is a drawing on a map that displays the map's orientation. On the other hand, a *compass* in math is what is used to draw a circle.

Nonfiction (Informational) Text Structures

Nonfiction text is often called informational or expository text. When students get to fourth grade, they are required to read a great deal of informational text and often have problems with comprehension because they may not have been taught the strategies needed. One strategy that aids in the understanding of informational text is to first identify the text structure. Text structure is important for comprehension because it lays the foundation for deciphering what is important in the text. For example, if the text structure is sequential, the author wants the reader to remember the order of events. Many times, authors will embed one text structure within another.

Teaching text structure can be done by pointing out and showing students when various text structures occur in a text. In addition, modeling and then having students write a particular text structure allows them to understand the structure. The following chart gives pertinent information on the main nonfiction text structures.

Informational Text Structures

Type of Text Structure	Description and Selected Signal Words	Author's Purpose	Example
Description or descriptive	Descriptive text can be included in fiction or nonfiction. Descriptive text, no matter the content, is very detailed and carefully describes a person, place, thing, or event. It contains specifically chosen adjectives and clear details. Signal words: *also, then, as, another, furthermore, a few, likewise, besides, several, many, in addition*	The author uses this description when details are important; these details can deepen understanding of what is being discussed.	The Eiffel Tower in Paris, France, is 1,063 feet tall and has an antenna at the very top. If the antenna were removed, the tower would be 984 feet tall.
Chronological (or sequential)	Chronological text structure must be written in the correct order, which can be arranged by occurrence of events, size, importance, and so forth. This can be a series of events that leads up to a conclusion. Signal words: ordinal numbers (*first, second*, and so forth), *next, until, while, last, soon, then, after, now, immediately, during, before*	This text structure is used when order is important, such as in historical events, scientific cycles, directions, or some form of ranking.	First, you open the car door. Then, you step in with your feet. Next, you sit on the seat.
Compare/contrast	Compare/contrast describes similarities and differences between two or more events, places, characters, objects, or other concepts. Signal words: *however, but, yet, instead of, even though, on the other hand, on the contrary, despite, still, in comparison*	Authors use compare/contrast for a variety of purposes. It can be used in the persuasive genre to show weaknesses in an opposing view. It can be used to compare today's society with past societies, and so forth.	Apples and oranges are more alike than the saying would imply. They both have skin, even though the orange has thick skin and the apple thin. They both are fruits and have small seeds. Despite the fact that an apple is red and an orange is, well, orange, they still have similarities.

Type of Text Structure	Description and Selected Signal Words	Author's Purpose	Example
Problem/solution	The author goes into detail to describe a particular problem, and counters that problem with the solution, solutions, or proposed solutions. Signal words: *one reason, to solve, a solution, the problem is, it was recommended, as a result, so that, something was wrong, this is a concern, now*	Authors use this text structure to inform readers of problems or possible problems in any area.	The people of Cleveland have been concerned because traffic has increased dramatically in the last 10 years. Many of the busy roads do not have sidewalks, and children and adults cannot walk safely. The town council applied for state grants, and a number of the busy roads now have sidewalks.
Cause/effect	The cause of the problem is given; what happened as a result of the problem is the effect. (The cause is the action; the effect is the result.) There can be several reasons identified as the cause, and there can also be several effects as a result. Signal words: *for this reason, in order to, as a result, because, consequently, so that, therefore, on account of, thus*	Authors use cause and effect to show a relationship between two or more occurrences. In persuasive text, the author can select the information pertinent to her own bias.	Susan has to study for the Praxis (5203) because she is taking it on Saturday. For this reason, she is not going out to dinner with us tonight and will not be playing in the volleyball game on Saturday.
Enumeration	Enumeration is a list, usually elaborated on, that connects particular information. Enumeration does not need to be in any necessary order. Signal words: *also, then, as, another, likewise, furthermore, a few, besides, several, many, some, in addition*	Authors use enumeration when it is necessary to "list" and elaborate on facts, items, subcategories, important events, people, etc.	There are many flowering bulbs that bloom in the spring. Daffodils, which are usually yellow, make a nice spring garden. Also, hyacinths bloom about the same time and add color. Finally, crocuses bloom very early and are low to the ground.
Question-and-answer	As it sounds, the text is written first with a question and then with the answer. Signal words: *what, why, when, where, who, how, how many, in this instance, refers to, the conclusion, one may conclude, in this case, it could be that*	Authors use question-and-answer when they want to get straight to the point and make sure the reader has a clear understanding of the material.	Why do we have daylight saving time? The idea is to get the most out of the daylight and use less energy. This started around World War I to save money during wartime.

Main Idea and Supporting Details

Being able to recognize the main idea is fundamental to comprehending text. The main idea of a text is the central thought or overarching topic of a passage. The point of the passage, it tells what the passage is mostly about. Supporting details are facts, examples, reasons, or causes that support the main idea; they may provide background information. It is through the gathering of main ideas and supporting details that readers are able to summarize and review what is being said in the text.

Students need to be taught:

- The definition of main idea and supporting details.
- That supporting details relate back to the main idea and provide more information about the main idea.
- That the first sentence, the topic sentence, is often the main idea.
- That the main idea is the important idea, and the details support what is being said about the main idea.
- That some examples or facts given about the main idea are often interesting, but not important.
- How distinguishing what is important from what is interesting enables the reader to state the main idea and important supporting details.

Teaching students how to identify the main idea and supporting details:

1. Begin by reviewing the definitions.
2. Ask students to tell you how they would define *important* and *interesting.*
3. Model with a short passage how you would select important information in the passage. Underline the important statements or phrases, and explain why they are important.
4. Discuss the underlined portions, and explain how you would identify the main idea. Explain that the rest of the sentences are details that support the main idea.
5. Do guided practice by having the students identify the main idea and important details in another passage. Discuss and make sure the procedure is understood.
6. Using another small passage, have students apply this learning with a partner or on their own.

Close Reading and Comprehension

A close reading is an analysis of a short text that is thoughtful, critical, and focuses on details. The purpose of close reading is to gain a deeper meaning of the text as the reader thoroughly investigates it for form, purpose, craft, language, meanings, and so forth.

Close reading involves:

- short text or passages
- minimal to no pre-reading activities (i.e., activation of prior knowledge, building background, and teaching vocabulary)
- analyzing the short text for form, purpose, craft, language, meanings, ideas, concepts, and so forth
- text analysis strategies
- inference skills
- rereading for deeper meaning and annotations (to write thoughts and comments)
- examination of text graphics and text features
- returning to any areas that can be confusing
- answering text-dependent questions
- collaborative discussion

Teach your students to use close reading to give them skills that will make them independent, competent readers who can analyze text and answer text-dependent questions as they grasp the deeper meaning of the text. As students learn to employ close reading skills, they will be able to read and understand more complex text.

Model Lesson on Close Reading

Use the following passage for this lesson on the procedures used to teach the components of close reading.

> Anticipation was in the air. The trees waved to the crowd as the wind passed through. After a long, hot, dry summer, the cool air was a welcomed kiss upon the faces of the military families that lined the airfield. They could see the plane, the pilot dipping one wing making the plane look as if it was saying, "Hello, we're home." Overflowing with joy, Amelia looked around at the excited mothers, fathers, and children as the plane descended onto the airfield. With a tinge of sadness, Amelia realized that some families were missing.

Lesson: The teacher begins the lesson by reading the excerpt with the students, asking them to think about key ideas and details as she reads. They then discuss the text. Next, to explore the author's craft, the teacher models her thinking as she talks about the language the author uses, citing the phrase *trees waved* and *the cool air was a welcomed kiss*. When talking about the details in the text with her students, the teacher will lead them to see that the author is using personification in her writing. The teacher will then have students reread and annotate any other personifications and also underline and comment on other details that bring meaning to the text. As the class delves back into the text, students discuss the personification of the plane as seen in the sentence *Hello, we're home.* Next, the teacher asks students to discuss with each other what meanings they see in the text. Why were people at the airfield? Why are the families so excited? Why does Amelia have a tinge of sadness? The teacher might point out the word *tinge,* calling it an odd word for the author to choose, and asking the students, "What does it mean?" Finally, students and teacher will discuss what the author means by *some families were missing*. What is the deeper meaning behind this sentence? What is the author's purpose in telling us this?

In this lesson, students learn to use their prior knowledge and schema to interact with the text as they read. Close reading is modeled several times, after which students begin to practice with partners and, finally, solo.

Note: Practice in close reading should always include the use of small excerpts or passages, rereading, annotation, and text-dependent questions/discussions. In addition, the text is usually read at least three times. First for the big idea, then for craft and structure, and finally for deeper understanding.

Using Evidence from the Text to Support Predictions, Opinions, and Conclusions

Using evidence from the text in predictions, opinions, and conclusions is important because it enables teachers to see that their students have read and understood the text. The previously modeled close reading approach is one way students can be taught to use evidence from the text. Other techniques are presented here.

Supporting Predictions

Students use information from the text to make sound predictions. When students do not use information from the text, a prediction can become a wild guess. Using predictions is a good way to teach inference skills and create support for text-dependent discussions. With young students, the teacher begins making predictions by looking at pictures. As she shows pictures to a class or group, she asks, "What do you think is going to happen?" After the children answer, the teacher then asks, "What did you see that made you think that would happen?" This teaches children at an early age that predictions need to be supported.

Students then learn how to predict from text in the same way, but are asked "What did you read that made you think of the prediction?" Traditional graphic organizers for predictions have two columns: one for "What I predict" and one for "What happened." However, using support-based answers, the graphic organizer should have three columns," "What I predict," "What evidence did I have," and "What happened."

Supporting Opinions

A fact is something that is correct and true. On the other hand, an opinion states what someone believes, a judgment, or a way of thinking about something. When students give an opinion or make a claim, they need to be able to provide reasons to support the opinion. They should be able to state what fact in the text gave them their idea and then explain how the text supports the idea. By giving a supported opinion, students learn to analyze text and think about what the author is saying, thereby arriving at a much deeper meaning.

Supporting Conclusions

A conclusion is an idea, a judgment, or a decision that is reached by reasoning. As do opinions, reasoning needs to be sound in order to come to a relevant conclusion. As students read, they use inference to construct meaning and draw conclusions about what is being read. Students need to be able to support their conclusions with evidence from the text. Consider the following sentence: "During recess time, Sarah, whose knee was bleeding, ran to the nurse's office crying." From this sentence, students can draw the conclusion that Sarah fell on the playground. There is support from the text: It was recess time, Sarah's knee was bleeding, and she was crying. All three of these pieces of text support the fact Sarah most likely fell on the playground. Students are taught this skill in the same way: by going to the sentence level to find support for a conclusion they have made.

Digital Media and Their Impact on Comprehension

Digital media are any type of media that are in electronic or digital formats. Anything that is in an audio, video, or photo presentation can be encoded for digital media. Using digital media can give students support in their reading, but in some situations, it may actually jeopardize comprehension. For instance, if students can click on a bird in the picture and hear it sing, this can interrupt the comprehension and get the student off task. Comprehension is important no matter the text type.

Digital media offer both challenges and rewards, as detailed in the following table.

Note: Students must be made aware of the types of web addresses that indicate a valid site (one where content is evaluated for correctness). URLs ending in ".edu" and ".gov" are considered valid sites.

Types of Digital Media

Media	Description	Advantages	Disadvantages
Podcasts	Audio files that can be listened to anytime.	Can be downloaded. Student can receive information and also create podcasts.	Information could be wrong. Audio only, no visuals.
Discussion board	Online repository where people can post and respond.	Students can write opinions, ideas, and so forth.	Most discussion boards are public, and that can cause problems. Some sites have private discussion boards, which are safer.

Media	Description	Advantages	Disadvantages
Apps	Usually a game format or digital manipulative for learning, or an app that allows instant connection.	Very motivational for children. Great for practicing skills.	Some app formats are too game-like and do not foster enough learning.
Electronic books	Software or a purchased online source that houses books at all levels. Interactive—can have words read and defined, provide phonics aid, and can be linked to more information. E-books can be storybook read alouds or interactive.	Some of the newer electronic software offers books on the same topic, but leveled for readers.	Some books have too many bells and whistles, which can distract students.
Digital magazines	Free online magazines that have articles, pictures, and videos.	Great content; images can be enlarged and copied for reports; content can be saved for a later resource.	Can't tell when new content is added; some sites have advertising; reading is not leveled or scaffolded in any way.
Blog	An online journal where the blogger posts and readers can respond.	Offers a real reason to write and global connections.	Some blogs can be outdated; student entries need to be monitored.
Wiki	Online resource that allows anyone to edit (this is known as an open source).	Various information can be found. Usually includes visuals.	Information can be inaccurate.
Videos "channels"	Online resources that offer videos on a variety of topics.	Give students a great view of concepts that may be difficult to understand. Good for ELLs too.	Videos can be long, so it is best to preview and select the portion to be shown.
Presentation sites	Sites like Voicethread, a resource to create picture stories.	Voicethread allows students to publish online, write, and include audio. Great for stories. Viewers must be invited, so site is safe.	Sites can be difficult to figure out how the product is to be created.
Live webcams	Sites such as Giant Panda Cam; allow 24-hour viewing.	Giant Panda Cam provides a live view of what is happening with the animal or habitats being watched. Great for observation.	Site needs to be teacher-approved; it can be tedious waiting for animal or some kind of action to appear.

Chapter 9

The Interdependence of Reading and Writing Development

Growth in reading promotes growth in writing, and vice versa. Studies have shown that children who read frequently tend to obtain scores that correlate with better writing. Wide reading promotes vocabulary growth, which results in more effective communication, whether in speaking or writing.

The Reading and Writing Connection

Connections between the reading and writing processes should be clearly explained to students, so as to aid in their understanding of the importance of each process. Connections include:

- Readers decode when they read a word, and they encode when they write.
- Reading can be used to reinforce word identification skills that translate into word spelling for the students. These skills include the development of word families that expand the students' writing vocabulary. (Example of a word family: *rank, crank, blank, lank,* and *bank*.)
- The more children read, the better they write.
- Texts become "mentor texts" or models for student writing.
- Studying the author's craft in texts aids students in using these same techniques in their own writing.
- Students learn as they read; this knowledge is transferred to their writing because it gives them something to write about.
- Reading various genres and text structures aids students in writing; conversely, writing various text structures and genres builds understanding in reading.
- While involved in the writing and reading process we see that writers read and reread. When children write and revise, they must continually read over what they have written. So, they are having more practice reading as they write.
- Writers and readers bring their own interpretation to the text as they construct meaning.
- Writers see their reading audience as the focus of their text.

Ways to Promote the Reading and Writing Connection

Teachers can help their students make the reading and writing connection in a number of ways:

- Have students study informational and fiction text structures in both their reading and writing.
- Use genre studies in which students are immersed in a particular genre to learn its characteristics; then, have students complete a writing assignment in that genre.
- Use mentor texts to show students the author's craft. For example, if the class is working on metaphors, share samples of metaphoric writing and analyze them with your students.
- Create classroom publications to allow students to both write their own texts and read those of their peers.
- Give students a writing assignment that focuses on a specific audience, such as directions for young children.

Promoting Reading Comprehension Through Written Responses

Reader response is a follow-up activity that teachers may assign after reading. These responses can be oral, like a group conversation in which children discuss the reading, or may consist of a written response. A written reader response should be engaging—anything from writing a postcard from the story setting to making a brochure sharing information learned from an informational text. A reader response needs to be more academic than fun—although no one rules out the fun.

When demonstrating comprehension through written responses, the student should provide a response that is closely connected to the event or information from the text. For example, if students are studying volcanoes, it's fun and informative to do the baking soda/vinegar experiment, and it does help students remember that a volcano erupts. This experience will be enhanced if students follow up the experiment with a written response, such as drawing a diagram of a volcano and writing an explanation of why the volcano erupts. This will result in a deeper understanding and promote better recall; plus, learning could be easily assessed.

Reasons to use written reader responses to promote comprehension:

- Written responses to reading take advantage of the reading/writing connection.
- When thinking about a written response, the reader must consider evidence in the text, think about what the text said, and reread; this deepens understanding.
- When writing a written response, the reader must think about the text, events, and information as he is writing, which also deepens understanding.
- A writer needs to reread and analyze his own written response and how it relates to the text.
- The writing assignment can give students the opportunity to ask questions or give opinions, depending on the nature of the reader response.
- Written responses allow readers to use new vocabulary and show understanding of the meaning and usage of the new words.
- Written responses allow the teacher to discuss interpretations privately with students and "unpack" thinking for better assessment of students' understanding.

Common reader responses in written format:

- Write journal responses: These can be anything pertinent to the text, such as a summary, a character description, an answer to a teacher's question, or what might be in the main character's diary.
- Write a letter to the character, perhaps giving advice.
- Choose five vocabulary words from the chapter (or book) that you can use in writing about a key event in the chapter (or book).
- Create a postcard from one of the characters.
- Explain how the character changes in this chapter (or book).
- Write three important facts from the text.
- Draw a cartoon about the text and include dialogue.
- Write a summary of events, containing facts and information from the text.
- Use graphic organizers for various purposes (story mapping, predictions, character analysis, and so forth)
- Write answers to inferential text-dependent questions.
- Make predictions: Pre-reading—what you think will happen and why you think it will happen; during reading—what clues do you have and how do they affect your prediction; post-reading—what actually happened and why the prediction was right or wrong.
- Do Readers' Theater skits written as a retelling of a story.
- Create a learning log, a journal type of writing that contains facts and concepts learned from the text.
- Create diagrams with labels and explanations.
- Write a book report and include a "Why you should read" section.
- Write a book review with a critique.
- Create a podcast, in which students write out the script and read to record.
- Do a cloze activity (filling in the blanks) or writer's frame—used mainly with younger children or struggling readers.

- Create a flap book or accordion book with selected criteria for the book.
- Do compare-and-contrast writing: character, theme, animal, and so forth.
- Write a poem—any genre of poetry that invites a well-thought-out response.

Developmental Stages of Writing

When children learn to speak, you hear the stages: first the cooing, then the babbling, and later the one- or two-word statement. A parallel type of development occurs in writing. A child begins writing with scribbles, which could be pictures, or sometimes recognizable pictures, or a scramble of letters that make no sense—to us. Children usually draw before they write. Teachers should encourage a child to draw as much detail as possible so they can see what the child has envisioned.

A few years back, I walked over to the writing center in a preschool where a 4-year-old had just finished "writing" his postcard. I took a few seconds to admire the scribbled lines across the index card, and asked the child if he would read it to me—and, of course, he did, rattling on and on! (This also showed me that the young boy understood that print has meaning.) As you will see by the developmental stages of writing detailed in the following table, there is a continuum of growth, and that is what is important for the Praxis (5203).

Developmental Stages of Writing

Developmental Stage	Description
Prephonemic Stage (some call this the scribbling stage)	The child writes with scribbles and drawings. Sometimes some of the scribbles can be identified as letters, as the child "pretends" to write.
Early Phonemic Stage (some call this letter-like symbols and/or strings of letters)	The child begins writing with a beginning or ending sound. Child might label a picture, such as a "b" for bunny; copy letters from print sources, such as STOP; or write "sentences" with letters or letter combinations representing words. (Example: *IPB* for *I play basketball.*)
Letter-Name Stage (some call this the Beginning Sounds Emerge Stage)	Usually, the beginning and ending letters are used to represent a word. (Example: *BL* for *ball.*)
Transitional Stage	The child uses beginning and ending letters; he may not include a vowel or all vowels, but other letters appear within the word. The transitional stage is easier for the adult to read, and the child uses "inventive spelling." (Example: *Mi bik iS brKn* for *My bike is broken.*)
Conventional Writing Stage	The child now writes the majority of words with conventional spelling. Most experts say that inventive spelling should end around third grade, and conventional spelling of common words should be expected on all final drafts in writing.

Adapted from http://www.mecfny.org/wp-content/uploads/2015/06/StagesofWritinghandout.pdf

Developmental Stages of Spelling

There are a few models for the developmental stages of spelling. The one presented here seems to be the most prevalent; it was derived from the research of Charles Read and Edmund Henderson in the early 1970s. This model has five stages (some models have as many as eight) and shows progress from preschool to conventional spellings and covers development for most elementary students. Bear, Invernizzi, Templeton, and Johnston add two more stages for advanced and older students: syllable and affixes spelling, and derivational relations spelling. In both of these stages, as the complex stage names indicate, students are becoming sophisticated spellers.

Developmental Stages of Spelling

Developmental Stage	Description
Precommunicative Stage	Letters are used to spell words, but there is no order, and no words are recognizable. (Example: *XPQTRD*)
Semiphonetic Stage	The child sometimes uses single letters to spell, and sometimes uses a couple of consonant letters. (Example: *I rD b* for *I ride my bike.*)
Phonetic Stage	Some words are recognizable while others are not, but if read phonetically, they can be understood. The child is using inventive spelling for some words. (Example: *My brthr is bigr thn me* for *My brother is bigger than me.*)
Transitional Stage	More words are spelled with conventional spelling, but some inventive spelling is still being used, and spelling rules may be employed but misused. The child usually recognizes that words have vowels. (Example: *I hurd my rite hand yesterdy* for *I hurt my right hand yesterday.*)
Correct Stage or Conventional Stage	The child is using conventional spelling, but may make some errors with irregular and unfamiliar words.

Word Strategies for Spelling

Teaching common orthographic patterns is considered the best way to teach spelling to young learners. (Back to roots here: *ortho* comes from the Greek root *ortho,* meaning "correct," and *graphos* means "writing.") Children need to be able to use common orthographic patterns to aid in their spelling.

In the early grades, both phonics and spelling are taught with onset and rimes and word family combinations. Children work with word families such as *cat, mat, hat* and *cut, hut, rut.* As the children advance in their spelling, the onset and rime patterns become more complex: *clock, mock, dock* and *night, fight, light.* Teaching word families gives children strong exposure to common orthographic patterns and strengthens their recall for spelling these words correctly. The reading and writing connection also plays a part in this, as generalizations in phonics aid in spelling. Although there are usually exceptions to most generalizations and rules, common spelling rules do help as a guide to correct spelling and should certainly be taught. You may remember many of the following common spelling rules from when you were in elementary school.

Common Spelling Rules

- Write "i" before "e," except after "c," unless it sounds like /a/ as in *neighbor* and *weigh.* (Examples: *belief, thief, sleigh*)
- When a one-syllable word ends in a single consonant, double the consonant when adding a suffix that begins with a vowel, such as *-ed, -ing,* or *-er.* (Examples: *bat→batted, batting, batter*)
- When a word ends with a silent "e," drop the "e" before adding a suffix that begins with a vowel, such as *-ed, -ing,* or *-er.* (Examples: *bike, biked, biking, biker*)
- If a word ends with an "e" and the suffix begins with a consonant, keep the "e." (Examples: *safe→safely; hope→hopeless*)
- To make most nouns and verbs plural, add an "s." (Examples: *mats, locks, caps*)

- When "y" is at the end of the word, if a vowel comes before the "y," just add "s" to make the word plural. (Examples: *boys, toys*)

- When a "y" is at the end of the word, if a consonant comes before the "y," change the "y" to "i" and add "-es" (or change the "y" to "i" before adding any suffix except a suffix that begins with "i"). (Examples: *candy→candies, lady→ladies, happy→happiness*)

- If a word ends in "ch," "s," "sh," or "x," add "-es" to make the word plural. (Examples: *witches, dresses, dishes, lynxes*)

- For words that end in "f," change the "f" to a "v" and add "-es" to make the word plural. (Examples: *wolf→wolves, loaf→loaves*)

Suggestions for Teaching Spelling

- Teach through onset and rimes (what we commonly call "word families").
- Have children work with other common word patterns from the common spelling rules.
- Use mini-lessons prior to writing to teach common orthographic patterns.
- Teach spelling through word study, using common spelling words. For example, have students "make words" by manipulating letters into the pattern or rule that you are teaching. For example, when teaching the "at" word family, give the students the letters "a," "t," "b," "f," "h," and "m." They can then rearrange the letters and make the words *bat, fat, hat,* and *mat.*

- Teach spelling through writing as children polish their writing piece to its final draft. Also, assess writing to see which spelling rules most children are not using correctly, and provide some directed lessons and practice on the particular rules or patterns where improvement is needed.

- Use word sorts. For example, give students nine words, three ending in "it," three ending in "at," and three ending in "et." Then have the students sort and say the words. This aids students in recognizing common word patterns.

- Play spelling games, such as which group can write the most words ending with "ack." This will reinforce the rules or patterns students are learning.

- Use a word wall for support while playing thinking games, such as "I'm thinking of a word on the wall that begins with 'm' and rhymes with *night*" (*might*).

Teaching Writing Mechanics

Writing mechanics are considered the correct use of capitalization, punctuation, and correct spelling. They are conventions of print that don't exist in oral language, but are used when reading. Correct usage of words is also important, but that is usually categorized under the grammar umbrella.

Mechanics are important to meaning. Take a look at the following sentences:

"There's the mean pig Julie. Watch out."

Or

"There's the mean pig, Julie. Watch out."

As you can see, these sentences show two different meanings. The placement of the comma is important! (No one would want to be Julie in the first set of sentences.)

In order to teach writing mechanics, you need to know them. If you have any reservations in this area, there are countless sites that show correct writing mechanics and grammar. These include sites such as grammarbook.com and grammarly.com. One popular site, quickanddirtytips.com (also known as "Grammar Girl"), also includes writing tips in podcasts.

How and When to Teach Writing Mechanics Effectively

- Teach through mentor texts. When reading, point out to students the author's use of writing conventions, for example, how the author uses quotation marks when writing dialogue.

- Model writing mechanics on a whiteboard, using whole class stories or nonfiction retellings and having students provide input into the writing.

- Teach during the final drafts of the writing process (see "Steps in the Writing Process," below). Students should focus on content first, and then mechanics—especially in the primary grades.

- Teach during writing conferences (see "Conferencing: Offering Students Feedback on Their Writing" on page 72). When conferencing with students about content, discuss mechanics as well. You may find through analyzing students' writing that several students need instruction on the same skill; therefore, there can be a whole class mini-lesson or small group instruction to address these needs.

- Using a writers' workshop format is very effective. In this format, the writing process is in a constant cycle and instruction is integrated into the process. The teacher conferences with students and teaches with mini-lessons on such things as grammar and writing techniques.

- Utilize the mini-lesson format, which uses short direct instruction to teach a skill or strategy. Teaching mechanics with a mini-lesson involves explaining the mechanic (i.e., sentences begin with capital letters), showing examples of the mechanic in use, modeling how to use the skill, and having the students practice the skill.

- Teach the mini-lesson, and use it as a focus during writing. Explain to students that you will be zeroing in on the correct use of the particular skill (i.e., sentences begin with capital letters) when you check over their writing.

- Teach through critical analysis. Show students model sentences or whole text, and analyze how the author uses conventions to help supply meaning to the text. For example, if the author is using a metaphor, discuss how that adds to the literary sense of the piece.

- To aid in correct spelling, if students are writing about the same topic, have the students brainstorm words they might use and write them on a whiteboard for reference.

The Writing Process and Promoting Writing Development

The writing process has five main components: prewriting, drafting, revising, editing, and publishing. The process brings students from initial brainstorming to a finished product and is guided by conferencing with either the teacher or peers.

Steps in the Writing Process

Step	Description
Prewriting	This is the initial stage of the writing process when students brainstorm. It can be done solo or collaboratively, as students talk through their ideas, or by actually sketching out the ideas.
Drafting	This is the beginning stage of writing, when the student writes the first (and then later) drafts.
Revising	Revising continues through each draft. This is when the writer looks at the content of what is being said. Conferences during the revision stage focus on questions of clarity, voice, organization, content, and so forth. The focus is not on writing conventions, although many writers revise and edit as they continue with their drafts.

(*continued*)

Step	Description
Editing	Editing is when writers look at the mechanics—the conventions of writing. The focus at this point is on making sure all capitals, end marks, paragraph breaks, and so forth are appropriate for the particular text.
Publishing	A final draft that is to be published in some way should have no mistakes. Not all pieces of writing need to be brought up to final draft, but some definitely should. The publishing can be done in myriad ways, such as a compilation of writings to be sent home to parents or published on a class website, writings to be put up on the hallway bulletin board or wall for all to see, a class blog or other digital media sharing, or sharing in the school library or public library.

As students complete the five steps in the writing process, teacher and peer conferencing should be taking place. In conferencing, students get feedback on their writing. Peer conferencing is acceptable, but students need to be taught how to peer conference with respect, praise, and positive, constructive comments. Students also need to be taught the importance of accepting constructive criticism.

The teacher conference is usually conducted one-on-one; the teacher asks the student to explain further about something in his writing and to clarify and/or answer questions readers may have. The teacher also helps the student work on organizing his writing. Conferences initially focus on revising what is being written to promote understanding for the reader, awareness of the intended audience, and use of authors' crafts.

Promoting Writing Development

To promote writing development, teachers should:

- Always be respectful of student writing, and foster an inviting classroom environment.
- Begin with chart writing with young children to model, and accept and praise what they write.
- Use the Language Experience Approach (LEA) for younger children. With this approach, the class or child dictates what is to be written regarding some shared or solo experience.
- Build in peer conferencing and teacher conferencing.
- Do collaborative writing projects, such as brochures or posters. This can be done in a variety of ways.
- Have children do journal writing; respond to their writing to show that they have you as an audience. Do not correct a child's journal, but be sure to model back correctly anything the child has written incorrectly.
- Have children use learning logs, a type of journal used to document their learning. The log can have results of experiments, facts and opinions about content, and so forth.
- Have children use a "writer's notebook," where they jot down ideas and starters to be used later.
- Build children's choice into your writing assignments.
- Whenever possible, give children real reasons to write. Letter writing: Put a mailbox in your classroom, and allow the children to "mail" to each other using the proper letter format. Or, children could complete written applications for classroom jobs such as line leader or whiteboard eraser.
- Write across the curriculum, not just in "writing class." For example, if the class is studying the water cycle, students can label a diagram of the water cycle, write a persuasive essay on the need for clean water, or write an explanation on how a water filtration system works.
- Have a writing center that contains various writing tools, from letter stamps to grocery list paper, that will make students enthusiastic about writing.

Traits of High-Quality Writing

When teachers score children's writing, they discuss the various traits of writing, usually getting students to focus on improving one trait at a time. The most commonly used traits are ideas, organization, voice, word choice, sentence fluency, and conventions. These are explained in the chart below, along with teacher expectations for each. Note that expectations will increase in complexity at each grade level.

Characteristics of High-Quality Writing

Writing Trait	Explanation	Expectations: What teachers look for in these areas. The expectations vary, depending on grade level.
Ideas	Ideas are the main message, the content of the writing and all the details to support the main message.	Strong ideas, supporting details, clear message.
Organization	The structure of the piece—how the writer chooses to format the structure of the writing, such as compare-contrast or chronological order.	Writing piece is easy to follow, logical, has a clear and engaging beginning, and shows coherence. There is sufficient information for clarity, ideas easily bridge from one to the next, and the writing reaches an ending that brings everything together.
Voice	How readers hear the writer as he is speaking to them.	Engaging, expressive, and shows sense of audience. Adds distinctive flavor to the writing. Writing shows emotions and feelings.
Word choice	Using colorful and precise language that interests the reader.	Uses imagery; precise words are carefully chosen; may use senses; may use figurative language; enhances content.
Sentence fluency	The flow of the language within the writing.	Sentences are coherent, vary in length, proceed easily from one to the next, and are well crafted.
Conventions	Mechanical correctness: spelling, punctuation, capitalization, paragraphs, use of correct grammar.	Mechanics and grammar are strong; writing shows a high standard in using traditional spelling and conventions.

Author Voice

The author's voice is a nuance of his writing that distinguishes it from other authors' writing. It may be direct speech, soft-toned, touchy-feely, enthusiastic, or sprinkled with catch phrases. There is uniqueness in the written words. Through writing, the author says "I am writing and speaking to you."

The following terms describe literary devices that can enhance voice and add details to the author's voice:

- **Alliteration:** Words beginning with the same consonant sound, written in a series. Example: *The dumb dog digs dirt.*
- **Ellipsis:** Used in a narrative when the author omits information and the reader fills in the gaps. Example: *Sally went to bed early because she was tired. . . . The next day at school she was full of energy.*
- **Hyperbole:** An exaggeration. Example: *Wow, that ice cream cone is a mile high.*
- **Imagery:** The use of descriptive or sensory words and phrases to create an image in the reader's mind. Example: *The waves seemed to roll over one another as they hit the pristine sand on the beach.*
- **Metaphor:** A hidden or implicit comparison, saying that one thing is another. Example: *She is a princess.*

- **Mood:** An emotional attitude conveyed in the story by the author. Example: *You could hear the children's laughter. The bright sun brought warmth and cheer to the crowd. Everyone was anticipating the parade's arrival.*
- **Onomatopoeia:** A word that sounds like what it represents. Examples: *buzz, hiss.*
- **Personification:** Giving human characteristics to animals or objects. Example: *The spooky house, with windows for eyes, was a haven for the homeless.*
- **Simile:** A comparison of two things using *like* or *as.* Example: *That lady is as sly as a fox.*
- **Symbolism:** Use of a person, place, thing, or event to represent something else. Example: *All the world's a stage.*
- **Theme:** The message the author is trying to send. Examples: *Be kind to others; walk in another man's shoes; family comes first.*
- **Tone:** An overall feeling or effect in the story, created through words or literary devices. Example: *The place, like her life, was chaotic. Stuff was everywhere and her mind was no different. Thoughts swirled all over the place and landed in a mess.*

Conferencing: Offering Students Feedback on Their Writing

Conferencing is a teachable moment. Although a teacher can conference with groups, it is best to conference with a student privately, when possible. When discussing the student's writing, teachers should praise particular texts or aspects, so as to keep the child motivated and comfortable about writing, but should also offer goals for improvement. A conference should only take a few minutes, and should include a discussion of one or two aspects of the student's writing, such as the content, the craft, the form, and, eventually, the mechanics.

Steps in the writing conference:

1. Sit side by side, and make the situation comfortable.
2. Begin with comfortable questions like "How is it going?" "What can I do to help?"
3. Read the part of the piece being worked on, and move into focusing on what the student is doing well.
4. Focus on one or two traits, and discuss these areas with the student.
5. Teach the student what he should do to improve this particular writing piece. Don't fix the writing for him—help the student, so he can apply this knowledge to the next piece he writes.
6. Follow up with the student as he revises the writing piece to make sure that new knowledge is clearly understood.

Useful conferencing techniques:

- Focus on the student as a writer and the work he is doing.
- Ask focus questions and make comments to get feedback from the student. The teacher may say things like: "Can you tell me more about X?" "I'm a bit confused here. Can you explain this event more thoroughly?" "Who is your audience? I can hear your voice in this piece, but something seems different in this section; let's talk about that." If you have a concern that the student is not writing correct facts, ask the student to check his resources to make sure he has accurate information.
- Do not zero in on all the errors. Select one or two areas where you can teach/discuss, and hope to see improvement at the next conference.
- Keep it brief; the student needs to write, and the teacher needs to move on to the next conference.
- Jot down anecdotal notes about the student and his progress.
- With older students, use peer editing prior to teacher editing; train students in peer-editing techniques.

- If a group of students seems to be weak on "leads," meaning they have no idea how to begin their writing piece, give a mini-lesson to that group, then conference on each lead. A mini-lesson could also be used if students are having problems transitioning from one paragraph to the next.

- Use consistent language at each conference. Doing so will enable the class to have a common language about writing.

Instruments for Writer's Feedback

There are several tools a student can use to make sure his writing piece meets the assignment expectations.

- **Writing rubric:** A writing rubric, such as one with the six traits (see the "Characteristics of High-Quality Writing" chart on page 71), can be used to evaluate and score writing. A student may be strong in voice, but weak in mechanics. A conference should be used to discuss the evaluation on the rubric so students can be given goals for future improvement.

- **Self-evaluation checklist:** A self-evaluation checklist can be used independently. For younger students, it might focus more on mechanics, with questions like: "Did I use end marks?" "Did I use capital letters?" "Did I leave a space between words?" "Does my writing make sense?" For older students, a checklist can include some of the same mechanical aspects, as well as questions like: "Did I use a lead-in?" "Did I use appropriate vocabulary?" "Is the writing organized?" "Am I stating all the information that I want, and does it make sense?" "Did I use correct grammar?"

- **Peer-evaluation checklist:** A peer-evaluation checklist can be used for peer conferencing. Questions would be similar to those on the self-evaluation checklist above, but would be prefaced with "Did the writer."

- **Criteria checklist:** A criteria checklist can be used to make sure the writer is including all criteria in a specialized assignment. For example, if students were being assigned to write an informational book, although the teacher would most likely use a rubric for scoring, a checklist that lists expectations could be provided. A checklist for an informational book may include: title, dedication page, table of contents, an appropriate number of chapters, and/or a glossary.

Writing: Forms and Purposes

Writers write for a variety of reasons: to give information, amuse, reflect, sympathize, press ideas, explore an idea, give directions, judge, inquire, give an image—the list could go on and on. The three main reasons for why writers write are (1) to entertain, (2) to inform or teach, and (3) to persuade or convince. Writers use various forms depending on the purpose of their writing. These forms, in essence, are genres. Refer back to the "Common Genres and Characteristics" chart in Chapter 8, page 52. The "Characteristics" column lists the criteria that identify a particular genre.

Main Forms of Writing

The following main forms of writing can be found in different genres.

- **Narrative:** Narrative writing tells a story, as in a novel. For children, a narrative often takes the form of a personal essay. Usually written in the first person, narratives often position the writer as the main character, telling a personal story.

- **Descriptive:** Descriptive writing creates a picture or a detailed explanation describing a person, place, thing, or event. The writer uses visual words; older writers may use metaphors, similes, and symbolism.

- **Persuasive:** Persuasive writing tries to convince the reader of the author's viewpoint and is written to express an opinion about something. This writing is often biased. It includes another point of view, but uses what appears to be logical reasoning and facts against this other point of view in order to support the writer's view of the situation.

- **Expository:** Expository writing is informational text that contains facts. It can be written with various text structures such as compare/contrast or chronological. See the "Informational Text Structures" chart in Chapter 8, page 58.

- **Creative:** Creative writing can be described as anything interesting to read. This could be poetry, short stories, plays, and so forth. This form is used as an avenue for fun, as facts do not need to be included.

Other Common Forms of Writing

These following forms are not mentioned in the genre or text structure charts in Chapter 8, but they are commonly used. Please note that there are dozens of other forms of writing not included here, such as various forms of poetry, obituaries, editorials, and advertisement.

- **Monologue:** A written account of one person speaking; written in the first person, usually as if the writer is thinking aloud.
- **Picture Book:** Contains plot and characters, or can be informational text. Pictures aid students in word identification and comprehension. The pictures may also include information not presented in the written text.
- **Short Story:** Usually contains characters, setting, a problem, attempts to solve the problem, and a solution.
- **Interview:** Recounts questions and answers from a given interview.
- **Play:** Contains dialogue, scenes, actions, sometimes a narrator, and directions on speaking and performance.
- **Letter:** Has traditional format with greeting, body, salutation, and signature. Format can vary depending on the purpose of the letter; a business letter format is different from that of a friendly letter.
- **Comic Strip:** Actions are shown in drawings, and thoughts and dialogue are written in balloons.
- **Memoir:** A first person narrative that recalls a significant personal event or events.
- **Folklore:** A story, usually based on fact, that is passed down from generation to generation.

Use of Mentor Texts

Mentor texts are used by teachers as a model of what is being written. Sometimes the mentor text can be a complete book or a collection of books. Other times, the mentor text can consist of selected sections or paragraphs of books that model a particular type of writing the students need to work on. If the teacher's goal is to get her students to write better character descriptions in their stories, she might select four or five different books that have wonderful character descriptions.

When using a mentor text, the teacher reads the selected piece and shows it on a projector; the class then analyzes the author's craft. Using the mentor text below, a character description from E. B. White's *Stuart Little* (1945), the reader gets quite an accurate picture of the Littles' second son:

> "He was only about two inches high; and he had a mouse's sharp nose, a mouse's tail, a mouse's whiskers, and the pleasant shy manner of a mouse. Before he was many days old he was not only looking like a mouse but acting like one, too—wearing a gray hat and carrying a small cane."

The teacher would read the humorous description and ask students to examine it. The teacher could facilitate with leading questions like: "What descriptors does the author use to describe Stuart?" "Can you visualize what Stuart looks like?" "What does the author say about Stuart's personality?" In this way, the teacher leads students into seeing that a good character description gives vivid details about the character's appearance and personality. Regarding this passage, the teacher could also discuss the author's craft of using humor to describe Stuart, and ask the question, "How could E. B. White have described Stuart without elaboration?" (*He looked like a mouse.*) The teacher could also ask, "Although we all know what a mouse looks like, how does E. B. White's description help us get a better picture of the character?" This mentor text would be followed up with two or three more examinations of character descriptions, serving as mentor texts, from other books.

Chapter 10

Reading and Writing as Tools for Inquiry and Research

When you teach children to do research, you are teaching them a lifelong skill. It is often recommended that students begin their research by looking at the "big idea." Research can be guided by inquiry-based learning principles. Inquiry-based learning begins with the teacher posing questions or assigning problems that need answers. The students then research and investigate to find the answers. For example, a big idea question might be: Is Earth's climate changing? From that point, the teacher might guide students into researching such ideas as extreme flooding or melting icebergs.

Teaching Students to Effectively Use a Variety of Research Sources

Note: All research techniques should be modeled and practiced before students do them independently.

Print

If students are to use print resources (books, encyclopedias, magazines, brochures) for research, a number of skills and techniques need to be taught and practiced before getting into the actual research:

- How to locate information in a book by the table of contents and the index.
- How to skim by looking for key words to locate the information needed.
- How to slow down and reread if information is confusing.
- How to use close reading techniques to analyze texts.
- How to write comments via annotations, either on the text copy or with sticky notes.
- How to highlight important information that relates to the research topic or question.
- How to recognize important facts and distinguish them from interesting details.
- How to do a simple citation (book/author).
- How to take good notes with important information, citing the source.
- How to know if the material is accurate and the author/source is credible. (See "Selecting and Evaluating Print and Digital Media Resource Materials" later in this chapter.)

Electronic Media

Digital media has an abundance of information on every topic. Students need to learn how to evaluate the accuracy of the information and the credibility of the source. Students should be taught the following:

Note: For younger children, or to scaffold, the teacher should preselect online resources and explain how the sites were selected.

- How to recognize whether a particular website and other sources have accurate information. (See "Selecting and Evaluating Print and Digital Media Resource Materials" later in this chapter.)
- How to use search engines to get the best resources.
- That online videos need to come from acceptable sites. Although many include accurate facts, some videos are merely observational. Using online videos as resources can be time-consuming.
- That some media sites, like instaGrok, will instantly make a semantic web that leads to sources of information and videos.

- To bookmark, save, and copy and paste information for future use.
- That some sites, such as Google Docs, can be used for collaborative writing.

Interviews

When conducting an interview—whether in person, by phone, or using digital media such as FaceTime or Skype—there are certain caveats to be aware of and clear protocols to follow:

- The person to be interviewed must have the expertise the student is seeking.
- Interview questions have to be written prior to the interview, so that the interviewee's time is not wasted.
- Some of the research must be completed prior to the interview in order for the student to create carefully worded open-ended questions for the interview.
- The student needs to preset a date and time to meet.
- The student needs to be prepared with questions, writing utensils, and a camera or recorder if wanted. (*Note:* The student must request the interviewee's permission to record the interview.)
- The student needs to begin the interview with polite introductions and should use good listening skills.
- The student needs to take notes and show interest in what is being said.
- The student needs to end the interview politely, thanking the interviewee for his time.
- As a follow-up, the student should send a thank-you note.

Observation

As I sit here writing about using observation for research, I am watching the Smithsonian's National Zoo's Panda Cam 2. One of the pandas, Mei Xiang or Bei Bei, is sleeping on the large rocks. The environment seems to be a small mountain with lots of big rocks to climb and big pieces of wood lying around. It appears to be cloudy and breezy in the nation's capital. I can see that the zookeepers feed the panda bamboo, and that the panda moves just a bit while sleeping, like a human. It is now around 6 o'clock in the evening. I don't know if pandas are nocturnal and sleep all day, or if the panda is just napping. So goes the power of observational research.

In the above scenario, the researcher (me) learned new information and also came up with a question about the sleeping habits of pandas. When students observe, whether it's using a live cam to watch bald eagles or a ruler to measure the growth of a plant, they are gathering information about their topic that can be synthesized into the research or become the focus of the research.

When performing observational research in the classroom, students should:

- Use an observation form to guide their observations. First and second graders will most likely use a teacher-provided observation form for all observational research. By third grade, students should be able to collaborate with their teacher to create the observation form, or they can simply take notes.
- Take photos or draw pictures to show observational data. Students can capture screen shots from live cams.
- List the time and date for all observational data.
- Note any changes and underline them to indicate importance.
- Follow a designated time duration for observations so the data collected doesn't become overwhelming. Examples: in plant growing, once a week for 4–6 weeks; in panda viewing, twice weekly for 10–15 minutes.
- When the observation window is over, review and summarize their notes for important details to synthesize into their findings from other sources.

Teaching Research Skills

Modeling is the essence of good teaching. The following procedure is one way that research can be conducted. There are many effective ways of teaching research. In all effective methods, the teacher either (1) models with a project first, and then has the students do a project; or (2) models each step before it happens, has the students practice with the teacher, and then the students do the step independently. During the various steps, the teacher must oversee students' work to make sure they are on the right track.

One Model for Conducting Research

1. As a class, decide the "big idea" for your research.
2. Students do background reading, independently or shared, to help come up with the big idea.
3. As a class, turn the big idea into the "big question," and then generate a list of smaller questions about the topic.
4. Model how the smaller questions can help organize the research project.
5. Direct students to gather resources: print, electronic media, interviews with experts, or observations.
6. Model how specific information is found in the resources. Model such techniques as looking at the table of contents, looking in the index, skimming as you look for information to answer the big question or smaller questions, deciding what is important as opposed to what is interesting, highlighting, making annotations, and other various techniques of good research as the need arises.
7. Direct students on how to decide if graphics are needed in the final report in order to make a point clear.
8. Have students write important information on index cards, or digital notes, along with reference citation(s). Model a simple citation, such as title and author or title and website. Show the students how to categorize their index cards by smaller questions to organize for the first draft.
9. Model as needed as students bring their writing up to final draft.

Using Technology to Conduct and Create Final Research Projects

A book could be written on this section, as there are myriad technology sources available on the Internet and in software to aid in research. It is not possible to list all of the available resources, but they are categorized for you below. Please note that the online resources named here were available at the time of this writing.

Technology Sources

Research aids:

- Sites with the domain extensions .edu and .gov are recommended for research. The Library of Congress website is an excellent site for primary sources.
- ReadWriteThink.org has capabilities to aid students in making timelines, outlines, and so forth.
- Mapmaking or map finding sites, such as MapQuest, Google Earth, Google Sky, or Google Map Maker.
- Semantic webs for brainstorming, such as instaGrok (finds sources) or ReadWriteThink.org.
- Live cams are good observational resources for animal research. Do a search on the animal or place wanted to see if a live cam might be available.
- Search engines, such as Gooru, that search reputable websites only.
- Telecommunication sites for interviewing, such as Skype, FaceTime, or Google Hangouts.

Writing aids:

- Collaborative writing sites, such as cooltoolsforschools or Storybird.
- Online applications that are depositories for information to be retrieved later, such as Evernote.
- Categorizing tools, such as Coggle or Text 2 Mind Map, that display and categorize information, which helps in paper organization.
- Annotation tools, such as Diigo or Kami, that allow for highlighting and annotating.

Presentation Programs

- Writing software, such as Microsoft Word, can be used for papers.
- PowerPoint or Prezi publishing software can be used to create presentations that can be displayed on an overhead projector.
- VoiceThread allows slides, print, and voiceover; it can be set privately for class use.
- Students can publish finished research on a class blog site via a blogging service such as Blogspot.
- Students can publish on a class website such as Weebly.
- Various sites, such as wikiHow, allow you to start a wiki where you can upload your presentation.

Selecting and Evaluating Print and Digital Media Resource Materials

The following are some guidelines and suggestions that teachers can share with their students to help them select and evaluate resource materials.

Print Resource Materials

- Primary sources are original documents from history. They can be a historical document like the U.S. Constitution or an audio recording from a person living through the Great Depression. When using primary sources, the source needs to be on topic and authenticated in some way.
- Informational books are usually reviewed by more than the author so information should be correct. However, note that for science topics, the book's publication date is important, as the information can be outdated.
- Magazines often contain advertisements that look like credible sources. Students need to be cognizant of looking for the word "advertisement" on the page.
- Newspaper articles are based on what is perceived to be true, but they are an acceptable source and can also be a primary source for historical events.
- Online children's magazines, such as *National Geographic Kids* and *TIME for Kids,* are considered credible sources.
- Maps, photographs, and prints can be used for research, although students must be aware that some map information can be outdated.
- Students need to know that persuasive materials contain bias and do not contain all information needed.
- Award-winning books can be good resources. There are a number of awards given for nonfiction books, such as the NCTE Orbis Pictus Award for Outstanding Nonfiction for Children and the ALSC Robert F. Sibert Informational Book Medal. Books that have received these awards are considered outstanding publications of nonfiction works.

Selecting Digital Media Resource Materials

Worthy selections:

- When selecting a site, ones that have domains that end with .edu or .gov are considered to have the most correct information.
- The American Library Association has a list of recommended websites, which are considered credible for research.
- Author sites are usually credible, but beware, as some are just marketing sites put together by publishers or marketers.
- Online e-books should be previewed by the teacher before being used for research; anyone can self-publish a book online.

Cautionary advice:

- Students need to be taught to look at the date of materials, as some online sources are outdated, but don't disappear.
- If the site design is too complicated, it is best to find an easier site to navigate.
- Poor writing conventions (spelling, punctuation, etc.) on a site indicate that it is probably not a credible site.
- Wikis, such as Wikipedia, allow anyone to write in them. These are not considered good sources to use as a citation, although information can be gleaned from reading the wiki. The information must be substantiated elsewhere.
- Blogs are not considered good research sources, as anyone can write anything.
- Radio and television broadcasts may not be accurate, as they may contain bias.

Research is highly respected in education. When someone quotes research, others listen. Research writing should stay on topic and be cohesive and engaging. When teaching students to research, whether using print sources, digital information, or both, it is important that students understand that facts need to be thorough and accurate. Sources need to be vetted so only credible ones are used.

Chapter 11

Assessment for Optimal Growth

Assessments, both formal and informal, are an important part of teaching reading. They are used to identify starting points for instruction and monitor student progress, and can help guide you in how best to help your students meet or exceed grade-level reading expectations. Teachers are held accountable for students' academic growth.

Formal Reading Assessments

Standardized tests are formal assessments. They have standardized measures, meaning that research has been done related to expectations for a certain age or grade group, so that statistics are available to support the expectations and allow for comparison of results. The data are standardized, and scores appear as percentiles, stanines, standard scores, or grade-level equivalents.

Standardized tests are created in two formats: norm-referenced and criterion-referenced.

- **Norm-referenced test:** This format compares students with other populations and gives a percentile score that "ranks" the student at a percentile against other students. If a student receives a score in the 75th percentile, this means that the child scored higher than 75% of the students who took the test, and lower than 25%. The norm would be at the 50th percentile, so receiving a score in the 75th percentile places the student above the norm.
- **Criterion-referenced test:** In this format, the test is set up to measure against certain criteria. The child is not compared with other test-takers, but is evaluated based on the content being measured on the test. For instance, a criterion-referenced reading test can test word attack knowledge, vocabulary, homophones, contractions, comprehension, and so forth.

Some standardized tests are a hybrid, a mix of norm-referenced and criterion-referenced. In this case, the test is set up in sets of "batteries" or content matter, where each of the content areas has been "ranked" for percentiles.

Scoring

Standard deviation refers to a range that indicates the child could have performed better or worse on a given day. Through mathematical calculations, the standard deviation gives a range for a student's test score. This tells us how spread out scores can be from a test. If the mathematically computed standard deviation is 3 and the norm is the 50th percentile, then the standard deviation is 3 in either direction. A child who scores 47 to 53 would be considered in the norm by use of the standard deviation. Or, if a child scores a 73, on any given day his scores could have been 70 to 76, as the standard deviation is the range above and below the actual score.

A stanine is a 9-point scale used for normalized test scores, with 1 to 3 considered below average, 4 to 6 average, and 7 to 9 above average. Therefore, a student whose scores land in the 4 to 6 stanine is considered to be in the average range, 5 being the average.

Determining Test Validity and Reliability

A test is valid if it measures what it says it will measure. For example, if an assessment says it is measuring inferential comprehension, but it only asks literal questions, the assessment is not valid. (Literal questions ask for what was said directly in the text, not what was inferred.)

A test is deemed reliable if it would produce the same results with a different set of people in a different setting. If you can give the California Achievement Test to third graders in California, Kentucky, Florida, and Massachusetts and get about the same curve with each state's results, the test is considered reliable.

Checking Your Understanding

Read each of the following statements and determine if it describes validity, reliability, a criterion-referenced test, or a norm-referenced test. Explain your answer.

1. A student is in the 47th percentile for this standardized test.
2. This norm-referenced test was given in New York, Missouri, and Oregon, in both rural and urban areas. The student scores in all of these areas were comparable.
3. There is some concern about this test because it asks for alphabetical order in a question that says it is measuring inference.
4. From the testing results, the teacher can see that Brendon needs to work on his word identification skills, vocabulary, and inferential comprehension.

Answers

1. Norm-referenced test: The test has been set against the normal curve, and this student has 46 percent of the students below him and 53 percent above him.
2. Reliability: The test is normed and has been given in various locations in order to assure its reliability, and scores are comparable in all locations.
3. Validity: The issue at hand is whether alphabetical order measures inferential comprehension. In order to be valid, a test must measure what it says it will measure. As illustrated by this statement, the test is not valid.
4. Criterion-referenced: The test results have pinpointed content in which Brendon has a weakness.

Monitoring Students' Reading and Writing Progress

Monitoring a student's reading and writing progress is an ongoing process. Three concepts are described in the chart below: progress monitoring, how assessment guides instruction, and formative assessment. To aid in your understanding of these concepts, a concrete example is provided, using a scenario with a child named Sarah.

Concept	Description and Purpose	Scenario
Progress monitoring	Progress monitoring is used to ensure that "no child is left behind." Scores from assessments are recorded, student weaknesses are identified, instruction is given, and, finally, a follow-up assessment will show whether progress has been made. This is a continual cycle in both reading and writing to ensure all students learn. The teacher must keep excellent records about a child's progress, and persistently use formative assessment to ensure the child continues to improve.	Sarah has been assessed using a running record, and the teacher has found her to be weak in identifying multisyllabic words.
Assessment guide instruction	The idea behind this concept is that a child is assessed in some form and goals are set from the results of the assessment. Instruction is then aligned to the goals that were set.	A goal for Sarah would be instruction that improves her ability to identify multisyllabic words. Sarah would be taught chunking skills and morphemic analysis (looking for smaller words or word parts that are known to the reader), and perhaps to use context cues more frequently to aid in word identification.

(continued)

Concept	Description and Purpose	Scenario
Formative assessment	When teachers monitor progress, children are assessed in different ways as a daily practice. When a teacher sees that a child is struggling in an area, she uses this formative assessment information to set goals for improvement in the weak areas. In addition, if a teacher sees that a child is "breezing" through the concept and skills being studied, the teacher knows it is time for that child to be given more challenging tasks.	After Sarah has been working with her new strategies to identify multisyllabic words, Sarah's teacher listens to her read. Sarah is given a text in which she can use her new skills to identify multisyllabic words. If Sarah does well in this formative assessment, it will be time to create new goals for her. If she does not do well, a different approach will need to be used for her instruction. (This is all within the cycle of progress monitoring.)

Reading Levels

As discussed in Chapter 6, the three reading levels are defined as follows:

- **Independent:** When a child can read 95% or more of the words correctly in a text, and shows excellent understanding of the text, this is the child's independent level and is considered too easy for the child to be challenged.

- **Instructional:** When a child reads 90–95% of the words correctly in a text, and shows good understanding of the text, this is the child's instructional level—what is called the "just right" reading level for the child's optimal learning.

- **Frustration:** When a child reads 89% or less of the words correctly in a text, and shows minimal understanding of the text, this indicates that the text is too difficult for the child.

Vygotsky and the Zone of Proximal Development

These levels are important because they help determine the most optimum level for instruction. As mentioned in Chapter 8, Lev Vygotsky, a learning theorist with a sociocultural approach to cognitive development, posited that cognitive development depends on a zone of proximal development (ZPD). To simplify, the ZPD is a range in which a person can learn. If something is too difficult (frustration level), the learning curve does not allow true learning to occur. If something is too easy (independent level), a person can't "learn" what he already knows. Therefore, the ZPD is at the instructional level, where someone can be taught by a more learned individual. This is because at that level, there is enough to learn—but not so much as to be frustrating. As a person learns the new material, the ZPD shifts forward, and the learning cycle continues at the new instructional level.

Informal Reading Assessments

Informal assessments are used almost daily in the classroom and are driven by content and performance; they are not standardized like formal assessments. Although there is usually some standardization of the procedures, scoring in informal assessments is often subjective. If a teacher is concerned about a student's understanding of contractions, an informal assessment could be given. The student might end up with a score of 9 out of 14; in this case, the goal would be to increase the student's individual score. The teacher could choose to group lower-scoring students together in a skills group and use small group instruction to improve each student's performance. In the case of a rubric, weaknesses and strengths would be identified in particular areas and goals would then be generated from that assessment.

Types of Informal Assessments

The following list is not exhaustive, but it gives an overview of the various informal assessments that are being used in classrooms today.

Early literacy assessments:

- **Letter identification:** Very young students should be assessed to see if they can identify the letters by name and letter/sound identification.

- **Concepts of print:** The teacher will ask a student if he can show her the concepts of print, such as a book's title, a sentence, end marks, and so forth. (For a more complete list of the concepts of print, see Chapter 4.)

- **Phonemic awareness:** In this assessment, students are told a word orally and asked to blend, separate, segment, or substitute sounds.

- **Retellings:** A retelling is when a child tells the listener what a story or informational text was about. In a story retelling, a teacher might be using a rubric to score the child's retelling (oral or written) and be looking for inclusion of the following: characters, setting, problem, attempts to solve, solution, inferences, and voice or mood, depending on the expectations and grade level. Retellings are usually scored with a checklist or rubric.

- **Running records:** A student reads a passage orally, and the teacher codes the miscues (errors) made. Miscues include omitting a word, pronouncing a word incorrectly, appealing for help, and substituting a word. If a student corrects an error, this is called self-correction, and is not counted as a miscue. Teachers analyze running records in order to ascertain word identification needs and reading levels of students. (For more on running records, see Chapter 6.)

Assessments used at all levels:

- **Portfolios:** A portfolio is an orderly and systematic collection of a student's work. The work is selected carefully to show student progress, or lack of progress. For example, the working portfolio may show a scored writing sample from weeks 1 and 5, in order to explain the goals that were set in week 1 and the progress made by week 5. Any of the assessments that will be discussed in this section can be part of a working portfolio. (A showcase portfolio, on the other hand, is work that the student and teacher select as best examples.)

- **Rubric:** A rubric is used to score work and represents what is expected from a student at that grade level in the content or skill being assessed. It is usually structured like a grid, with the work divided by the criteria expected, such as voice, content, or word choice in writing. Then, a thorough explanation of what is expected is explained in boxes that are arranged in a continuum of developing to proficient. Scoring for each criterion can range from unacceptable to acceptable to target and is represented in gradients that run the gamut from "best" to "needs to do better." A student could be scored at the target level in voice, but do poorly in content. The separate scores for various criteria allow for formative assessment data and goal setting for students.

- **Spelling inventories:** Made popular by their book *Words Their Way,* authors Donald R. Bear, Marcia Invernizzi, Shane Templeton, and Francine Johnston offer a spelling "test" for students. The results show what spelling patterns individual students are weak in. Teachers can then group the students by skills needed and use formative assessment for progress monitoring.

- **Informal reading inventories (IRIs):** Although considered informal assessments, many informal reading inventories (IRIs) have been normed by grade levels and have standardized directions for administration. An IRI usually consists of grade-level word lists to assess word recognition levels and grade-level passages to assess reading comprehension, along with word recognition to obtain a student's grade level for reading. The passages can be read orally and miscues can be recorded, or the IRI can constitute a silent comprehension check. IRIs are usually used as one measure to decide what level book a child should read for "just right" reading.

- **Cloze procedure:** This is an assessment where every fifth or sixth word is left blank. The student reads the text, and, using context and semantic cues, tries to fill in the blank with the correct word or a synonym. The cloze procedure can also be used to assess reading level and the student's use of syntax (structure of language) and semantics (meaning) to select words to place in the blanks. Once the student fills in the blank, only the exact replacement word is scored as correct. If the text is at the child's instructional level, then 40–59 percent of the words would be correct. Sixty percent and above is independent; below 40 percent is frustration level.

Assessing the affective domain (dealing with feelings and emotions):

- **Attitudinal survey:** This is an informal gathering of information about students' attitudes on various subjects, such as speaking, reading, and writing. A survey might ask questions like "Do you like to read at home?" This question would be pinpointing whether the student likes recreational reading, whereas "Do you enjoy reading at school?" would focus on academic reading. (If you search online for "elementary speaking, reading, and writing attitude surveys," you will find dozens of examples.)

- **Interest inventories:** This is a series of questions that teachers ask students in order to get to know them a bit and to see what they might be interested in reading or writing about.

Using Diagnostic Reading Data to Differentiate Instruction

Differentiation occurs in a classroom when a teacher matches a student with the materials and instruction needed to aid in improvement. This process can be used with a struggling reader who needs slower paced instruction or for a gifted student who knows the material being taught and deserves the opportunity to learn. To differentiate instruction, data need to be collected and analyzed at predetermined intervals. This information is then used to differentiate instruction in the classroom; progress monitoring must also be documented. A teacher must always be ready to take a student to the "next step," meaning that when progress is shown, the work must become more complex so that learning continues. Or, if progress is not apparent, then the instruction needs to be altered so that the student can learn. Regular progress monitoring ensures that students are learning at the optimal level and pace.

What Will Data Tell You?

Data Source	What Can Be Determined
Norm-referenced test	Where each child performs compared to others in his age group and grade. Depending on the type of test, student needs can also be determined.
Criterion-referenced test	Specifically scored to pinpoint strengths and weaknesses with respect to the content the test is assessing (letter/sound correspondence, mechanics, comprehension, and so forth). A child can score at the "ceiling" level, meaning that he scored better than the limits of the assessment.
Informal assessment	Myriad information depending on the assessment, as noted previously in the list of informal assessments. If a rubric in fluency is used, a child's data might say the child is weak in speed, but strong in expression.
Group/class data	If each child in the class had the same assessment, class data exist, but the data must be organized as such. Class data are used to group students for specific needs. The scores are analyzed by class to form instructional groups, such as leveled reading groups, writing strategy groups, or word enrichment groups. In the case of word attack concerns, if seven students in a class are showing on a criterion-referenced assessment that medial vowels are problematic, then these seven students would be in a group where skills and strategies are taught that will help identify medial vowels sounds.

Ways to Differentiate

The main reason teachers gather data is to place each child where he can receive optimal learning in a group, class, or individual setting. This is done through differentiation.

Tiers of Differentiation

Carol Tomlinson is considered the "mother" of tiered differentiation and has written extensively about differentiated instruction. "Tiers" basically means "levels." In differentiation, an activity is "cloned" to an easier or more complex level so that all students can learn at the level in which they need instruction. Tomlinson states that differentiation occurs in three basic ways: through content, process, and product. Although teachers differentiate what students are doing, the desired outcome or objective of the lesson does not change.

- **Content:** Differentiation through content means that the materials or information is differentiated in tiers to meet the learners' needs.

  Example: The desired outcome is for students to learn about ants and ant colonies. Students would be given leveled books with at least three levels: one for the struggling readers, another for the on-grade readers, and finally, a more complex text for the students who need a challenge. The information required for the outcome to be met would be included in the easiest text, but the other two levels would also contain that information, plus more detailed or complex information.

- **Process:** Differentiation through process means that the instruction is tiered to meet the needs of the learner.

  Example: The desired outcome is student improvement in inference skills. During group time, the teacher will be more explicit with the struggling group as she explains and models how, together, they can infer what the author is saying and use support from the text. With the on-grade level group, the teacher models her inferences and support, and then has the students work together to discuss other inferences and support gleaned from the text. For the advanced group, the teacher explains that she wants the students to read and state at least three inferences from the chapter and the supporting evidence. The teacher models with one example to ensure all students understand.

- **Product:** Differentiation through product means that the end result would be tiered.

  Example: The desired outcome is to have students write directions. A teacher would have the struggling readers write directions for a three-step art project, the on-grade group would write directions for a five-step project, and the group that needs a challenge would write directions for a seven-step project. The key is that all students would be writing directions at different levels of difficulty.

Curriculum Compacting

In curriculum compacting, a child "compacts out," which means that an assessment has been made that shows the child already knows the material being studied. Once that has been ascertained, the teacher gives the child a project, or allows him to choose an individual project (or group project, if there is more than one child compacting out), that will foster new or extended learning related to the topic or goals.

Interest

Interest triggers motivation. If children are highly motivated to learn something, they will work harder and "go beyond" in their learning. Often, because of their interest, they have more background knowledge on a topic, which places them at a higher level of learning at the outset.

Learning Centers

Learning centers can be chosen by interest or assigned by need. They can be supplied with materials to differentiate learning, and the time needed at the center can be set differently for each child. For example, a word work center could have manipulatives for struggling students to make the "ent" word family (such as *bent, cent, dent, lent, rent, sent, tent, went*). The middle level students would have a cloze activity (fill in the blank) in which they would put one of the "ent" words into a sentence like "The campers put up their _____." The highest level group would be told to use the "ent" family words and write their own sentences.

Multiple Intelligences

Developmental psychologist Howard Gardner is known for his theory of multiple intelligences. This theory states that we are not all smart in the same way, and that there is not just one type of intelligence. When differentiating for the various intelligences, teachers can give students a choice of an activity that capitalizes on their strength. Gardner has identified the following eight different intelligence types:

1. **naturalistic:** Smart with items in nature; seeing patterns in the natural.
2. **bodily-kinesthetic:** Learns through hands-on experiences; tactile.
3. **musical-rhythmic:** Learns musical instruments easily; learns through music and rhythm.
4. **intrapersonal:** Strong with inner thoughts; understands self.
5. **interpersonal:** Friendly; understands the needs and feeling of others.
6. **logical-mathematical:** Smart with math, reasoning, and logical thinking.
7. **verbal-linguistic:** Strong with the use of language to present ideas for various purposes.
8. **visual-spatial:** Creates and learns from visual images; thinks spatially and three-dimensionally.

Scaffolding

This term is derived from the word *scaffold,* a raised wooden platform used to work on out-of-reach areas. In the classroom, teachers provide scaffolding for students by asking guided questions, giving partial answers, or breaking up a lesson into smaller parts. The idea is that as students become better at the skill, teachers can take the "scaffold" away. Scaffolding is a major part of Vygotsky's zone of proximal development, where teachers scaffold learners to work in a slightly challenging context.

Reading or Writing Workshop

When students are reading or writing more independently of the teacher, the class can be taught "workshop" style. Books and writing topics are often self-selected; they are supported with flexible group mini-lessons on content the teacher deems necessary from analyzing different works. Although reading and writing workshops are driven by student interest, the teacher is very much the leader in the classroom as she facilitates learning, monitors progress, and informally assesses students to offer mini-lessons in their areas of need.

Literature Discussion Groups

There are two main ways to discuss literature in the classroom: literature circles and reciprocal teaching. Both are described in detail below.

- **Literature circles:** Students are given roles such as discussion director, vocabulary finder, clarifier, visualizer or artist, questioner, and so forth. Students are trained in their roles so that groups will be productive.
- **Reciprocal teaching:** Grouping in which students have four major strategies that guide their discussion: summarizing, clarifying, question generating, and predicting. These strategies are first modeled and then practiced before groups are allowed to operate without teacher guidance. In older grades, a student leads the group discussion.

Flexible Grouping and Guided Reading

Flexible grouping and guided reading are similar ways to differentiate, as guided reading groups should be flexible. These methods are described in detail below.

Flexible Grouping

Flexible grouping allows the teacher to differentiate instruction to maximize student learning. Students are brought together in small groups to get instruction that is matched to their needs based on assessments. Progress monitoring is the key to flexible grouping. The premise of flexible grouping is the ability of the teacher to switch students from one group to another, depending on the level and needs of the student. Students do not stay in the same group; some advance faster than others, and a student is not kept in a group where he knows the content being taught. As students advance, they move within the learning groups or move to a newly created group. With effective teaching, the level of all students should always be advancing. Flexible grouping is as it is named—flexible in the content being taught and in student composition, as the needs of students are always changing.

Flexible grouping could be used for, but is not limited to, the following:

- leveled reading groups (discussed more in "Guided Reading," below)
- writing groups depending on need, focusing on instruction in a particular trait in writing
- word identification skills
- reading skills and strategies
- vocabulary instruction
- English Language Learners (recognize that ELL students themselves may be at different levels, depending on their knowledge of the English language and of the content being taught)

Guided Reading

Guided reading is a form of flexible grouping that enables the teacher to teach small groups of students on the same reading level and often with the same needs. Components of guided reading include the following:

- Students are grouped by assessment level; a group of six students is considered an optimal group size.
- Assessment is continuous; it may include daily observations, running records, and IRIs.
- Groups meet for about 20 minutes to read with teacher scaffolding, discuss the reading, and participate in daily skill or strategy focus.
- Three to four guided reading groups are recommended per class.
- Small group size allows the teacher to get to know students as readers and to design instruction to their needs. When a student progresses beyond other members in the group, that student is moved to the appropriate reading level group.
- When a reading group meets with the teacher, the other groups are kept well occupied with an academically focused task such as centers, literature discussion groups, independent reading, or reader response work.

Response to Intervention

Response to Intervention (RTI) programming began with the reauthorization of the Individuals with Disabilities Education Act (IDEA) in 2004. RTI requires scientifically research-based instruction and usually includes three tiers. (*Note:* These tiers differ from the three tiers in Tomlinson's differentiation mentioned earlier in this chapter.) The tiers or levels indicate the instructional organization and what services will be offered to students at each level. The use of RTI is to make sure all possible steps have been taken to ensure a child does not get further behind and to make certain that only the neediest students are identified for special education.

Most RTI models contain three tiers, which look like this:

- **Tier 1:** Classroom instruction is from the teacher. Progress is monitored; differentiated instruction supports all learners. This means that all students get high-quality, scientifically research-based instruction. Students who do not progress adequately are moved to Tier 2 for supplemental instruction. (About 80 percent of all students fall in Tier 1.)
- **Tier 2:** Students receive help from both the teacher and specialists. The intervention and support are focused on what is needed most and supplement classroom instruction. Progress is monitored. Instruction in this tier is based on needs; specific interventions are made by either a teacher, a specialist, or a coach, usually in small groups. Students who do not show enough progress are moved to Tier 3; students who show more than adequate progress are moved back to Tier 1. (About 15 percent of all students fall in Tier 2.)

- **Tier 3:** Students who struggle the most are placed in Tier 3. The intervention is intensive, with targeted instruction from specialists or coaches. Students at this level often get one-on-one instruction. If students are not successful at this level, they are referred for special education services. (About 5 percent of all students fall in Tier 3.)

Assessment is a crucial and continual part of all literacy instruction. It is a teacher's responsibility to assess students, monitor their progress, and adjust instruction for their optimal growth. Assessments can be formal or informal. The diagnostic information gleaned from assessments is used to group students and make individual goals. Lessons are differentiated in a variety of ways to help students meet the designated goals. During this time, the teacher continues to monitor progress and, using effective practices, adjusts instruction when needed.

Chapter 12

Test-Taking Strategies

Chapter 1 prepared you for studying for the Praxis (5203). Chapters 2–11 contained the material to be studied. The main focus of this chapter is to prepare you for the actual taking of the test. To start, review the three-day countdown for some last-minute test-preparation tips. Then learn how to use this book's two practice tests to simulate a real testing experience. There are recommendations to help you take the two practice tests in this book as if you were at the test site. Why? Simulation can help a person become a bit more comfortable in uncomfortable or unusual situations. The last section of this chapter gives you some tips for test day.

Countdown to the Praxis (5203)

The following timeline is recommended as you prepare for your test.

Three Days Before the Test

Go to www.ets.org/praxis and look for tidbits and helpful suggestions. There could be updates that are important to your test-taking experience. Watch any videos, read any updates, and check your "My Praxis" account.

There are three constructed-response questions on the Praxis (5203). Take some time to focus on this question type. Think about how you might begin any of your essays for the constructed-response questions. While you don't know in advance what the questions will be, there are some generic beginnings that can get you started, such as:

- After reviewing the material on . . .
- The teacher's notes suggest . . .
- When looking at the information provided, . . .
- In the case of this particular student, it appears . . .
- According to reading research and theory, . . .
- When analyzing the available assessment(s), . . .

Think about appropriate transitional phrases to begin your concluding essay paragraph. Again, it needs to fit the particular question, but some generic endings include:

- In conclusion, the evidence offered in this . . .
- The final point that is important to state . . .
- To summarize, . . .
- Finally, in support of what was said, . . .

You have 2½ hours to complete the Praxis (5203). Decide how much time you will need to write three short essay responses. Think about how much time you will need to answer 90 selected-response questions. Think carefully about what will work for you. If you are undecided, try the following approach:

1. Answer the constructed-response questions first. They are the most laborious and take lots of thinking. Give yourself no more than 60 minutes, which allows 20 minutes for each short essay response. This is not a lot of time. But you are prepared with beginning and ending phrases to get you started. **Remember:** The constructed-response questions account for approximately 25% of your score. Be sure to save enough time to answer the 90 selected-response questions, which account for 75% of your score.

2. After 60 minutes, switch to the selected-response questions. You now have 90 minutes left, and you are hoping to devote 10 to 20 of those minutes to go back and check your constructed responses and any

uncertain questions. When you start the selected-response questions, look at the time and calculate what time it will be in 45 minutes. You want to be at least halfway through the selected-response questions at that point. For example, if you start the selected-response questions at 10:00 a.m., you will want to be at least on question 45 by 10:45 a.m. With all the studying you've done, you will most likely be further along—which is good, as it will give you time to review your writing and perhaps some of the confusing selected-response questions.

3. Try this timing breakdown on one of the two practice tests in this book, and then tweak the timing as needed to make a timing plan for test day.

Two Days Before the Test

If unexpected complications have kept you from studying for the Praxis (5203), you have a problem. But don't panic. It's time to react. If you need to pull an all-nighter, do so two nights before the test. Do not stay up all night the night before the test.

If you have adhered to your study plan, just review, at this point. Review, study, and make sure you have everything clear in your head. When reviewing the reading content, focus on what you consider your weaker areas. Go over your notes. Make yourself confident.

Finally, if you overeat like this author does when she's anxious, put all (okay, most) of your junk food in a basket, and ask your neighbor to hold it for 48 hours. Seriously, you don't need a stomachache when taking the test!

The Night Before the Test

- Check on the Praxis website for any updates.
- Verify your test center location (do so through your "My Praxis" account).
- Even if you are going to use a GPS, if you have never been to the test site, look it up on a map to make sure that you have a visual of where you are going.
- Print your admission ticket, and have it ready to bring with you.
- Assemble your identification documents.
- No personal items are allowed. No one at the site will take responsibility for any personal items.
- Put your ID and admissions ticket (and map, if needed) in a place where you will remember to take them (in the car if necessary!).

You do need to think about your physical health as you prepare for the test. Make sure you have decent meals the night before and the morning of the test. You want to go into that test room feeling physically and mentally alert.

Figure out what time you need to go to bed in order to get 8 hours of sleep, and stick to that bedtime.

The Morning of the Test

- Eat. This might be the one time that a doughnut might help.
- Dress comfortably. Layers might be useful, in case the testing center is too hot or cold for you.
- Watch your liquid intake so you are not uncomfortable.
- Get to the testing center early. Expect a line.

How to Take the Practice Tests to Simulate Real Testing

Pretend that the practice tests in this book are real tests, and study as if you were going to a test center to take the actual Praxis (5203). Use the study approach that you have decided is the best for you. If there is any topic that is still not clear to you, do an online search. You want to go into the test knowing and understanding this material. When you feel confident that you have studied well enough and can do well on the Praxis (5203), it is time to take the practice tests.

When taking the practice tests, try to mimic test-day conditions:

- Place yourself at a table or desk with a computer or laptop to answer the constructed-response questions.
- Have two or three pencils ready to use to fill in the selected-response bubbles on the provided answer sheets.
- Set a timer for 2½ hours.
- Pace yourself. Use the plan you made previously (in the "Three Days Before the Test" section). *Remember:* 90 questions, 3 essays. So, if you plan to spend 60 minutes on the essays and 70 minutes on the selected-response questions, that leaves you 20 minutes to review.
- Decide which question type you are going to tackle first. Many students prefer to do the writing first because that seems to take the greater amount of energy. Decide what time limit you will observe.
- Start the selected portion of the test, stop at the previously decided time, and go to the second part.
- If there is time left at the end, use it to review what you have written. Check over conventions, spelling, and sentence structure.
- Stop when the timer goes off. Do not exceed the 2½-hour testing time when taking the practice tests.

After you take both practice tests, you will have a better idea of how long each portion of the real test will take you, so you can plan your test-taking time accordingly. Furthermore, after scoring the practice tests, you will know if there are any areas you need to review again before taking the actual test. This will help give you a focus as you review prior to taking the Praxis (5203).

Constructed-Response Tips

Remember the points on the Praxis (5203) scoring rubric for scoring the writing (see page 11): Make sure you have answered all parts of the question. Your response needs to be clear, with supporting details, and must show strong knowledge of the reading content.

In your essay writing, don't just throw in reading terminology. If you are using a reading term, either define it or support it in your response. Here is an example of how this should be done:

> You are asked to analyze a running record. The running record shows that a child reads the following words with short vowel sounds: *beat, tail, boat, bait,* and *pail.* With analysis, you can see that the child needs to learn that vowel digraphs say the long sound of the first vowel. In your essay response, you may write "Since all of the words with vowel digraphs ("ea" in *beat,* "ai" in *tail,* "oa" in *boat,* "ai" in *bait,* and "ai" in *pail*) had errors, the child's weakness is in vowel digraphs. A vowel digraph is when two consecutive vowels make one sound."

Test Day

At the test center, you will have 30 minutes to complete a tutorial before you start the timed test.

When the test begins:

- Check the time. You have 2½ hours (150 minutes) for this test.
- Go to the section you plan to start with.
- Remember your timing plan. When should you be done with the constructed-response questions? The selected-response questions?
- Divide that time mentally in order to pace yourself.
- When the first section is done (constructed response or selected response), begin immediately with the other section, remembering to consider timing and to pace yourself.
- Keep calm and test on.

After the test:

Don't start second-guessing yourself and beating yourself up. It is what it is. Congratulate yourself for your great preparation! Now, go to your neighbor's house and get that junk food. You deserve it!

Chapter 13

Practice Test 1

Answer Sheet

(Remove This Sheet and Use It to Mark Your Answers)

Selected-Response Questions

1 Ⓐ Ⓑ Ⓒ Ⓓ	46 Ⓐ Ⓑ Ⓒ Ⓓ
2 Ⓐ Ⓑ Ⓒ Ⓓ	47 Ⓐ Ⓑ Ⓒ Ⓓ
3 Ⓐ Ⓑ Ⓒ Ⓓ	48 Ⓐ Ⓑ Ⓒ Ⓓ
4 Ⓐ Ⓑ Ⓒ Ⓓ	49 Ⓐ Ⓑ Ⓒ Ⓓ
5 Ⓐ Ⓑ Ⓒ Ⓓ	50 Ⓐ Ⓑ Ⓒ Ⓓ
6 Ⓐ Ⓑ Ⓒ Ⓓ	51 Ⓐ Ⓑ Ⓒ Ⓓ
7 Ⓐ Ⓑ Ⓒ Ⓓ	52 Ⓐ Ⓑ Ⓒ Ⓓ
8 Ⓐ Ⓑ Ⓒ Ⓓ	53 Ⓐ Ⓑ Ⓒ Ⓓ
9 Ⓐ Ⓑ Ⓒ Ⓓ	54 Ⓐ Ⓑ Ⓒ Ⓓ
10 Ⓐ Ⓑ Ⓒ Ⓓ	55 Ⓐ Ⓑ Ⓒ Ⓓ
11 Ⓐ Ⓑ Ⓒ Ⓓ	56 Ⓐ Ⓑ Ⓒ Ⓓ
12 Ⓐ Ⓑ Ⓒ Ⓓ	57 Ⓐ Ⓑ Ⓒ Ⓓ
13 Ⓐ Ⓑ Ⓒ Ⓓ	58 Ⓐ Ⓑ Ⓒ Ⓓ
14 Ⓐ Ⓑ Ⓒ Ⓓ	59 Ⓐ Ⓑ Ⓒ Ⓓ
15 Ⓐ Ⓑ Ⓒ Ⓓ	60 Ⓐ Ⓑ Ⓒ Ⓓ
16 Ⓐ Ⓑ Ⓒ Ⓓ	61 Ⓐ Ⓑ Ⓒ Ⓓ
17 Ⓐ Ⓑ Ⓒ Ⓓ	62 Ⓐ Ⓑ Ⓒ Ⓓ
18 Ⓐ Ⓑ Ⓒ Ⓓ	63 Ⓐ Ⓑ Ⓒ Ⓓ
19 Ⓐ Ⓑ Ⓒ Ⓓ	64 Ⓐ Ⓑ Ⓒ Ⓓ
20 Ⓐ Ⓑ Ⓒ Ⓓ	65 Ⓐ Ⓑ Ⓒ Ⓓ
21 Ⓐ Ⓑ Ⓒ Ⓓ	66 Ⓐ Ⓑ Ⓒ Ⓓ
22 Ⓐ Ⓑ Ⓒ Ⓓ	67 Ⓐ Ⓑ Ⓒ Ⓓ
23 Ⓐ Ⓑ Ⓒ Ⓓ	68 Ⓐ Ⓑ Ⓒ Ⓓ
24 Ⓐ Ⓑ Ⓒ Ⓓ	69 Ⓐ Ⓑ Ⓒ Ⓓ
25 Ⓐ Ⓑ Ⓒ Ⓓ	70 Ⓐ Ⓑ Ⓒ Ⓓ
26 Ⓐ Ⓑ Ⓒ Ⓓ	71 Ⓐ Ⓑ Ⓒ Ⓓ
27 Ⓐ Ⓑ Ⓒ Ⓓ	72 Ⓐ Ⓑ Ⓒ Ⓓ
28 Ⓐ Ⓑ Ⓒ Ⓓ	73 Ⓐ Ⓑ Ⓒ Ⓓ
29 Ⓐ Ⓑ Ⓒ Ⓓ	74 Ⓐ Ⓑ Ⓒ Ⓓ
30 Ⓐ Ⓑ Ⓒ Ⓓ	75 Ⓐ Ⓑ Ⓒ Ⓓ
31 Ⓐ Ⓑ Ⓒ Ⓓ	76 Ⓐ Ⓑ Ⓒ Ⓓ
32 Ⓐ Ⓑ Ⓒ Ⓓ	77 Ⓐ Ⓑ Ⓒ Ⓓ
33 Ⓐ Ⓑ Ⓒ Ⓓ	78 Ⓐ Ⓑ Ⓒ Ⓓ
34 Ⓐ Ⓑ Ⓒ Ⓓ	79 Ⓐ Ⓑ Ⓒ Ⓓ
35 Ⓐ Ⓑ Ⓒ Ⓓ	80 Ⓐ Ⓑ Ⓒ Ⓓ
36 Ⓐ Ⓑ Ⓒ Ⓓ	81 Ⓐ Ⓑ Ⓒ Ⓓ
37 Ⓐ Ⓑ Ⓒ Ⓓ	82 Ⓐ Ⓑ Ⓒ Ⓓ
38 Ⓐ Ⓑ Ⓒ Ⓓ	83 Ⓐ Ⓑ Ⓒ Ⓓ
39 Ⓐ Ⓑ Ⓒ Ⓓ	84 Ⓐ Ⓑ Ⓒ Ⓓ
40 Ⓐ Ⓑ Ⓒ Ⓓ	85 Ⓐ Ⓑ Ⓒ Ⓓ
41 Ⓐ Ⓑ Ⓒ Ⓓ	86 Ⓐ Ⓑ Ⓒ Ⓓ
42 Ⓐ Ⓑ Ⓒ Ⓓ	87 Ⓐ Ⓑ Ⓒ Ⓓ
43 Ⓐ Ⓑ Ⓒ Ⓓ	88 Ⓐ Ⓑ Ⓒ Ⓓ
44 Ⓐ Ⓑ Ⓒ Ⓓ	89 Ⓐ Ⓑ Ⓒ Ⓓ
45 Ⓐ Ⓑ Ⓒ Ⓓ	90 Ⓐ Ⓑ Ⓒ Ⓓ

CUT HERE

·CUT HERE·

Time: 2½ hours

Selected-Response Questions

90 questions

1. A kindergarten teacher is working with a small group of children. She says the word *cat* to the students. Then she puts her left hand on her right shoulder and says /k/, and then moves her hand to her elbow and says the short /a/ sound. Finally, she brings her left hand down to her right hand and says /t/. She repeats the word *cat* and the motions, having the students follow her example. She does this with the words *tap, had, mat,* and *rag.* What is the teacher's main purpose in this lesson?

   A. She is segmenting to teach students the short sound for the letter "a."
   B. She is segmenting to teach students the long sound of the letter "a."
   C. She is segmenting to teach students phonemic awareness of various letter sounds.
   D. She is segmenting sounds to have children match the sounds to the individual letters.

2. Which of the following best describes how language acquisition and writing development are acquired?

   A. Language acquisition begins at birth, whereas writing development begins with formal schooling.
   B. Both follow a linear progression in which children grow through appropriate milestones.
   C. Language acquisition is learned through modeling, whereas writing development is taught through effective instruction.
   D. Writing helps children to learn the basic structure of oral language.

3. What are the four types of vocabulary that we process daily?

   A. Babbling, sentences, listening, and writing
   B. Receptive, expressive, speaking, and listening
   C. Telegraphic, sentences, pragmatics, and phrases
   D. Speaking, listening, reading, and writing

4. Mrs. Moniz is reading a picture book to her first-grade class. She is careful to stop and explain unfamiliar words. She points to pictures that will help in explaining new concepts. She stops after her explanation and has students discuss the new vocabulary or concept. What is the teacher's main reason for doing this?

   A. The teacher wants to ensure that her young students are grasping the letter-sound correspondence as she introduces new words.
   B. The teacher is using effective instruction by having her students actively participate in the learning of unfamiliar words and new concepts.
   C. The teacher is modeling how pictures can aid in comprehension of new words.
   D. The teacher is modeling good book-handling skills as she progresses from page to page and points at the pictures.

GO ON TO THE NEXT PAGE

5. Which of the following statements best describes why oral vocabulary is important for reading comprehension?

   A. The use of accurate oral language is important in student discussions about the text being read.
   B. Students' oral language is important for understanding what the teacher expects and, therefore, impacts their understanding of how to complete a reading task.
   C. The more oral vocabulary the students know and understand, the deeper and more accurate their comprehension will be when reading.
   D. Limited oral language enables students to learn more words through wide reading, therefore improving comprehension.

6. The teacher is doing shared reading with a small group of students in her kindergarten class. As she reads, she is taking the pointer past each word to the end of the line. Then the teacher carefully takes the pointer to the next line and continues to follow the text as she reads. On which concept of print is the teacher focusing?

   A. The directionality of print
   B. Beginning, middle, and ending of a book
   C. Where a sentence begins and ends
   D. What defines a word

7. In his read aloud, a teacher is reading a fourth-grade level book to his second-grade class. Which of the following statements best describes the purpose of reading a fourth-grade level text to second graders?

   A. The teacher is reading a higher level text in order to model more complex sentences.
   B. The teacher understands the importance of using predictable books in teaching beginning readers, and wants his students to grasp how predictable books can aid in learning new words.
   C. Reading a fourth-grade text to second graders allows for deeper comprehension, as the concepts are more difficult for these younger students.
   D. The teacher has chosen a higher grade level book to expose his students to the vocabulary in order to increase their listening and speaking vocabularies.

The following scenario is used to answer the next <u>two</u> questions.

   A fifth-grade classroom teacher has her students create a "pop-up" card (an accordion fold under a message or picture, so the message or picture "pops up" when opened) for a character of their choice in the book they are reading. She stresses that the card's message must contain a fact or imply a character trait so that the card is meaningful to the character.

8. What might be the purpose of a teacher having students write a "pop-up" card for a character?

   A. The ability of the students to show in sequence what is happening to the characters in the text
   B. The ability of the students to employ vocabulary learned from the text
   C. The ability of the students to analyze a character for wants, needs, or motives
   D. The ability of the students to explicate the message of the text

9. After the project is completed, the teacher has the students write out the directions for making a "pop-up" card. What text structure is the teacher having the students practice in this exercise?

   A. Compare/contrast
   B. Sequential
   C. Problem/solution
   D. Description

GO ON TO THE NEXT PAGE

10. Which of the following word groups demonstrates that a suffix can have a different sound, although the meaning remains unchanged?

   A.   *recorder, baker, plumber*
   B.   *swimming, bending, contemplating*
   C.   *alteration, complication, amplification*
   D.   *wanted, baked, whisked*

11. A fifth-grade class is studying the settlement of the prairie states. The text thoroughly describes everyday life on the prairie, from raising animals to making candles. The teacher wants the students to understand the challenges of pioneer life as compared with life today.

Which of the following student activities would be most effective in aiding students' understanding of the hardships of pioneer life as compared with modern-day living?

   A.   Write an essay that describes the hardships faced by pioneers that settled in the prairie states.
   B.   Complete a Venn diagram that compares the daily life of prairie state pioneers with that of modern people.
   C.   Write a play that students can act out that portrays the hard work and work ethic of the prairie state pioneers.
   D.   Read an article on the art of making candles and their use in pioneer times.

12. A teacher is working with a group of fourth-grade English Language Learners. When discussing the reading, the teacher mentions that the main character was *dog tired*. The students look up at the teacher in confusion. What is the best technique for the teacher to use to aid the ELL students in their understanding?

   A.   Explain what a homograph is, explain what *dog tired* means, and use a synonym for clarity.
   B.   Define *dog tired* and be careful in the future not to use confusing terms.
   C.   Explain the use of idioms in the English language, discuss the character, and ask what *dog tired* might mean.
   D.   Continue on with the lesson, and explicitly teach the term *dog tired* at a later time.

13. Which word below contains two morphemes?

   A.   *nation*
   B.   *baker*
   C.   *impracticality*
   D.   *table*

14. Look at the following passage. Which particular trait of writing would be the best for a teacher to have students focus on when they read this passage?

   She was beyond cute. Her hair, a deep black, was pulled back into two pigtails that accented the loose curls around her small face. The bright pink shorts and flowered top spoke of gaiety and potential fun. But it was her smile, with the two missing front teeth, that stole our hearts as Sarah skipped toward us.

   A.   Organization
   B.   Conventions
   C.   Ideas
   D.   Voice

GO ON TO THE NEXT PAGE

15. When reviewing a standardized test, Mrs. Lee sees that Daniel, a third grader, is in the 47th percentile for word usage. She is not surprised, as she has noticed that Daniel sometimes uses words incorrectly in his writing, but she has not noticed that in his oral language.

Which one of the following statements best describes what Mrs. Lee should do for Daniel?

A. Mrs. Lee should administer a spelling test to Daniel that contains targeted morphemes; from there, she should place him appropriately in the correct skills group for targeted morphemes and the lower reading group.

B. The 47th percentile is a concern. Daniel should be recommended for further testing to see if he needs more support from specialists within the system.

C. Since the 47th percentile is still in the middle range, Daniel's progress is average. Using flexible grouping, Mrs. Lee should place Daniel in a group working with morphemic activities and correct usage of various morphemic structures.

D. Daniel should be placed in a writing group that is focusing on writing organization and word choice.

Use the following writing sample to answer the next two questions.

I wnt to the str to git a nu bik and I hd a lot of fn becz Mom git me sm icrem

16. The child's writing evidences that the child knows which of the following?

A. Sentence conventions
B. Beginning and ending sounds
C. Words contain vowels
D. Vowel-consonant-silent "e" spellings

17. The child's writing evidences that the child could most use which of the following?

A. Instruction in the appropriate use of capital letters
B. Work with consonant letter sounds to ensure proper letter-sound correspondence
C. Making word activities with word families
D. Work with irregular spelling patterns

18. A teacher listens to Jerome, a second grader, read a decodable book. Although Jerome reads the words correctly, he seems to sound out most words, which causes his reading to be slower than expected for his grade level. Which of the following would be the most appropriate strategy for the teacher?

A. Have Jerome make a word list of the more complicated words in the text and practice them on index cards.

B. Have Jerome work with the irregular words in the story and make up sentences using these words.

C. Place Jerome in a flexible group working with decoding words and the letter-sound correspondence.

D. Have Jerome reread the text a number of times for a variety of reasons, such as to get used to reading aloud by reading to a partner, or to select interesting sentences.

Use the following passage to answer the next two questions.

Kayla was in a pensive mood. She had a sense of foreboding, as if something was going to go wrong. As she walked down the street, a feeling of déjà vu overtook her. The surroundings seemed sterile. Nothing looked messy or out of place; no litter, no graffiti, no people. A chill ran down her spine. It seemed so familiar, yet different. Whatever the cause, Kayla had a sense of discomfort.

GO ON TO THE NEXT PAGE

19. Mr. Markin is planning his reading lesson for his fifth-grade level reading group. He has decided that two vocabulary words in the passage should be explicitly taught prior to the reading. Which two words would best be taught explicitly during pre-reading?

    A. *pensive, déjà vu*
    B. *foreboding, déjà vu*
    C. *graffiti, sterile*
    D. *familiar, sterile*

20. Which two vocabulary words in the previous passage would be the best for Mr. Markin to use for morphemic or structural analysis?

    A. *pensive, déjà vu*
    B. *surroundings, sterile*
    C. *foreboding, discomfort*
    D. *graffiti, whatever*

21. A classroom teacher is using text sets to teach her students about land forms. The books cover some of the same information but are at different reading levels. Students are reading their books with a partner and stopping every other page to discuss what was read. What is the teacher's main purpose in having students stop and discuss?

    A. To build fluency as they discuss the vocabulary in the text
    B. To clarify any confusing areas as they discuss the text
    C. To ensure students don't skip a page as they read
    D. To let students read independently and answer questions

22. Mrs. Finch is worried about her lowest reading group. Although they can read decodable books, their reading is slow and without expression. Mrs. Finch has decided that she needs to work with the students using a different instructional activity. Which of the following reading modes would be best for Mrs. Finch's group at this time?

    A. Shared reading
    B. Partner reading
    C. Silent reading
    D. Choral reading

23. Mrs. Conant's second-grade class students are studying animals, habitats, and adaptations. Mrs. Conant's objective is to have her students understand that animals have adapted to their environment. One of the vocabulary words used in the book is *camouflage*. Which of the following instructional activities would be most effective to ensure that students understand the word *camouflage* and the concepts of animals adapting to their environment?

    A. Mrs. Conant should explicitly teach the word *camouflage,* promoting a clear understanding of the multiple definitions of the word to enable students' deeper understanding of the concepts.
    B. Mrs. Conant should preview the text with the students, discussing bold words and captions, stressing the section of the text that focuses on camouflage.
    C. Mrs. Conant should explicitly teach the word *camouflage,* using only the text definition, then preview the text and focus on *camouflage,* discussing the pictures that show animal adaptation by camouflage and having partners discuss this.
    D. Mrs. Conant should begin the lesson with a semantic web surrounding the term *animal adaptation*. As students volunteer words associated with animal adaptation, Mrs. Conant should make sure the word *camouflage* is included in the semantic web.

GO ON TO THE NEXT PAGE

24. Which of the following groups of words demonstrates that different letters and letter combinations can represent the same speech sound?

    A. *shut, chick, stripe*

    B. *fork, tough, graph*

    C. *major, minor, mentor*

    D. *gift, given, girl*

25. Which of the following is the most accurate description of explicit teaching of writing conventions?

    A. When teaching end marks, give students a paper with a variety of statements and questions. Ask them to read each of the statements or questions and put a period, exclamation point, or question mark at the end.

    B. When working with reading groups, point out the end marks and ask students to explain why the author used a period, exclamation point, or question mark.

    C. While doing close reading, tell students to notice the use of end marks in the text. Ask them to circle the periods, question marks, and exclamation points to discuss their uses with their skills group.

    D. In a mini-lesson format, explain the use of periods, exclamation points, and question marks. Model the use of each for the students. In a writing assignment, tell students they must use at least two of the end marks. During conferencing and editing, make sure end marks have been used correctly.

26. Which of the following words has three phonemes?

    A. *tuck*

    B. *important*

    C. *bracket*

    D. *gnu*

27. A class is preparing to read a complex text about the cause of the Revolutionary War. The teacher activated prior knowledge through a semantic web, but found that the students were limited in their knowledge of the Revolutionary War. The best technique to support students' comprehension of this complex text would be to

    A. read the text to the students, stopping to discuss difficult vocabulary words.

    B. assign the students the reading selection and have them write their questions as they read.

    C. have students read a small portion of the text, discuss the text in partners, then have a class discussion about the concepts prior to reading the next section.

    D. make a graphic organizer for students to fill in as they read the text independently, then have students discuss the filled-in graphic organizer in small groups.

28. Which of the following will NOT aid in fostering cultural responsiveness in a teacher's instruction?

    A. Encourage students to express themselves and explain cultural expectations when acceptable.

    B. Understand that a teacher should not communicate high expectations to all students, as it might frighten them.

    C. Encourage learners to analyze and discuss the multiple perspectives of various cultures.

    D. Build collaborative activities into classroom instruction.

GO ON TO THE NEXT PAGE

29. A teacher is doing shared reading in a first-grade class using a big book about a young boy who loses a tooth. As the teacher reads, she has the class discuss the pictures and predict what is happening in the book. When the main character loses his tooth, the teacher has her students talk with partners about when they lost a tooth. Which of the following best describes the teacher's purpose in using partner talk?

A. Predictions enable students to interact with the text and use inference skills to determine what is going to happen.

B. Discussing the pictures aids students in understanding unknown vocabulary words.

C. Talking about losing a tooth gives students an attention break and allows them to refocus as the teacher reads.

D. A connection to the text allows students to be actively engaged with the text and deepens their understanding of the events in the text.

30. It is important for a standardized test to be evaluated for reliability. Which of the following best describes what is measured when evaluating a test for reliability?

A. The questions have been checked for correct content to ensure that no question is erroneously counted wrong.

B. The timing of the test is standard at all test sites and the directions are to be read as written.

C. The test measures the skills or content it says that it will measure.

D. The test will get the same results with a different set of people in a different setting.

31. Think of the reading lesson in sections of before, during, and after. The following choices offer strategies to be used in reading lessons before, during, and after. Choose the answer choice that best shows the strategies in the correct order: one strategy for before reading, one for during reading, and one for after reading.

A. Before—summarize; During—question; After—work with vocabulary

B. Before—set a purpose; During—self-monitor; After—summarize

C. Before—question; During—set a purpose; After—predict

D. Before—set a purpose; During—build background; After—infer

32. Read the following scenario.

Using two index cards, the teacher covers the words *Mike, his,* and *bike* in the following sentence:

Mike rode his bike.

The teacher explains that *rode* is one word in the sentence. The teacher then visually counts all the words in the sentence, saying there are four words in all. Next, the teacher isolates, by covering the other words (*Mike, rode,* and *bike*) and proceeds in the same fashion, explaining that *his* is one word in the sentence, counting all the words in the sentence, and noting that there are four words in all.

Which of the following best describes what the teacher is trying to teach?

A. Phonemic awareness

B. Concepts of print

C. Phonics

D. Word usage

33. Mrs. Nelson writes the following words on the whiteboard: *pail, beat, boat,* and *pie.* She reads each word separately and asks the students what long vowel sound they hear, and then circles the first vowel in each word. She explains the phonics generalization as follows: "When two vowels do the walking, the first one does the talking." She has the students watch and listen to the song with that theme from YouTube. She then writes the words *goat, bait, read,* and *lie* on the whiteboard and has students read each word, say the long vowel sound, and explain why that sound is heard.

Which of the following best describes what the teacher is teaching in this scenario?

A. Vowel identification
B. Vowel digraphs
C. Vowel diphthongs
D. Long vowel sounds

34. It is important for a standardized test to be evaluated for validity. Which of the following best describes what is being measured when a test is said to be valid?

A. The test measures the skills or content it says it will measure.
B. The test has been given a number of times to students in the Illinois schools and the students' scores have been comparable across the state.
C. The test will get the same results with a different set of students in a different setting.
D. The test has at least four answer choices to choose from and only one of them can be correct, although there is always one answer choice that is considerably close to an acceptable answer.

35. In a second-grade social studies class, students are learning about community organization. They read the following passage:

A city is a place where lots of people live. A city has apartments, and many people park their cars on the street. A city has buses, sometimes lots of subway stations, and maybe even a big airport. A city usually has a mayor and a city council. They make the city's laws and decide how much taxes will be. But a town is much smaller and does not have as many people in it. It may have bus stops and one subway station. Sometimes a town has an airport for small planes. A town can have a mayor, but often laws and taxes are decided by the town council.

Which of the following best describes the text structure of this passage?

A. Description
B. Cause and effect
C. Problem and solution
D. Compare and contrast

Use the following scenario to answer the next <u>three</u> questions.

Mr. George, a fourth-grade teacher, has his students read the following passage. He sets the purpose for reading by telling the students to think about how Jacob and Aiden help each other.

Late in the afternoon, Jacob and Aiden were headed to the baseball field to practice. Jacob was the team's main pitcher and wanted to practice his curve balls. Aiden wanted to practice his batting, as he had struck out in the last two games. Jacob and Aiden threw the ball back and forth for a warm-up. Then Aiden picked up the bat, and Jacob headed to the pitcher's mound. Jacob threw the first pitch and Aiden swung and missed. Aiden missed the second pitch. Jacob tried not to smile as he prepared to throw the third pitch. As the ball came toward him, Aiden paced himself perfectly, swung with all his might, and the ball flew low inside the field, right near first base. Both boys grinned. Jacob knew that if a player had been on first base, Aiden would be out. Aiden was happy because he saved face; although he might have gotten out, at least he hit the ball.

GO ON TO THE NEXT PAGE

36. Mr. George is working on text-dependent inferential skills with his students. Which of the following questions is a text-dependent inferential question?

    A. When did Jacob and Aiden go to the baseball field?

    B. How would you feel if you had struck out in your last two baseball games?

    C. Why did Jacob try not to smile as he threw the third pitch?

    D. Why were both boys satisfied with the ending pitch?

37. After the reading, Mr. George focuses on *pitcher* as a multiple-meaning word. He asks the students what the word means in this passage and then if they know any other meanings for the word. What is the best term for the type of word Mr. George is referring to?

    A. Homograph

    B. Euphemism

    C. Synonym

    D. Homophone

38. Next, Mr. George reads the following sentence from the passage, "Aiden was happy because he saved face; although he might have gotten out, at least he hit the ball." He directs the students to the phrase *saved face* and asks what they think it means in the context of the passage and holds a discussion on its meaning. Which of the following best describes what Mr. George is teaching the children in this scenario?

    A. Acronyms

    B. Affixes

    C. Idioms

    D. Compound words

39. Which of the following is NOT considered an effective technique in close reading?

    A. Building background

    B. Rereading

    C. Annotating

    D. Collaborative discussion

40. Mrs. Florence's sixth-grade class, while studying the colonial era, was given the explanation and criteria for a research project on this topic. Students were instructed to use three online sources for their research. Which of the following best describes what Mrs. Florence should do to ensure that her students know how to select online sources with accurate and appropriate information?

    A. Mrs. Florence should give the students a list of appropriate websites that can be used for research on the colonial era.

    B. Mrs. Florence should show her students how to use a search engine in order to find a variety of information on the colonial era.

    C. Mrs. Florence should teach her students how to find appropriate sites that are credible and have accurate information.

    D. Mrs. Florence should start the students off by having them look up their topic on Wikipedia.

41. Mr. Benson was looking closely at Jared's assessment folder. For the standardized test, he saw that Jared was in the 83rd percentile for vocabulary and the 54th for comprehension. Jared's writing showed adequate vocabulary and use of conventions, although there was not a strong voice. The running record was on grade level, but the file showed that Jared did not do well in summarizing what he had read. With this information, which of the following pairs of approaches would be best for Mr. Benson to use as he begins Jared's instruction?

    A. Word study with an emphasis on structural analysis; modeling of voice in writing

    B. Phonics instruction with a focus on digraphs and diphthongs; summarizing strategies

    C. Vocabulary instruction; visualization techniques

    D. Comprehension strategies; modeling of voice in writing

GO ON TO THE NEXT PAGE

42. A number of students in a first-grade classroom were having difficulty with high-frequency words that were phonetically irregular. Which of the following techniques would be best for the teacher to implement with these students?

  A. Using a word wall with high-frequency sight words, continually adding new words, and referring to the word wall frequently for reinforcement

  B. Having students make a word book by putting word families of common spelling patterns together on different pages of the book for easy reference

  C. Using decodable and predictable texts for free reading and reading instruction

  D. Having students collaboratively discuss phonetically irregular words and list the words for further review

43. Which of the following statements describes explicit instruction?

  A. Students are given minimal instruction, but the teacher supports students as they work.

  B. The instruction begins with the teacher setting the purpose of the lesson.

  C. Students are to explore the given material and choose two important points.

  D. The instruction begins with students generating questions for inquiry.

44. Mrs. Bishop has been noticing that her students have recently been asking her to repeat information that she said previously. This has been disruptive to the class. Which of the following techniques should Mrs. Bishop use to address this concern?

  A. Have students think of two questions as Mrs. Bishop is talking.

  B. Write down the information so students can refer to it.

  C. Call on students that appear not to be paying attention and give them a direct question about what she was just talking about.

  D. Work with students so they are looking at her when she speaks and ask them to give her nonverbal cues that they understand.

45. Which of the following is an effective technique for English Language Learners?

  A. Speak loudly so that your words are enunciated for the students.

  B. When coming to a word that the students may not know, write it out.

  C. When making an important point, have students repeat what you have said.

  D. Ask questions that can be answered with one or two words.

46. The following are examples of what a teacher may have students do when working with words. Which of the following shows the teacher is focusing on phonemic awareness?

  A. The teacher asks students to put the short /a/ sound in the word *pot* and say the new word.

  B. The teacher asks students to identify the letters in the word *bank*.

  C. The teacher dictates the word *cake* and asks students to write down the letters they hear.

  D. The teacher asks students to say what letter begins the words *door, dad,* and *duck*.

47. Which of the following is the best instructional technique to help students develop an understanding of the author's purpose?

  A. Using a short piece of copied text, have students highlight metaphorical language as the text is read out loud. Then during rereading, have the class stop and discuss the metaphorical meaning.

  B. Expose students to a variety of texts; as a new genre is introduced, discuss the criteria for the new genre.

  C. Read a persuasive text while making a list on a two-column chart—one side with the pros given by the author, the other side with the cons given by the author.

  D. Read two different texts on the same topic and model how to synthesize the information.

GO ON TO THE NEXT PAGE

48. Which of the following is NOT an effective method of feedback to help students through the writing process?

    A. Teacher conferencing
    B. Peer editing
    C. Writing checklists
    D. Final draft scoring

49. A second-grade teacher has had her eye on Noah, who seems to be struggling a bit with his reading. She did a running record as Noah read from the text. Below is a sample showing what the text said and what Noah read.

    Text: Yesterday, that bird flew to its nest in the barn.

    Noah: Yes that bird flied to its nest in the back.

When the teacher questioned Noah about what he had read, he said, "The bird flied to its nest." Using this information, the teacher could best meet Noah's needs by

    A. working with vocabulary strategies to enhance comprehension.
    B. looking at the beginning and ending of the word to read through the word.
    C. stressing metacognitive strategies such as asking "Does this make sense?"
    D. teaching strategies for multisyllabic words.

50. Mrs. Clark is having Emma separate the beginning sound of short words from the ending sound. So, Emma says *st-ick* for *stick*, *p-at* for *pat*, and *dr-op* for *drop*. What best describes the skill Emma has mastered?

    A. Separating onsets from rimes
    B. Identifying short vowel sounds
    C. Being able to sound out unknown words
    D. Blending of letter sounds

51. A third-grade teacher was beginning a lesson on the forms of water. The teacher asked students what they knew about the different forms of water and wrote down their replies on the whiteboard. The words given were: *wet, snow, rain, liquid, ice,* and *hail*. As the students continued to provide more terms, the teacher asked them to group the words into categories, such as connecting *rain* with *liquid,* and then asked the students to explain why they formed a particular group. Why would the teacher have students take these steps prior to reading a text on the forms of water?

    A. To help the students identify terms that are related to water
    B. To activate prior knowledge and aid in understanding by using schemata to categorize information on the topic
    C. To assess students' ability to categorize information
    D. To make connections to personal life for deeper understanding of content

52. Jessica, a second grader, is reading to her teacher. The teacher can't help but notice that Jessica's reading is slow and laborious. What should the teacher assess first in order to determine learning goals for Jessica?

    A. Fluency
    B. Letter identification
    C. Decoding skills
    D. Metacognitive strategies

53. Some students are having difficulty with letter identification and cannot name all of the letters. Which of the following would be the best strategy to promote growth in this area?

    A. The teacher begins with the short /a/ sound and goes through a series of short /a/ words.
    B. The teacher has students look at the posted alphabet as she says each letter's name.
    C. The teacher begins a shared reading session by naming the letters in the book's title.
    D. The students, using a tablet app, trace a letter as the teacher is saying the letter's name.

GO ON TO THE NEXT PAGE

54. Which of the following would be considered an informal assessment that shows a child has reached the initial level of phonemic awareness?

    A.   The student can look at a word and blend the letter sounds together to form the word.

    B.   The student can listen to a single-syllable word and identify the beginning sound.

    C.   The student can state the number of syllables in a word.

    D.   The student can identify the letter at the beginning of a single-syllable word.

55. Mrs. Barker has been doing a writers' workshop with her students. Although she has seen some improvement in their writing, she is getting highly discouraged. She is finding that she cannot conference with the students enough, and they need more help in writing more meaningful thoughts. This is slowing student progress and causing behavioral issues, as children interrupt others while they wait for a teacher conference. She is feeling overwhelmed. Which of the following strategies would be the most effective to implement in this writers' workshop?

    A.   Initiate peer editing and conferencing during writers' workshop.

    B.   Conference with some students while others are doing their math.

    C.   Have students begin to use a self-editing checklist and initial each section.

    D.   At the beginning of class, have students tell the teacher what words they need and write a list on the whiteboard.

56. A third-grade teacher has one student who is a nonreader, but the student has good comprehension of oral directions and information. The class is gathering background knowledge on a simplified research project. What is the best way for the teacher to proceed with this particular student?

    A.   Have the student work on a decoding app while the other students are doing the research project.

    B.   Have the student cut out pictures that focus on the research topic.

    C.   Assign the student a topic for which there are first-grade level books in the classroom.

    D.   Have the student listen to a podcast on the chosen research topic.

57. Which text structure would the signal words *as a result* pertain to?

    A.   Chronological

    B.   Cause and effect

    C.   Compare/contrast

    D.   Description

The following scenario is to be used with the next <u>two</u> questions.

Mr. Gomez is working with fifth-grade students on the following passage:

> For two days now sadness had enveloped the whole town. Laughter would sometimes emerge from a young child. People talked in whispers, as if the kidnapper had bugged telephone poles and sidewalks. Everyone hoped, everyone feared. Tommy was a ray of sunshine, their ray of sunshine, and his disappearance had dampened spirits like no other town event.

GO ON TO THE NEXT PAGE

58. Mr. Gomez has the students read the passage twice and asks them to turn and talk (partner talk) about what is taking place in the passage. Mr. Gomez shows the passage on an overhead projector or SMART board and discusses the following questions with the students:

What mood is the author portraying in this passage?

What does the author mean by *sadness enveloped the whole town*?

What is the significance of people in public talking in whispers?

What does *ray of sunshine* mean? What is meant by *dampened spirits*?

What kind of strategy is the teacher modeling in this scenario?

A. Shared reading
B. Structural analysis
C. Theme and literary devices
D. Close reading

59. Mr. Gomez then asks the students an inferential question. Which question below would be the best text-based inferential question for Mr. Gomez to ask?

A. How many days has the town been silent?
B. How would you feel if someone was kidnapped from your town?
C. What did the author mean when he wrote *Everyone hoped, everyone feared*?
D. Should people have let their children laugh?

60. If you were to begin teaching your fourth-grade class structural analysis, which of the following groups of words would be best to use?

A. *matter, batter, splatter, shatter*
B. *appeared, appearing, disappear, reappear*
C. *through, shoe, flew, blue*
D. *laughing, barked, recall, unimportant*

61. Which of the following strategies should a teacher use first when a new English Language Learner is admitted to her classroom?

A. Speak slowly and enunciate carefully.
B. Welcome the student by asking about his background.
C. Talk normally so the student can get used to the rhythm and speed of the teacher's speech.
D. Buddy the child with another student to practice his English.

62. A group of second-grade students is reading slowly and without expression. The teacher has informally assessed the students and has determined the need for techniques to improve fluency. Which of the following is the most effective approach for the teacher to use with this group?

A. Have students reread their books silently.
B. Implement Readers' Theater.
C. Teach students chunking.
D. Have students read in a group, reading one at a time.

GO ON TO THE NEXT PAGE

63. Sarah retells the story of Cinderella for her classroom teacher. Sarah says, "Cinderella didn't have any money and needed a dress for the ball. She was sad, so the fairy godmother came and gave her a dress. Cinderella helped her sisters get ready. She had animals as friends because she was nice. She went to the ball and had a lot of fun. Then she married the prince."

Sarah's failure to mention the glass slipper in her retelling is evidence of which great weakness in her reading development?

    A. Sarah may have problems with inferential comprehension.
    B. Sarah may have a problem with working memory.
    C. Sarah may have some concerns with literal comprehension.
    D. Sarah may have a concern with sequence.

64. On the Woodcock Reading Mastery Test, a norm-referenced reading test, one student received a score in the 98th percentile in the vocabulary domain. Which of the following best describes what this information tells us about the student?

    A. The student did better than 98% of the students in the age/grade level who have taken the vocabulary section.
    B. The student got 98% of the vocabulary words correct.
    C. The student was able to get 98 of the vocabulary words correct.
    D. The test is not valid because a student should not be able to receive a score in the 98th percentile.

65. When a teacher gives students instructional level books to read as they are taught a unit of study, the teacher is differentiating by

    A. content.
    B. process.
    C. product.
    D. instruction.

66. Which of the following is NOT conducive to a culturally responsive classroom?

    A. Children are taught that respect for other cultures is an expectation in the classroom.
    B. Invite all children to be learners and express that all participation is valuable.
    C. Make sure books in the classroom are about American culture so ELL students will get to know our culture.
    D. Teach children that cultural differences make the world more interesting.

67. A sixth-grade teacher assigns a persuasive piece of text as independent reading for the class. Which of the following post-reading activities would best promote an analysis of the information given in the text?

    A. Have students respond in writing, discussing their own opinion about the topic.
    B. Have students fill in a T-chart with the pros and cons of the topic being discussed.
    C. Have students look up the author's background.
    D. Have students write five things they learned from the text.

68. Why is the ability to blend phonemes orally important to the development of reading?

    A. It helps students to determine syllables within words.
    B. It helps students to understand new words in context.
    C. It aids students in connecting a sound to a letter for decoding purposes.
    D. It allows students to distinguish onset from rime.

GO ON TO THE NEXT PAGE

69. As Mrs. Yu reads a book to her class, she shares her thoughts. She reads the text that says, *Polar bears live near the shore and on sea ice. Polar bears hunt for seals on the ice.* Mrs. Yu then says, "I knew polar bears lived in the cold, but it says here that they hunt for seals. Polar bears must eat seals. I didn't know that." She reads on, *The main food for polar bears is seals.* She then says, "I was right, they do eat seals." She reads on, *Sometimes polar bears catch a seal when it surfaces, and sometimes they swim beneath the ice to catch a seal.* Mrs. Yu continues to unpack her thinking as she says, "I knew polar bears could swim, but they must be really good swimmers to be able to swim under ice."

This teaching activity is most likely to help improve students' reading by

   A.   increasing students' listening vocabulary.
   B.   modeling metacognitive strategies so students can follow how she comprehends.
   C.   sharing strategies to work with content area vocabulary.
   D.   sharing her thoughts about the narrative text.

70. Kaylee read the text with her group. When Kaylee gave the teacher her summary of the text, it was not in order and contained some interesting details. What best describes the first goal that should be set for Kaylee?

   A.   Kaylee needs instruction on how to summarize lots of information.
   B.   Kaylee should be taught to employ prediction techniques prior to reading.
   C.   Kaylee should be taught explicitly how to differentiate interesting details from important facts.
   D.   Kaylee should be given some self-monitoring strategies to improve her reading.

71. A teacher is working with students on a unit on plant life. After discussing some information from the text, the teacher is concerned that one student is having a problem with the vocabulary and the surrounding concepts. Which of the following describes the procedure that would best benefit this student?

   A.   Instead of having the student read silently, read the book to the student.
   B.   Work with the student on chunking strategies to help him read multisyllabic words.
   C.   Have the student look up the words in the glossary and write the definitions.
   D.   Use a guided word sort and have the student sort the concept words into various categories.

72. A teacher is working with her young students in a shared reading group. As she reads a big book to them, she moves her finger across the page and points to the word she is reading. Which of the following concepts of print best describes what this teacher is modeling?

   A.   Where a sentence begins and ends
   B.   Directionality
   C.   That spaces exist between words
   D.   Number of words in a selected sentence

73. A sixth-grade class is studying a unit on the United States government. Enrico, a Spanish-speaking ELL student, is struggling with understanding the three branches of government and gets the responsibilities of each confused. Which of the following activities would best help Enrico to understand these concepts?

   A.   Have Enrico read the material in Spanish.
   B.   Give Enrico a graphic organizer to study that has the three boxes, each box labeled with a branch of the government and listing the duties of that branch.
   C.   Select a lower-level book so Enrico can read it to learn the duties of the three branches of government.
   D.   Make a chart with the three branches of government, using visual cues, and have Enrico reread the text and fill in the duties of each.

GO ON TO THE NEXT PAGE

74. A fifth-grade class is reading a novel in which the young girl character says, "My mom talks about my grandpa all the time. I never did meet my grandpa, as Mom says he's *gone to the happy hunting ground*. I don't know why he's there because I wonder if he knows how much my mom misses him." The teacher explains that the character's confusion about her grandfather is caused by the mother's expression, which is called a

    A. hyperbole.
    B. metaphor.
    C. euphemism.
    D. palindrome.

75. A sixth-grade teacher is beginning a 3-week unit on nutrition. Which types of words would be the most appropriate for the teacher to select for explicit pre-reading instruction?

    A. Multisyllabic words with familiar sounds
    B. Polysyllabic words with irregular spellings
    C. Affixes and root words
    D. Words that are challenging because of concepts within the text

76. By the time children are in kindergarten and first grade, their oral language has seen tremendous growth since birth. Which statement below best describes what should be expected by age 5?

    A. Language structure is usually in place.
    B. Children use short speech to send a message.
    C. Pragmatics are as expected.
    D. Speech usually centers on a want.

Use the following information to answer the next <u>three</u> questions.

The following Informal Reading Inventory (IRI) was used with a second-grade class. Part I, Word List, is read aloud to the teacher, who codes errors. The same is done with Part II, The Passage. The passage section is followed by comprehension questions, which students answer and the teacher scores as being at the frustration, instructional, or independent level. If a student scores at the frustration level on the word list or on the comprehension questions, then further assessments are needed, as it appears that the child is not reading at a grade 2 level.

Part I: Word List
puppy
really
wanted
think
something
skip
moved

Part II: The Passage
    Luke was happy because he had a new puppy. Luke's mom said he could name the puppy. Luke wanted a really good name, but he couldn't think of one. Then the puppy did something very silly. When the puppy moved, it looked like he was skipping! So, Luke named the puppy Skippy.

GO ON TO THE NEXT PAGE

77. One of the students read the word list and got all words correct except for the word *wanted*. When he read the passage, he was able to read all the words correctly. But after reading, the student did not score at the instructional level when answering the comprehension questions. Which of the following best summarizes one result of the assessment for this child?

   A. The student appears to be reading at grade level, and the teacher should begin the student with grade 2 level books.

   B. This assessment indicates the student has strong metacognitive skills, as he was able to read *wanted* correctly in the passage.

   C. According to this assessment, the student is proficient in phonics, but struggles with comprehension.

   D. It appears the student has limited ability to read multisyllabic words.

78. Another student read the word list and got *wanted* and *moved* incorrect, but was at the instructional level. When reading the passage, he got *wanted, moved, couldn't,* and *skipping* incorrect. His passage reading and comprehension questions were at the instructional level. Which of the following best summarizes one result of the assessment for this child?

   A. The student should be placed in a higher grade level book in order to read more challenging material.

   B. The student should be placed in grade 2 level books and placed in a skills group on multisyllabic words.

   C. The student should be placed in grade 2 level books and placed in a skills group on word tenses and affixes.

   D. The student should be placed in a higher grade level book and placed in a skills group on contractions.

79. Another student read the word list and missed five of the seven words, yet she only missed two words in the passage and received an independent level for the passage. Which of the following best summarizes one result of the assessment for this child?

   A. The student is relying too much on phonics, which is problematic for comprehension.

   B. The student is proficient at reading words with affixes, which fosters better comprehension.

   C. The student is proficient in decoding skills, but needs comprehension strategies.

   D. The student is able to use context cues to identify words, but shows a weakness in decoding.

80. It is the spring of your graduation year and you have just been hired to teach a first-grade class. You are so excited and plan to spend part of your summer perusing library and yard sales for books for your classroom. Since many, if not most, of your students will be ready for beginning level readers, what criteria should you mainly look for in the books that you purchase?

   A. The books should use natural language and contain decodable and repeated words.

   B. The books should have rich language and lots of connections.

   C. The books should have complex vocabulary and an assortment of diagrams.

   D. Pictures should not give away the words in the book, but enhance comprehension.

81. An ELL is reading a text that contains the following: *Sam sat and watched. The bugs flew. The worms crawled.* But the student reads, "Sam sat and watched. The bug flew. The worm crawled." Of the following, what question should we be asking ourselves about this student's errors in reading?

   A. Should the student be given strategies that ensure he reads through the word?

   B. Does the student know the sound of the letter "s"?

   C. Does the student know that an "s" on the end of a word can indicate that a word is plural?

   D. Does the student know what bugs and worms are?

GO ON TO THE NEXT PAGE

82. Amanda, a first grader, started at a new school today. Amanda sat quietly at her new desk and seemed somewhat shy. The new teacher, anxious to get to know Amanda, sat down next to her to talk. Amanda explained why they had moved to the new town and what her mother and father did for work. When asked, she talked about her favorite television show and series books. She said that the characters in *The Boxcar Children* series were "creative" and "delighted" her. From this informal interview, what might the teacher glean about Amanda's home life and past literary experiences?

   A. Amanda is often alone and has lots of time to read.
   B. Amanda watches a great amount of television because her parents work.
   C. Amanda has been exposed to rich vocabulary and reading is encouraged in the home.
   D. Amanda is lonely and talks a lot when given the opportunity.

83. A fourth-grade teacher was working on comprehension with a group of students. The students read the sentence *Tim came in from recess with a red face and his fists clenched.* When the teacher asked the students what this might mean, Johnnie answered, "His face was red." What might this response imply about Johnnie's comprehension?

   A. He needs some strategies for evaluative comprehension.
   B. He needs some strategies for pragmatics.
   C. He needs some strategies for literal comprehension.
   D. He needs some strategies for inferential comprehension.

84. Mrs. Thomas is working with fifth-grade English Language Learners that have recently arrived from an African country. All the students have attended school and have literacy skills in their own language. She has the students working on identifying body parts, such as head, arms, legs, and fingers. Which of the following is the most effective way to teach these students this vocabulary?

   A. Hand out pictures of the different body parts and have the students match them to the correct word.
   B. Have students point to the body part, say the word together after the teacher models, and then say the word to a partner.
   C. Show pictures of the body parts on slides and have students identify each body part.
   D. Give the students picture cards with the body part and the word. Have them pick a card and say the word to a partner.

85. Which of the following types of assessment would be best to help pinpoint specific literacy needs for students?

   A. Criterion-referenced test
   B. Norm-referenced test
   C. Running record
   D. Showcase portfolio

86. Which would be considered one of the most important reasons to have students complete a written reader response for a text they have read?

   A. It is easier to assess students' understanding of text with a written reader response.
   B. Oral reader responses do not provide teachers an adequate picture of students' thinking.
   C. A written reader response gives students the opportunity to use newly acquired vocabulary.
   D. When writing a reader response, the reader must think about the text, events, and information as he is writing, which deepens understanding.

87. What is the best way to teach young learners spelling?

   A. Have students copy sentences from books they have read and engaged in.
   B. Teach common orthographic patterns.
   C. Teach a few challenging spelling patterns.
   D. Use a word wall for reference during writers' workshop.

GO ON TO THE NEXT PAGE

88. Which of the following is an example of explicit teaching?

    A. The teacher gives the students five words and asks that they put them in alphabetical order.

    B. The teacher shows the word *ball,* states that it begins with /b/, and repeats the sound.

    C. The teacher gives the students ten word cards and asks them to do a free sort.

    D. The teacher puts labels on items around the room for children to read (light switch, whiteboard).

89. Read the following passage:

    I tell you that guy could jump as high as a kite can fly. Well, he must have been 10 feet tall with shoes at least size 20. I had to take thirty steps to keep up with one of his.

What literary device is the author using?

    A. Simile

    B. Personification

    C. Imagery

    D. Hyperbole

90. Mr. Carson was preparing his students to write a memoir about something poignant that happened in their life. During read aloud time and for their leveled reading texts, Mr. Carson was using memoirs written by various authors. Which statement below best describes Mr. Carson's purpose in doing this?

    A. He wanted the students to see the rich vocabulary in the books.

    B. He was using the memoirs as mentor texts.

    C. He knew that reading memoirs would be motivating and interesting to his students.

    D. He was selecting certain passages to show how literary devices are used.

GO ON TO THE NEXT PAGE

Constructed-Response Questions

3 questions

Constructed-Response Question #1

Eric read the following text to his teacher. The plain text shows the original verbiage. The bold type shows the teacher's marking as she coded the reading. Look carefully at the following and answer the questions below.

---

         side   **birth SC**
Sara ran down the <u>sidewalk</u> to her friends. It was Sara's <u>birthday.</u> Sara was happy to see her friends.

  wet   **sim**
The <u>weatherman</u> had said it was going to be a nice day so her friends brought their <u>swimsuits</u> to go into

          gramma
the pool. Sara's <u>grandmother</u> said she would watch them while Sara's mom made the food. They were

       cake   **it**   **in the house**
                   ^   ^
going to have <u>cupcakes</u> and eat <u>them</u> <u>inside</u>. Sara had a wonderful time at her birthday party.

Coding
Substitution (error) has what the student said above the word.
SC means self-correction.
^ means an insertion.

Analyze the above miscues. Using evidence from the teacher's coding, state one strength that Eric has as a reader, and one weakness. State a learning goal for Eric and how you might instruct Eric to attain that goal.

Constructed-Response Question #2

A fifth-grade teacher is introducing a leveled book on the expansion of the U.S. West to a group of students. She shares her premade KWL chart and has the students brainstorm what they know about the western expansion. She then gathers questions and writes them under the W on the chart. The teacher then takes out a map and discusses the outlined western territory. She provides a short slideshow that contains pictures of what settlers used for transportation and some of the hardships they encountered. These pictures are discussed with the students. After finishing the KWL, the teacher explicitly teaches two vocabulary words from the text. She then previews the text with the students. Finally, she allows them to choose a place in the room to read the text with a partner.

Why can we be certain that these partners will be able to read and comprehend this text successfully?

Constructed-Response Question #3

A third-grade teacher has been observing her students carefully. She has noticed that the students who read fluently also show a greater comprehension of the text than the nonfluent readers. She has also concluded that their writing skills are stronger.

Explain why this observation makes sense.

Answer Key

1. C	**19.** A	**37.** A	**55.** A	**73.** D
2. B	**20.** C	**38.** C	**56.** D	**74.** C
3. D	**21.** B	**39.** A	**57.** B	**75.** D
4. B	**22.** D	**40.** C	**58.** D	**76.** A
5. C	**23.** C	**41.** D	**59.** C	**77.** C
6. A	**24.** B	**42.** A	**60.** B	**78.** C
7. D	**25.** D	**43.** B	**61.** A	**79.** D
8. C	**26.** A	**44.** D	**62.** B	**80.** A
9. B	**27.** C	**45.** D	**63.** C	**81.** C
10. D	**28.** B	**46.** A	**64.** A	**82.** C
11. B	**29.** D	**47.** C	**65.** A	**83.** D
12. C	**30.** D	**48.** D	**66.** C	**84.** B
13. B	**31.** B	**49.** B	**67.** B	**85.** A
14. D	**32.** B	**50.** A	**68.** C	**86.** D
15. C	**33.** B	**51.** B	**69.** B	**87.** B
16. B	**34.** A	**52.** C	**70.** C	**88.** B
17. C	**35.** D	**53.** D	**71.** D	**89.** D
18. D	**36.** C	**54.** B	**72.** B	**90.** B

Answer Explanations

Selected-Response Questions

1. **C.** This is the only answer that does not introduce letter-sound correspondence. The teacher, in this scenario, is not working with letters (choices A, B, and D), just sounds, so the answer would be phonemic awareness.

2. **B.** Both language acquisition and writing development follow a linear progression in which children grow through appropriate milestones. Remember, most language structure is learned prior to age 5.

3. **D.** Speaking, listening, reading, and writing are the four types of vocabulary that we process daily. In choice B, receptive languages are listening and reading; expressive languages are speaking and writing, making this answer choice redundant.

4. **B.** The teacher is using effective instruction by having her students actively participate in the learning of unfamiliar words and new concepts. Although some of the answer choices, such as modeling good book-handling skills (choice D), explicitly refer to discrete activities, the main reason is active student participation for understanding.

5. **C.** The more oral vocabulary the students know and understand, the deeper and more accurate their comprehension will be when reading. Choices A and B do not refer specifically to comprehension. Choice D refers to limited oral language, but that will inhibit comprehension, not help it.

6. **A.** The directionality of print. The teacher is not focusing on story parts (choice B), does not explicitly state where a sentence begins or ends (choice C), and does not stress each word (choice D).

7. **D.** The teacher has chosen a higher grade level book to expose his students to the vocabulary in order to increase their listening and speaking vocabularies. The sentences may or may not be more complex (choice A), the book is not necessarily predictable (choice B), and vocabulary knowledge is needed to understand higher level concepts (choice C).

8. **C.** The ability of the students to analyze a character for wants, needs, or motives. There is no request for sequence (choice A), text vocabulary (choice B), or text message (choice D).

9. **B.** Sequential. Directions would need to be written in sequential order. While the steps will be descriptive (choice D), the text structure itself is sequential.

10. **D.** *Wanted, baked, whisked.* When the suffix -*ed* is added to *want,* it is pronounced /ed/, as a second syllable: *want-ed.* The suffix -*ed* in the words *baked* and *whisked* is pronounced /d/, and they remain one-syllable words.

11. **B.** Complete a Venn diagram that compares the daily life of prairie state pioneers with that of modern people. The goal is comparison, and the other three answer choices delve deeper into pioneer life, but do not compare and contrast.

12. **C.** Explain the use of idioms in the English language, discuss the character, and ask what *dog tired* might mean. *Dog tired* is an idiom and, therefore, would be especially confusing to ELLs. The teacher should make sure students understand that idioms exist, and teach students how to figure out their meanings.

13. **B.** Two parts of the word *baker* have meaning: *bake,* to cook in the oven, and -*er* meaning "one that does." *Nation* (choice A) is a single morpheme (the smallest unit of language that has meaning), *impracticality* (choice C) has multiple morphemes, and *table* (choice D) is a single morpheme.

14. **D.** Voice. The author's craft most apparent in this passage is voice, as the imagery is plain. In order to focus on ideas (choice C) that show support, the passage would need to be longer. And although the organization (choice A) is fine, again a longer passage should be used to focus on organization. Conventions (choice B) is not the best choice because there is not a great mix here for modeling different conventions used in writing.

15. **C.** Since the 47th percentile is still in the middle range, Daniel's progress is average. Using flexible grouping, Mrs. Lee should place Daniel in a group working with morphemic activities and correct usage of various morphemic structures. Spelling (choice A) is not the same as word usage, but centers more on phonics. The 47th percentile is not a concern, so Daniel should not be recommended for further testing (choice B). Although additional writing and drafting texts could help Daniel with word usage, this is not necessarily a focus (choice D).

16. **B.** Beginning and ending sounds. The writing does not show proper sentence conventions (choice A). The majority of the words do not contain vowels (choice C), and the VCe spelling pattern (choice D) is not being used, as in *bik*.

17. **C.** Making word activities with word families. Right now, the greatest need for this child is to learn that all words contain at least one vowel, and using the making-word-families strategy teaches children that they must have a vowel in their words. The child seems to have conquered capitalization (choice A) and consonant letter sounds (choice B). Focus on irregular spelling patterns (choice D) should come later.

18. **D.** Have Jerome reread the text a number of times for a variety of reasons, such as to get used to reading aloud by reading to a partner, or to select interesting sentences. Jerome is having a problem with reading speed, so he needs practice rereading the same words. The slow reading did not seem to be caused by more complicated words (choice A) or irregular words (choice B), and he does not need phonics (choice C), as he is decoding correctly.

19. **A.** *Pensive, déjà vu.* There is not enough context to explain or give an idea of what these two words might mean. You could insert *happy, sad,* or *bad* to replace the word *pensive* and it would still make sense in that particular sentence, although *happy* could be eliminated as the reader continues to read. There is also nothing in the context to really explain what *déjà vu* means. The meaning of *foreboding* (choice B) is hinted at with the phrase *as if something was going to go wrong; graffiti* (choice C) is not important to the meaning of the passage; the meaning of *sterile* (choices C and D) is hinted at with the phrase *Nothing looked messy or out of place,* and the word *familiar* (choice D) can be figured out by the phrase *yet different.*

20. **C.** *Foreboding, discomfort.* Morphemic or structural analysis has students analyze parts of words, their meaning, and derivatives. *Pensive* (choice A) could be considered, but not *déjà vu. Surroundings* (choice B) could be considered, but not *sterile. Graffiti* should not be used, and the two words in *whatever* should already be known by students reading at this level (choice D).

21. **B.** To clarify any confusing areas as they discuss the text. Remember, text sets are sets of books about the same content or by the same author. Reading text sets with a partner and stopping every other page to discuss the content will not build fluency (choice A), although the students may discuss the book's vocabulary. Also, the discussion will not ensure that the students don't skip a page (choice C), and finally, there was nothing in this scenario about answering questions (choice D).

22. **D.** Choral reading. Choral reading, if done correctly, involves rereading and practice in order to read correctly. This would improve reading rate and the use of expression. Shared reading (choice A), where the teacher reads a book with the students, would model correct prosody (expression) but not necessarily have students practice reading. Partner reading (choice B) would allow oral reading, but then both students would be hearing the other read laboriously and without expression. Silent reading (choice C) may help with reading rate, but not with expression.

23. **C.** Mrs. Conant should explicitly teach the word *camouflage,* using only the text definition, then preview the text and focus on *camouflage* and discuss the pictures that show animal adaptation by camouflage and have partners discuss this. Multiple definitions should not be taught at this time (choice A). While previewing the text is a good strategy, it is not enough to ensure that students know the word *camouflage* prior to reading (choice B). Creating a semantic web would provide exposure to the word, but students need more if they are to truly understand the word and the concept (choice D).

24. **B.** *Fork, tough, graph.* The /f/ (f sound) is spelled with the letter(s) "f," "gh," and "ph." None of the other combinations have variant spellings of a letter sound.

25. **D.** In a mini-lesson format, explain the use of periods, exclamation points, and question marks. Model the use of each for the students. In a writing assignment, tell students they must use at least two of the end marks. During conferencing and editing, make sure end marks have been used correctly. The key to selecting the correct answer is noticing the word *explicit* in the question prompt; *explicit teaching* means direct instruction. Having students practice end marks without instruction doesn't work (choice A), pointing out end marks during reading is exposure but not explicit teaching of their use (choice B), and having students circle and discuss end marks is not explicit discussion (choice C), but perhaps could be used for a review.

26. **A.** *Tuck.* You need to know that a phoneme is a letter sound and that a grapheme is a letter. The word *tuck* has three sounds: /t/ /u/ /k/. The "ck" is a consonant digraph that has one sound. The other answer choices do not apply; even though *gnu* (choice D) has three letters, it only has two phonemes: /n/ and /u/.

27. **C.** Have students read a small portion of the text, discuss the text with a partner, then have a class discussion about the concepts prior to reading the next section. This makes them active participants in both the reading and discussion of the concepts. Although the other three choices could be somewhat beneficial, students need to learn to read complex text on their own, not have it read to them (choice A). Writing questions (choice B) or filling in a graphic organizer (choice D) would not ensure that students understood these difficult concepts.

28. **B.** Understand that a teacher should not communicate high expectations to all students, as it might frighten them. This is NOT culturally responsive. Teachers definitely need to communicate high expectations to all students.

29. **D.** A connection to the text allows students to be actively engaged with the text and deepens their understanding of the events in the text. The question does not ask about making predictions (choice A) or understanding vocabulary (choice B), but about connecting to the text with partner talk. If the teacher is using effective read aloud techniques, partner talk is not used for a "break" (choice C), but rather to foster active participation in the reading. This connection is a self to text connection; there are also text to text and text to world connections.

30. **D.** The test will get the same results with a different set of people in a different setting. Reliability refers to the results of test scores, ensuring that the test provides a reliable measure no matter if it is given in Wyoming, Tennessee, or Florida, for example. All tests should have correct content (choice A), and standardized means that the test-taking requirements are the same in all testing situations (choice B). The test measures the skills or content it says that it will measure (choice C) is the definition for validity.

31. **B.** Before—set a purpose; During—self-monitor; After—summarize. Setting a purpose prior to reading has been shown to increase comprehension. During reading, self-monitoring is when readers ask themselves if the text makes sense, and summarizing after reading helps readers to think about the information in the text. Regarding the other answer choices, questioning can be used during reading; vocabulary can be worked with before, during, and after reading; building background, if needed, should be done before reading; and inferences should be made during reading, although inferential questions used after reading can aid students in thinking about the text differently.

32. **B.** Concepts of print. One of the concepts of print is learning to identify and understand what a "word" is, and this scenario shows explicit teaching of that. It does not bring in sound only related to phonemic awareness (choice A); the teacher is not teaching phonics (letter-sound correspondence, choice C), nor is she discussing word usage (choice D), such as nouns. The teacher is simply stating that each word is just that: a word.

33. **B.** Vowel digraphs. A digraph is two letters that make one sound. Children at this stage can already identify the vowels, and a diphthong is a glided vowel sound as the "oi" in the word *oil*. While long vowel sounds (choice D) are being taught, this is not the best answer. Long vowel sounds also include open syllables, like the /o/ in *open* and VCe pattern such as in the word *take*. Based on the words the teacher uses in this lesson, vowel digraphs are the focus. Therefore, vowel digraphs is the best answer.

34. **A.** The test measures the skills or content it says that it will measure. For instance, if a test says it is measuring letter identification, it is not asking for the letter sound, but the name. If it is asking students to give the letter sound, it is measuring letter-sound correspondence (phonics) and not letter identification. Getting the same test results in a variety of settings with a variety of groups shows reliability (choices B and C). It doesn't matter how many answer choices there are to choose from, as long as only one of those answer choices is correct (choice D).

35. **D.** Compare and contrast. Although each part of the paragraph is descriptive (choice A), as it describes a city and a town, the overarching text structure serves to compare and contrast. Getting children to understand how a city and town are alike and different would be the goal of this passage. Also, the word *But* is a signal word for the compare and contrast text structure. There is no cause and effect (choice B) or problem and solution (choice C) in this passage.

36. **C.** Why did Jacob try not to smile as he threw the third pitch? This question asks the reader to infer; each student's answer could be different, but still correct. For example, Jacob knows that professional pitchers are not supposed to show emotion. Jacob didn't want Aiden to know he was happy because Aiden had made two strikes, which showed he was pitching well. Or, Jacob did not want to hurt Aiden's feelings, as Aiden already had two strikes. The questions about when the boys went to the baseball field (choice A) and why both boys were satisfied with the ending pitch (choice D) are literal, as the answers are in the text. The question "How would you feel it you had struck out in your last two baseball games?" (choice B) is not text dependent; most students could answer that question without reading the text.

37. **A.** Homograph. A homograph refers to two words that are spelled the same, but have different meanings and may not be pronounced the same. Two very different meanings of *pitcher* are "one who pitches" and "a jug from which a person can pour." A euphemism (choice B) is an expression or word that is substituted for something considered too harsh or vulgar. A synonym (choice C) is a word that means the same thing or nearly the same thing. Homophones (or homonyms, choice D) are two words that are spelled differently, but sound the same.

38. **C.** Idioms. An idiom is a group of words that have a different meaning than what is expected. This is the case with *saved face,* as it does not have the literal meaning "to save a face," but means "to keep oneself from being embarrassed." An acronym (choice A) is an abbreviation that is used as a word. An affix (choice B) is a beginning (prefix) or ending (suffix) added to a word to form a new word. A compound word (choice D) is two words put together to make one new word.

39. **A.** Building background is not considered an effective practice in close reading. Rereading (choice B), annotating (choice C), and having a collaborative discussion (choice D) about what is being read are all considered techniques of close reading.

40. **C.** Mrs. Florence should teach her students how to find appropriate sites that are credible and have accurate information. Teaching children to look for sites with .edu or .gov extensions, or reputable children's online magazines, is one effective way. Giving them a list of appropriate sites (choice A) does not teach the students how to find appropriate sites on their own. Using a search engine (choice B) is a beginning step, but not enough. Finally, sites such as Wikipedia are "open source"; they can be added to by anyone, so the information is not always accurate and reliable (choice D).

41. **D.** Comprehension strategies; modeling of voice in writing. The standardized test shows strength in word recognition. The running record shows that Jared is strong in word identification. The standardized test shows that although Jared is average in comprehension, he is not as strong there as he is in vocabulary. Poor summarization is an indicator of poor comprehension. Jared is weak on voice, so instruction in this area is appropriate. Jared does not need word study (choice A), phonics instruction (choice B), or vocabulary instruction (choice C) at this time.

42. **A.** Using a word wall with high-frequency sight words, continually adding new words, and referring to the word wall frequently for reinforcement. Common spelling patterns (choice B) and decodable words in predictable texts (choice C) are not the problem, and collaborative discussion on phonetically irregular words (choice D) would not be sufficient, and may not even be productive.

43. **B.** The instruction begins with the teacher setting the purpose for the lesson. Explicit teaching is direct teaching in which a teacher models and tells students what they need to learn. Explicit instruction is not minimal instruction (choice A); it is clear and thorough. Exploration (choice C), inquiry (choice D), and hypothesizing are good teaching techniques for different types of content, but they are not part of explicit instruction.

44. **D.** Work with students so they are looking at her when she speaks and ask them to give her nonverbal cues that they understand. The problem with this scenario appears to be poor listening skills. Students ask questions when they are confused, which may be caused because they didn't listen carefully. Mrs. Bishop needs to begin by teaching the students how to be good listeners. Asking questions is a technique used in forming good listening skills, but students shouldn't be forced to ask questions (choice A); instead, they should ask questions when they need something clarified. In some cases, providing written information for the students (choice B) may be useful, but that won't address the everyday problem. Putting students on the spot with questions (choice C) will also not alleviate their overall confusion.

45. **D.** Ask questions that can be answered with one or two words. You want to ensure that ELLs understand the vocabulary and information they are hearing. Speaking loudly (choice A) does not help with understanding unless there is a hearing problem. Writing out the word (choice B) will not help an ELL know what the word means, although it would eventually help with word recognition. Having any student repeat what is said (choice C) will not necessarily mean they understand it, although using an echo technique under certain circumstances may be feasible.

46. **A.** The teacher asks students to put the short /a/ sound in the word *pot* and say the new word. To answer this correctly you must know two things: the symbol /a/ stands for the short "a" sound and that phonemic awareness refers only to sounds; students do not need to know that letters exist. All the other answer choices include letter to sound correspondence, which is phonics, not phonemic awareness.

47. **C.** Read a persuasive text while making a list on a two-column chart—one side with the pros given by the author, the other side with the cons given by the author. This allows students to understand the author's viewpoint by noting which column has more entries. Metaphorical language (choice A) would be voice in writing, genre identification (choice B) is a skill but is not directly associated with author's purpose, and synthesizing information (choice D) is important but does not focus on author's purpose.

48. **D.** Final draft scoring. This means the writing process is over or there was not a writing process. Teacher conferencing (choice A), peer editing (choice B), and writing checklists or rubrics (choice C) are all forms of feedback that aid students in improving their writing.

49. **B.** Looking at the beginning and ending of the word to read through the word. Working with vocabulary strategies to enhance comprehension (choice A) would focus on word identification, but that's not where Noah is struggling. Although Noah read the sentence incorrectly, his interpretation does make sense, so stressing metacognitive strategies (choice C) is not the best approach. There was only one multisyllabic word in the sentence (*yesterday*), so teaching multisyllabic words (choice D) should not be an immediate instructional focus for Noah.

50. **A.** Separating onsets from rimes. Emma is not identifying short vowel sounds (choice B), although all of these words have short vowel sounds. We do not know if Emma has mastered sounding out unknown words (choice C) because we do not know if these words are known or unknown to Emma. This is not blending (choice D), but rather segmenting sounds.

51. **B.** To activate prior knowledge and aid in understanding by using schemata to categorize information on the topic. This is a tricky one. Choice A (to help the students identify terms that are related to water) is possible, but not the best selection since there many more terms they will learn such as solid, gas, evaporation, and so forth. They are giving the teacher Tier 1 words, not necessarily Tier 3 words. The students are categorizing (choice C), but that is not the best reason for why the teacher is having the students do this grouping exercise. Finally, choice D is incorrect because the students are giving words, but not personal stories. The information given does not let us know if the students are making personal connections.

52. **C.** Decoding skills. Jessica's slow and laborious reading shows that she needs to work on word identification and decoding first. Fluency (choice A) is not correct because the teacher can already tell that Jessica is not fluent, as she is reading slowly and laboriously. Jessica is reading words, so working on letter identification (choice B) is not necessary. The situation does not call for work on metacognitive strategies (choice D).

53. **D.** The students, using a tablet app, trace a letter as the teacher is saying the letter's name. This is direct instruction on one letter and allows kinesthetic movement to reinforce learning. Beginning with a short /a/ sound and going through a series of short /a/ words (choice A) is incorrect because the goal is not learning the short /a/ sound. Having students look at the posted alphabet while she says each letter's name (choice B) may not be an effective approach for most students. Starting a shared reading session with naming the letters in the book's title (choice C) would be reinforcement, but it is not the best strategy to teach letter identification.

54. **B.** The student can listen to a single-syllable word and identify the beginning sound. Choices A and D can be eliminated because they involve letter-sound correspondence and phonemic awareness is only sound. Choice C is incorrect because identifying syllables is a phonological awareness skill.

55. **A.** Initiate peer editing and conferencing during writers' workshop. The scenario states that students need help in writing more meaningful thoughts. Conferencing with some students while others are doing their math (choice B) might stop the writers' workshop problem but cause another in math. If the writing problem focused on mechanics or spelling, a self-editing checklist (choice C) or providing a list of words (choice D) could work.

56. **D.** Have the student listen to a podcast on the chosen research topic. Having the student work on a decoding app while the other students are doing the research project (choice A) could be feasible during reading time, but the student has good comprehension and needs to be given the opportunity to think like other third-grade students. Having the student cut out pictures (choice B) is not effective and minimizes learning in this area. Assigning the student a topic for which there are first-grade level books in the classroom (choice C) limits choice, but might be feasible—yet only after the student has gathered some background information through listening or viewing, and is familiar with vocabulary on the topic.

57. **B.** Cause and effect. *As a result* tells us that something happened and the effect is about to be stated. Chronological (choice A) is incorrect, as there is no indication of order. The signal words *as a result* also do not indicate a comparison (choice C) or a description (choice D).

58. **D.** Close reading. The teacher is guiding students through an analysis of a short piece of text that they have read at least twice. Shared reading (choice A) is what teachers do with a big book in front of primary classrooms. Structural analysis (choice B) refers to word structure. Theme (choice C) was not mentioned, and although the passage contains a metaphorical phrase (*their ray of sunshine*), that is not the emphasis in the discussion questions.

59. **C.** What did the author mean when he wrote *Everyone hoped, everyone feared*? "How many days has the town been silent?" (choice A) is a literal (fact) question. "How would you feel if someone was kidnapped from your town?" (choice B) is a "beyond the text" question and is not text dependent; you can answer that question without having read the passage. "Should people have let their children laugh?" (choice D) is an evaluative question because it is asking the reader to judge an aspect of the situation.

60. **B.** *Appeared, appearing, disappear, reappear.* These four words all have the base word *appear*. By analyzing both the structure and definitions of the words and the added affixes (*-ed, -ing, dis-,* and *re-*), a student can decipher the words' meanings. The group of words in choice A is a word family, choice C shows different ways of spelling the long "oo" sound, and choice D is a group of words with added affixes, but not the best way to teach structural analysis since they all have a different base.

61. **A.** Speak slowly and enunciate carefully. The student is new to this language and needs to hear clearly the words being said. The child is nowhere near ready for being asked about his background (choice B). At this early time, the ELL will not be able to focus on or get used to the rhythm and speed of the teacher's speech (choice C); the child will need to learn some key words before he can follow along at a faster pace. Pairing the child with another student to practice his English (choice D) is a nice thing to do and most likely would benefit the ELL, but we are asking about a strategy that the teacher can do, and the teacher will be ultimately responsible for the student's progress.

62. **B.** Implement Readers' Theater. This will enable children to reread and practice reading orally. The theater aspect will get them to read with expression as they increase the reading rate of the book they are using. Silent reading (choice A) will not help them with expression or necessarily with accuracy. Teaching students chunking (choice C) may or may not help this group; the information given doesn't detail the syllable structure of the words the students are having problems with. Choice D, having students take turns reading in a group (round-robin) does not ensure that they are reading with expression.

63. **C.** Sarah's omission of the glass slipper may indicate some concerns with literal comprehension. Actually, Sarah didn't mention a lot of things, which shows a lack of detail. This indicates that there could be problems with literal understanding. Choice A is incorrect because Sarah does show a bit of inference—she said Cinderella was sad, nice, and had fun, none of which are explicitly stated in the story. Sarah's retelling does not show that she has a problem with working memory (choice B); there is not enough evidence to judge her working memory. Sarah's omission of the glass slipper doesn't suggest anything about her ability to sequence (choice D).

64. **A.** The student did better than 98% of the students in the age/grade level who have taken the vocabulary section. The question states that this is a norm-referenced test and the 98th percentile tells you where this student was placed in comparison with others in his grade group.

65. **A.** Content. The leveled reading books would be considered the content of the unit, and since the teacher is giving students books that are at their instructional level, it is the content that is differentiated. Process (choice B) and instruction (choice D) mean basically the same thing. The instruction is part of the process. Finally, product (choice C) is what the students write or create as a response to a lesson.

66. **C.** Make sure books in the classroom are about American culture so that ELL students will get to know our culture. Classroom books should represent a variety of cultures. Choices A, B, and D are all considered culturally responsive.

67. **B.** Have students fill in a T-chart with the pros and cons of the topic being discussed. The other three answer choices do not have students analyze, and the question specifically asks which activities would best promote an analysis of the text.

68. **C.** It aids students in connecting a sound to a letter for decoding purposes. Blending phonemes has nothing to with determining syllables (choice A), they are not reading new words (choice B), and onsets and rimes are not being distinguished (choice D).

69. **B.** Modeling metacognitive strategies so students can follow how she comprehends. Mrs. Yu is reading just a small portion and vocabulary is not the focus of what she is teaching, so choices A and C are incorrect. She is reading an informational text, not a narrative (choice D).

70. **C.** Kaylee should be taught explicitly how to differentiate interesting details from important facts. The question asks what best describes the first goal that should be set for Kaylee. Kaylee needs to be able to determine what is important before she can be successful at summarizing (choice A). We have no way of knowing if her random summary was connected to predictions (choice B). The first goal would not be self-monitoring (choice D), although that could be considered later.

71. **D.** Use a guided word sort and have the student sort the concept words into various categories. Sorting words into various categories allows a student to focus on broader aspects of a word, including conceptual configurations. Reading to the child (choice A) does not focus on helping with concepts, chunking strategies (choice B) will not address concept confusion, and looking up words in the glossary and writing the definition (choice C) does not guarantee any understanding.

72. **B.** Directionality. The teacher's finger is moving across the page as she reads to show children in what direction she is reading the text. The scenario does not say she is stopping and pointing out beginnings and endings of sentences (choice A). The teacher is pointing to the words as she moves her fingers across the text, not to the spaces between the words (choice C). Finally, there is no counting of words within a sentence (choice D).

73. **D.** Make a chart with the three branches of government, using visual cues, and have Enrico reread the text and fill in the duties for each. Making a chart would prompt Enrico to interact with the material and think about the duties as he writes. Reading in Spanish (choice A) may not help him understand and will not help him in English reading proficiency. Using a graphic organizer that details the three branches (choice B) would be a great visual, but it's not the best strategy at this point. Finally, reading a lower-level text (choice C) will not give Enrico the same interaction with the text as writing down the duties will provide.

74. **C.** Euphemism. A euphemism is the phrasing of something that may be impolite or unkind in a more gentle way. The expression *gone to the happy hunting ground* means the grandfather is deceased. A hyperbole (choice A) is an exaggeration, which doesn't make sense with this example. A metaphor (choice B) describes one thing as being like another, and a palindrome (choice D) is a word that is spelled the same forward and backward, such as *mom*.

75. **D.** Words that are challenging because of concepts within the text. Since these words are important to the unit concepts, they need to be understood by the students. Choices A and B both refer to words with more than one syllable, but they may not be conceptually challenging. Affixes and root words (choice C) focus on structural analysis skills, not concepts within the unit.

76. **A.** Language structure is usually in place. Using short speech to send a message (choice B) usually happens at age 2½ to 3. Pragmatics (choice C) is an adult level concept, and speech focusing on a want (choice D) happens at around 20 months.

77. **C.** According to this assessment, the student is proficient in phonics, but struggles with comprehension. Choice A is incorrect, as the IRI scoring states that if a child is at the frustration level for either the word list or passage comprehension, then the result at this level is frustration. Choice B is incorrect because being able to correctly read one word in context is not enough information to assess metacognitive skills. Choice D is incorrect, as there is no support for this assessment result.

78. **C.** The student should be placed in grade 2 level books and placed in a skills group on word tenses and affixes. Choice A is incorrect, as children should be placed in their instructional level and grade 2 is this student's instructional level. Choice B is incorrect, as not all errors were multisyllabic words. Finally, choice D is incorrect, as grade 2 is the instructional level and only one contraction was incorrect; more assessment would be needed to see if contractions are a problem area.

79. **D.** The student is able to use context cues to identify words, but shows a weakness in decoding. The isolated words in the word list were mostly incorrect, but the student was able to correctly read those same words when they were in the context of the passage. Choice A is incorrect because there is no reliance on phonics and no problem with comprehension. Choice B is incorrect because we don't know what words were correct on the word list; we were not given that information. Choice C is incorrect because comprehension is not a concern.

80. **A.** The books should use natural language and contain decodable and repeated words. Books with rich language and lots of connections (choice B) would be confusing for many first graders. Most first graders are not ready for complex vocabulary and diagrams (choice C). Unlike choice D, we encourage beginning level books to have pictures that match the text to help beginning readers with word identification.

81. **C.** The student got only the plural words incorrect, so he may not know that you need to add the /s/ sound. Choices A and D seem like good choices, but the question asks about the student's errors in reading. He is reading through most words, and understanding the vocabulary focuses on comprehension, not word identification. Choice B should be eliminated because the student read the words *Sam* and *sat* correctly, and therefore does know the /s/ sound.

82. **C.** Amanda has been exposed to rich vocabulary and reading is encouraged in the home. The other three answer choices are speculation. There is not enough information to make these inferences.

83. **D.** He needs some strategies for inferential comprehension. Johnnie's response was literal, so he doesn't need strategies for literal comprehension (choice C); the sentence said that Tim's face was red. There is no evaluation in the question or answer (choice A), and we cannot judge pragmatics from this information (choice B).

84. **B.** Have students point to the body part, say the word together after the teacher models, then say the word to a partner. This is using modeling, tactile movement, and practice—all good. Matching the picture to the word independently of teaching (choice A) may cause words to be learned incorrectly, and there is no use of oral language, which is needed with ELLs. Choice C might be a good way to assess if the ELLs have learned the English words for body parts. Choice D has no modeling, so the students could mispronounce the word.

85. **A.** Criterion-referenced test. A criterion-referenced test is set to score certain skills such as vocabulary knowledge, letter sound knowledge, comprehension, etc. A norm-referenced test (choice B) shows the percentile a student is in and is a comparative measure. A running record (choice C) would give some information, but not all. Finally, a showcase portfolio (choice D) is just that, a showcase of a student's best work and will not necessarily show any deficiencies.

86. **D.** When writing a reader response, the reader must think about the text, events, and information as he is writing, which deepens understanding. Choice A is not true; understanding can be assessed with oral responses. The teacher can ask more questions during an oral response to get to the student's thinking, so choice B is incorrect. While a written response does give students a chance to use the new vocabulary (choice C), that would not be the most important reason to use written responses.

87. **B.** Teach common orthographic patterns. The key words in this question are *young learners*. First and second graders learn spelling through phonetically regular word families, such as *cat, mat, hat* or *last, fast, blast*. Having students copy sentences (choice A) does not work, as the words are too different and students might copy wrong. Teaching a few challenging spelling patterns (choice C) may be a good approach for older learners, but again the question asks about young learners, who may not be ready for patterns such as changing the "y" to "i" and adding "es." Finally, a word wall (choice D) is a great reference for writers' workshop, but the number of words up on the wall is limited.

88. **B.** The teacher shows the word *ball,* states that it begins with /b/, and repeats the sound. In explicit teaching, the teacher directly instructs what is to be learned. The other three answer choices are all viable activities in the classroom, but they have no direct instruction.

89. **D.** Hyperbole. Hyperbole is an exaggeration, such as the size 20 shoes. A simile (choice A) is when authors compare one thing with another using *like* or *as.* Personification (choice B) is giving human characteristics to animals or objects. Imagery (choice C) is the use of descriptive or sensory words and phrases to create an image.

90. **B.** The teacher was using memoirs as mentor texts. Mentor texts are used by teachers as models of what is being written. The key point in the question is that Mr. Carson is going to have his students write memoirs; the other answer choices, while viable for different reasons, do not focus on the teacher's goal for the students' writing.

Model Answers to Constructed-Response Questions

Before you begin writing an answer, you should remember what is expected to obtain a score of 3. To paraphrase expectations:

- Clearly and directly answer *all parts* of the question.
- Show reading content and your understanding. Be accurate in that content.
- Write a strong explanation—support what you say!

Then, analyze the question that the test is asking you to answer. Two strong responses are given for each constructed-response question.

Constructed-Response Question #1

Model Answer 1

The teacher's coding on Eric's oral reading indicates both a strength and a weakness in word identification skills. Eric's strength appears to be in recognizing beginning letter sounds. His weakness lies in his inability to read through to the ending of the word.

The coding shows that Eric made nine mistakes and two were insertions. Of the seven words with substitutions, six of the errors began with the correct letter sound. Eric read *side* for *sidewalk, wet* for *weatherman, sim* for *swimsuits, gramma* for *grandmother, cake* for *cupcakes,* and *in* for *inside.* In addition, on the one self-correction, he read *birth* for *birthday.* This clearly shows that Eric is using his phonics skills to recognize the initial phoneme.

On the other hand, the miscues indicate that Eric does not finish some words, specifically multisyllabic words. The errors of reading *side* for *sidewalk, wet* for *weatherman, gramma* for *grandmother,* and *in* for *inside,* along with the self-correction *birth* for *birthday,* clearly show that Eric is reading the initial syllable of the word, but does not follow through.

At this time, one instructional goal for Eric is to have him read through the words and to learn to "chunk" pieces of the word by reading parts of the word to make it whole. To begin the instruction, we would want to make sure that Eric recognizes a whole word. Then during instruction, we would want to point out multisyllabic words and discuss looking through the whole word and reading the initial letter sound, medial sounds, and the ending letter sound. Eric should be taught to look for known parts in the word. Finally, Eric needs metacognitive strategies to make sure what is read makes sense.

Model Answer 2

The record of Eric's oral reading shows that he has both a strength and a weakness in word identification. Eric's strength is that he is reading for meaning. Eric's weakness is that he does not recognize compound words.

When analyzing Eric's strength, there are a number of errors in which Eric read the word incorrectly, but it still made sense in what he was reading. For instance, Eric read *gramma* for *grandmother.* This clearly indicates that Eric understood the word *grandmother.* He also read *cake* for *cupcakes,* most likely because he knew it was a birthday party. Then he used the pronoun *it* in referring to *cake.* In that context, it was a noun-pronoun agreement and was syntactically correct. He then read *in the house* for *inside.* In the story, the word *inside* implies "in the house." Finally, Eric made one self-correction; by correcting *birth* to *birthday,* he showed his understanding of the gist of the story.

Eric's weakness in reading this material is shown in his errors of not recognizing compound words. Only one of Eric's substitutions was not for a compound word. In addition, the two insertions were to replace a compound word. Eric read *side* for *sidewalk, wet* for *weatherman, sim* for *swimsuits, gramma* for *grandmother, cake* for *cupcakes,* and *in the house* for *inside.* Even in Eric's one self-correction, the initial error was on a commonly used compound word.

For an instructional goal, Eric needs to learn to recognize and "chunk" compound words. A number of activities could aid him in this goal. Eric needs to learn that a compound word is two smaller words combined to make a new word that represents what is being talked about. For example, a cupcake is a cake the size of a cup. It would be advantageous for Eric to match two words together to form a compound word and draw a picture of the new word. In addition, when Eric is reading, the teacher should have him point out compound words and show how the words can be chunked for word recognition.

Constructed-Response Question #2

Model Answer 1

There are various reasons that students will be able to read this text successfully. The teacher has employed a number of effective instructional techniques to aid in her students' success.

First, using the KWL strategy activates prior knowledge and allows students to connect what they know about westward expansion with the new knowledge they will gain during reading.

Second, the teacher explicitly teaches two vocabulary words. Although we know that students learn most words through wide reading, explicit teaching of vocabulary is recommended when the word cannot be figured out in the text and if the concepts are difficult. Since the teacher has only selected two words to pre-teach, they were obviously chosen carefully.

Third, the teacher builds some background by making sure students know where the western territory was located. She also does a slideshow, showing visuals of what happened during that time period. The visuals would help all learners, but would be especially important to any English Language Learners.

Fourth, she previews the text with the students. This means that they look and discuss the titles and subtitles and any pictures or graphics that are in the text. They also discuss any words that may be in bold, as new vocabulary often is in children's textbooks. The preview allows students to get an overview of what they will be reading, which helps in their comprehension and recall.

These four instructional techniques scaffold students' reading and prepare for them to successfully read the text with a partner.

Model Answer 2

The lesson on the expansion of the U.S. West appears shows to be an effective lesson in many ways. The lesson includes a number of activities that would help students to successfully read the text during partner reading. The instruction is well organized and difficult concepts are pre-taught.

The lesson begins with the teacher finding out what the students already know about U.S. westward expansion as she uses a KWL chart. This activates prior knowledge, which will help the students in making connections to new learning. When we make connections from the known to the new, it helps us categorize information in our head for deeper understanding. Furthermore, the teacher then has the students ask about what they would like to learn about western expansion. This motivates students, as it sets a purpose for their reading.

Next, the teacher builds background for the reading, but she is not telling students what is in the text; she is giving them information that will help them understand what they will be reading. She shows visuals, a map, and other pictures of that era. This especially helps students with a visual learning style.

Then, the teacher teaches two vocabulary words that will also help fifth-grade students deal with the difficult concept of westward expansion. Pre-teaching minimal vocabulary aids students in their understanding of complex text. When students encounter these two words within the text, they will be able to read more fluently as they won't have to stop for word identification.

The teacher's next step is previewing the text. This means that she is going over all bold words, such as titles, subtitles, and sometimes new vocabulary, and previewing visuals in the text. Research has shown that previewing a text helps readers get a map of what they are reading and helps them remember more.

Finally, the teacher sends the students to a comfortable spot to read with partners. Reading with partners will help struggling readers and English Language Learners, if partners are chosen carefully. All of the techniques used by this teacher are examples of effective teaching.

Constructed-Response Question #3

Model Answer 1

The teacher's observations and conclusions can be supported by current research and theory on reading. A fluent reader can read accurately, show an age-level reading rate, and read with expression. Students who read fluently have a smooth reading pattern, as they do not have to stop and identify words. This fluent reading enables the students to focus on comprehension and not word identification.

It is not surprising that the more fluent readers have stronger writing skills. There is an interdependence of reading and writing development. What a student learns in his or her reading can transfer into his or her writing. When a student learns something new while writing, that is reinforced when reading. Since the more fluent readers have an easier time with word recognition, reading sentences in their entirety, and most likely decoding, these skills then transfer over to the writing area.

Model Answer 2

That the teacher has observed that fluent readers have better comprehension and are stronger writers makes a lot of sense, since there is a connection between reading and writing. We know that a fluent reader gets better at reading when he writes and gets better at writing when he reads.

When a student is fluent, this means that the student has a large vocabulary of sight words. These students know not just words that we think of as sight words, such as *was, were, like, is;* they also know grade appropriate or higher-level words by sight. This means that the student does not have to stop and decode a word to read it. When students must stop their reading to figure out what a word is, this interrupts the flow of their reading. When a student's reading is interrupted, the comprehension of the text is also interrupted, which decreases understanding. A fluent reader is able to concentrate on comprehending the text and not word identification.

The teacher's conclusion that the more fluent readers are also better writers is a logical conclusion. Since there is interdependence between reading and writing, when there is improvement in one area, it affects the other. Fluent readers can concentrate on the message of the text and how the author writes this message, which allows them to learn at a deeper level. Texts become mentor texts and models for good writing. Fluent readers can also concentrate on the author's voice and word choices. This learning then transfers into their writing.

Chapter 14

Practice Test 2

Answer Sheet

(Remove This Sheet and Use It to Mark Your Answers)

Selected-Response Questions

1 Ⓐ Ⓑ Ⓒ Ⓓ	46 Ⓐ Ⓑ Ⓒ Ⓓ
2 Ⓐ Ⓑ Ⓒ Ⓓ	47 Ⓐ Ⓑ Ⓒ Ⓓ
3 Ⓐ Ⓑ Ⓒ Ⓓ	48 Ⓐ Ⓑ Ⓒ Ⓓ
4 Ⓐ Ⓑ Ⓒ Ⓓ	49 Ⓐ Ⓑ Ⓒ Ⓓ
5 Ⓐ Ⓑ Ⓒ Ⓓ	50 Ⓐ Ⓑ Ⓒ Ⓓ
6 Ⓐ Ⓑ Ⓒ Ⓓ	51 Ⓐ Ⓑ Ⓒ Ⓓ
7 Ⓐ Ⓑ Ⓒ Ⓓ	52 Ⓐ Ⓑ Ⓒ Ⓓ
8 Ⓐ Ⓑ Ⓒ Ⓓ	53 Ⓐ Ⓑ Ⓒ Ⓓ
9 Ⓐ Ⓑ Ⓒ Ⓓ	54 Ⓐ Ⓑ Ⓒ Ⓓ
10 Ⓐ Ⓑ Ⓒ Ⓓ	55 Ⓐ Ⓑ Ⓒ Ⓓ
11 Ⓐ Ⓑ Ⓒ Ⓓ	56 Ⓐ Ⓑ Ⓒ Ⓓ
12 Ⓐ Ⓑ Ⓒ Ⓓ	57 Ⓐ Ⓑ Ⓒ Ⓓ
13 Ⓐ Ⓑ Ⓒ Ⓓ	58 Ⓐ Ⓑ Ⓒ Ⓓ
14 Ⓐ Ⓑ Ⓒ Ⓓ	59 Ⓐ Ⓑ Ⓒ Ⓓ
15 Ⓐ Ⓑ Ⓒ Ⓓ	60 Ⓐ Ⓑ Ⓒ Ⓓ
16 Ⓐ Ⓑ Ⓒ Ⓓ	61 Ⓐ Ⓑ Ⓒ Ⓓ
17 Ⓐ Ⓑ Ⓒ Ⓓ	62 Ⓐ Ⓑ Ⓒ Ⓓ
18 Ⓐ Ⓑ Ⓒ Ⓓ	63 Ⓐ Ⓑ Ⓒ Ⓓ
19 Ⓐ Ⓑ Ⓒ Ⓓ	64 Ⓐ Ⓑ Ⓒ Ⓓ
20 Ⓐ Ⓑ Ⓒ Ⓓ	65 Ⓐ Ⓑ Ⓒ Ⓓ
21 Ⓐ Ⓑ Ⓒ Ⓓ	66 Ⓐ Ⓑ Ⓒ Ⓓ
22 Ⓐ Ⓑ Ⓒ Ⓓ	67 Ⓐ Ⓑ Ⓒ Ⓓ
23 Ⓐ Ⓑ Ⓒ Ⓓ	68 Ⓐ Ⓑ Ⓒ Ⓓ
24 Ⓐ Ⓑ Ⓒ Ⓓ	69 Ⓐ Ⓑ Ⓒ Ⓓ
25 Ⓐ Ⓑ Ⓒ Ⓓ	70 Ⓐ Ⓑ Ⓒ Ⓓ
26 Ⓐ Ⓑ Ⓒ Ⓓ	71 Ⓐ Ⓑ Ⓒ Ⓓ
27 Ⓐ Ⓑ Ⓒ Ⓓ	72 Ⓐ Ⓑ Ⓒ Ⓓ
28 Ⓐ Ⓑ Ⓒ Ⓓ	73 Ⓐ Ⓑ Ⓒ Ⓓ
29 Ⓐ Ⓑ Ⓒ Ⓓ	74 Ⓐ Ⓑ Ⓒ Ⓓ
30 Ⓐ Ⓑ Ⓒ Ⓓ	75 Ⓐ Ⓑ Ⓒ Ⓓ
31 Ⓐ Ⓑ Ⓒ Ⓓ	76 Ⓐ Ⓑ Ⓒ Ⓓ
32 Ⓐ Ⓑ Ⓒ Ⓓ	77 Ⓐ Ⓑ Ⓒ Ⓓ
33 Ⓐ Ⓑ Ⓒ Ⓓ	78 Ⓐ Ⓑ Ⓒ Ⓓ
34 Ⓐ Ⓑ Ⓒ Ⓓ	79 Ⓐ Ⓑ Ⓒ Ⓓ
35 Ⓐ Ⓑ Ⓒ Ⓓ	80 Ⓐ Ⓑ Ⓒ Ⓓ
36 Ⓐ Ⓑ Ⓒ Ⓓ	81 Ⓐ Ⓑ Ⓒ Ⓓ
37 Ⓐ Ⓑ Ⓒ Ⓓ	82 Ⓐ Ⓑ Ⓒ Ⓓ
38 Ⓐ Ⓑ Ⓒ Ⓓ	83 Ⓐ Ⓑ Ⓒ Ⓓ
39 Ⓐ Ⓑ Ⓒ Ⓓ	84 Ⓐ Ⓑ Ⓒ Ⓓ
40 Ⓐ Ⓑ Ⓒ Ⓓ	85 Ⓐ Ⓑ Ⓒ Ⓓ
41 Ⓐ Ⓑ Ⓒ Ⓓ	86 Ⓐ Ⓑ Ⓒ Ⓓ
42 Ⓐ Ⓑ Ⓒ Ⓓ	87 Ⓐ Ⓑ Ⓒ Ⓓ
43 Ⓐ Ⓑ Ⓒ Ⓓ	88 Ⓐ Ⓑ Ⓒ Ⓓ
44 Ⓐ Ⓑ Ⓒ Ⓓ	89 Ⓐ Ⓑ Ⓒ Ⓓ
45 Ⓐ Ⓑ Ⓒ Ⓓ	90 Ⓐ Ⓑ Ⓒ Ⓓ

-CUT HERE-

Time: 2½ hours

Selected-Response Questions

90 questions

1. Mrs. Baron, a first-grade teacher, is reading a picture book with her class. As she reads, she stops and discusses unfamiliar vocabulary words and asks questions to check students' understanding. Mrs. Baron has students look at the pictures and then tell her what they think is happening. She is careful to make sure students understand that the pictures help convey the information in the book. What is the teacher's main reason for doing this?

   A. The teacher is modeling how pictures can aid in comprehension of new words.

   B. The teacher is modeling good book handling skills; as she progresses she shows students that reading goes from front to back.

   C. The teacher is engaging her students in the reading and, therefore, having them actively participate in the learning of unfamiliar words and new concepts.

   D. The teacher wants to ensure that as she introduces new words, her students understand that letters correspond to specific sounds.

2. Which of the following words contains two morphemes?

   A. *mountain*

   B. *playfully*

   C. *notice*

   D. *hopeful*

3. Mrs. Compton is working with a third-grade group of students on comprehension skills. The group reads the sentence "The baby stopped crying when the mother gave him the bottle." The teacher asks what this might mean. Sarah responds that the baby was now quiet. Joey says that the baby had been hungry, and since he was getting fed he stopped crying. What do these answers tell us about Sarah and Joey's comprehension of this sentence?

   A. Sarah gave a literal answer and Joey gave an evaluative answer.

   B. Sarah shows some inferencing skills, as she was able to glean that the baby had become quiet. However, Joey's response shows greater inference; most likely from prior knowledge, he associated the baby's crying with hunger and understood that the baby becoming quiet meant the bottle had satisfied this hunger.

   C. Sarah shows that she has deep understanding, as the sentence implies that the baby had quieted down. Joey, on the other hand, was inaccurate, as we have no way of knowing that the baby was hungry.

   D. Sarah shows misunderstanding, as she doesn't even mention that the baby might be hungry. Joey's response contains a deeper meaning.

4. Tricia, a first grader, is showing great difficulty in letter identification and cannot name all of the letters. Which of the following is the best strategy to promote growth in this area?

   A. The teacher works with Tricia on the sounds of letters "s," "a," and "t."

   B. The teacher works with Tricia, using word cards with common sight words such as *was, in, the,* and *can.*

   C. The teacher works with Tricia on one of the letters she needs to learn. She has Tricia trace the letter and say its name.

   D. The teacher gives Tricia an iPad app that has all the letters and their sounds and has her work with that for 5 minutes daily.

GO ON TO THE NEXT PAGE

5. Which of the following approaches most accurately describes the explicit teaching of end marks?

    A. When reading a book to the students, explain that an exclamation point means excitement and that a sentence ending with an exclamation point should be read with excitement.

    B. Show students a series of statements and questions containing no end marks. Go through each sentence and explain why you are adding a period, question mark, or exclamation point.

    C. During close reading, have students circle the end marks in the short section of text you are using.

    D. Tell students they are to write three sentences. One must have a question mark, one a period, and one an exclamation point.

6. Which of the following words has three phonemes?

    A. *compartment*

    B. *gnat*

    C. *nothing*

    D. *bee*

7. In a first-grade class, each child has Elkonin boxes on his desk. As the teacher says a word, the students are to put a token in the number of boxes corresponding to the number of sounds they hear in the spoken word. What can the teacher assess as she watches her students?

    A. Phonemic awareness

    B. Letter-sound correspondence

    C. Hearing ability

    D. Morphemic awareness

8. Below is a writing piece from a student.

We went to Grandma's. We had tacos. Grandma's table was full of food. We had corn on the cob. There wasn't enough room for everyone at the table. We got soda to drink. I had to sit on my dad's lap. That was funny. Then we had cake for dessert.

Which of the following writing traits would be the best for the teacher to have the student set as an initial writing goal?

    A. Organization

    B. Ideas

    C. Voice

    D. Word choice

9. The teacher has noticed that as Tasha reads orally, she often pauses to figure out words. Tasha is usually able to say the words, and when finished reading does comprehend what she has read. Of the following choices, which area of reading would best describe where Tasha needs help?

    A. Decoding

    B. Look-back strategies

    C. Fluency

    D. Vocabulary

Use the following writing sample to answer the next <u>two</u> questions.

I luv mi mom. Mi mom halpt me dres. she iz not mene. she iz grate.

10. The child's writing evidences that the child knows which of the following?

    A. Knowledge of sentence conventions

    B. Words contain vowels

    C. Sight words

    D. Phonics

GO ON TO THE NEXT PAGE

11. The child's writing evidences that the child could most use help with which of the following?

    A. Proper use of end marks

    B. Digraphs

    C. Sentence organization

    D. Diphthongs

12. Which of the following groups of words demonstrates that different letters and letter combinations can represent the same speech sound?

    A. *field, find, fit*

    B. *too, you, blue*

    C. *baker, teacher, plumber*

    D. *cucumber, cake, candy*

13. In preparation for his students reading a book in which a family experiences a hurricane, Mr. Su explains how a hurricane is formed and describes the damage it can cause. As Mr. Su discusses the scientific concepts behind the formation of a hurricane, he questions the students and asks for their feedback and interpretation of what he is teaching. Why is Mr. Su asking for student feedback as he is teaching?

    A. To ensure students score high on the follow-up quiz

    B. To make sure they know hurricane vocabulary prior to reading the book

    C. To aid in student analysis of the characters within the story

    D. To hold students accountable for listening

14. A group of fifth graders was reading an article on current election events. During discussion, the teacher noticed that Alicia, a fluent reader, was not participating as much as she normally did. When the teacher questioned her privately, Alicia admitted she did not understand a lot of what she had been reading. What could the teacher have done differently to help Alicia in her comprehension of the article?

    A. Pre-teach vocabulary and have the students read orally.

    B. Work with the students on letter sounds and blending.

    C. Have Alicia reread the article.

    D. Pre-teach vocabulary with the students and build background on elections.

15. Which of the following best describes the relationship between the acquisition of oral language and the development of writing skills?

    A. As children learn to identify letters orally, they learn to write letters.

    B. Learning language and learning to write both have developmental stages that follow a linear progression.

    C. Language develops when children are babies; writing does not begin to develop until formal schooling.

    D. Like oral language, beginning writing starts with small words.

16. Why is it important for children to have strong vocabulary in their oral language?

    A. Strong oral language skills ensure students will learn phonics.

    B. Strong oral vocabulary aids in word identification.

    C. Having a strong oral language vocabulary aids students in comprehension, as they read known words within the text.

    D. Strong oral vocabulary aids students in reading with expression.

GO ON TO THE NEXT PAGE

17. A kindergarten teacher is reading a big book with a group of children. As she reads, she points to each word. She shows students the spaces before and after the word and explains that the spaces separate one word from another in the sentence *Jess has a boat*. Using index cards the teacher covers the words *Jess* and *a boat* and explains that what the students see is one word: *has*. She then reads the sentence, "Jess has a boat." She explains that this sentence has four words. She then asks one student to come up and point to each word. What skill is the teacher working on?

    A. Concepts of print
    B. Alphabetic principle
    C. Encoding
    D. Structural analysis

18. Read the following passage.

Noah thought the beach looked beautiful as he walked carefully over the small rocks toward the sand. The waves in the water reflected tiny rainbows. As he drew closer to the water, Noah realized the beauty was deceptive, as he could see a film of gasoline on the water's surface. As he looked farther out, he found the trail of gasoline led to a boat where a man was working on the engine.

Which of the following best identifies the text structure the author uses in the above passage?

    A. Problem/solution
    B. Description
    C. Cause and effect
    D. Chronological

19. A teacher is working with a group of English Language Learners. As she reads through their writing, she sees that the students are writing things such as *there* for *they're*, *pale* for *pail*, and *right* for *write*. Which of the following is the best instructional goal for the teacher in order to help these students?

    A. Teaching homophones
    B. Teaching homographs
    C. Teaching contractions
    D. Teaching idioms

20. As Mr. Janson reads a big book to his kindergarten class, he puts his finger on the book and points to the area where he is reading, sliding his finger along the sentence. He then slides his finger to the next line and continues to read as he moves his finger with the print. What concept of print is the teacher focusing on?

    A. What defines a word
    B. Where a sentence ends
    C. Directionality of print
    D. That print carries meaning

21. Read the following text.

Michael thought I was kidding. I mean, he really thought I was kidding. He said to me, "No way, man. Get outta here." Then he just laughed. Really, who is this guy to be laughing at me? So, I took out my cell phone and told him to turn around and I took a picture. I plopped my cell in front of his face. Then he saw it! Someone had written on the back of his shirt, "I'm an idiot." Michael wasn't laughing anymore!

Of the following, which best labels the writing trait that could be modeled with the above paragraph?

    A. Word choice
    B. Voice
    C. Ideas
    D. Sentence fluency

GO ON TO THE NEXT PAGE

22. Ms. Clark is concerned about her lowest reading group. They read very slowly and without expression. She needs to employ a strategy that will help them improve in this area. Which of the following instructional strategies should Ms. Clark implement to help these students?

   A. Readers' Theater
   B. Increase silent reading time.
   C. Focus on visualization skills.
   D. Use word cards to increase vocabulary skills.

23. Mrs. Gomez felt that too many students needed to have writing conferences with her, and the students were making easily remedied mistakes. She felt her students were making careless errors and were not putting effort into editing their work. She had given them scoring rubrics, but this was not working. What would be the best strategy for her to try next?

   A. Carve more hours out of the school day for writing workshop.
   B. Use a variety of texts.
   C. Teach students how to use spell-check.
   D. Give students a self-evaluation checklist.

24. Mr. Samson is preparing to work with his sixth-grade students as they read Longfellow's poem "Paul Revere's Ride." He is concerned about their understanding of the poem, as it contains high-level vocabulary and unfamiliar geography. Which of the following activities should Mr. Samson use to help the class comprehend this poem?

   A. Build intensive background on the Civil War and where it was fought.
   B. Pinpoint on a map of Massachusetts where the towns in the poem are located.
   C. Have the students read the poem with a partner.
   D. Use close reading techniques such as selecting complex lines of the poem to discuss.

25. What are the four different types of language that children and adults use daily?

   A. Receptive, expressive, thinking, and talking
   B. Listening, speaking, reading, and writing
   C. Pragmatics, receptive, expressive, and telegraphic
   D. Sentences, stories, facts, and opinions

Use the following assessment results for the next <u>two</u> questions.

The following spelling inventory results are from a pre-test and a post-test.

Word Given	Pre-test	Post-test
1. beach	bech	beach
2. candy	kande	kandy
3. driver	driveor	drivor
4. pail	pale	pail
5. cane	kane	kane
6. baker	bakor	bakor
7. easy	ese	eesy

GO ON TO THE NEXT PAGE

26. In which two areas did the child improve?

    A. Learning that "y" says the sound of long /e/ at the ends of words and diphthongs

    B. Learning that the letter "c" can say the sound of /k/ and "or" says the /er/ sound

    C. Digraphs and diphthongs

    D. Learning that "y" says the sound of long /e/ at the ends of words and digraphs

27. What would you consider to be a good instructional goal for this student?

    A. Working with the suffixes *-er* and *-y*

    B. Working with diphthongs

    C. Working with the vowel, consonant, silent "e" (VCe) phonics rule

    D. Working with the hard and soft sounds of the letter "c"

28. When a teacher gives students leveled reading responses depending on their ability, the teacher is differentiating by

    A. content.

    B. process.

    C. product.

    D. instruction.

29. As Sarah, a first grader, writes in her daily journal, she says each word out loud. The teacher hears Sarah quietly say "like," then "/l/ /i/ /k/" as Sarah first segments the sound and then writes the letter on her paper. The teacher smiles as she sees Sarah has written the letters "l," "i," and "k." Which of the following best describes what Sarah is doing as she writes in her daily journal?

    A. Blending

    B. Decoding

    C. Separating onsets from rimes

    D. Encoding

30. Mrs. Crone's fourth-grade class is about to read a book on energy, a very difficult concept required in her district at this grade level. During pre-reading, Mrs. Crone completes a semantic web with her students. What is the best reason for doing this activity with her students?

    A. To determine whether she should have the students read a book on energy

    B. To help students bridge from what they know to what they will learn

    C. As a way to start close reading with her students

    D. In order to get all students at the same starting point

31. Mrs. Clive, a third-grade teacher, has just completed a couple of assessments with one of her reading groups. When looking at the results, Mrs. Clive noticed that Jerome and Katelyn have progressed beyond the other five students in their reading group. She decided to place Jerome and Katelyn in the next higher group, but first she will group students by books they have chosen and are interested in reading. Which of the following best describes the techniques used in Mrs. Clive's classroom organization?

    A. She has leveled reading groups in her classroom.

    B. She has skills groups in her classroom.

    C. She holds reading workshops in her classroom.

    D. She uses flexible grouping in her classroom.

GO ON TO THE NEXT PAGE

32. ABC Elementary School has adopted the Response to Intervention (RTI) program and has implemented the three-tier model. Eric, a second-grade student, had been getting by with the teacher's help through differentiation techniques. Recently, the teacher has noticed that Eric is not keeping up with his peers, so she has decided to move Eric into a tier that will offer him more help. In which tier will Eric be placed?

    A.   Tier 0

    B.   Tier 1

    C.   Tier 2

    D.   Tier 3

33. In which of the following groups of words do all three words contain a vowel digraph?

    A.   *pail, mail, fail*

    B.   *boa, oar, goat*

    C.   *to, through, blue*

    D.   *weight, tight, receipt*

34. Mr. Conrad is doing word work with his sixth-grade students. Together, they have made the following semantic web.

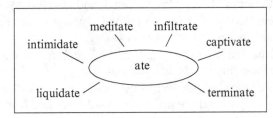

Which of the following best represents the skill Mr. Conrad is working on?

    A.   Phonemic awareness

    B.   Syllabication

    C.   Morphemic analysis

    D.   Prefixes

35. Bonita has recently moved to the United States mainland from Puerto Rico and has just begun fourth grade in a school that does not have a lot of ethnic diversity. Mrs. Painter was dismayed when she witnessed two girls making fun of Bonita's accent. Although she took the girls aside and explained that they were being unkind, Mrs. Painter knew she had to do more. She chose some books on Puerto Rican and Hispanic culture to use as read alouds, and to have Bonita teach the class a few Spanish words, such as please and thank you. Which of the following best describes Mrs. Painter's purpose in doing this?

    A.   To make sure all students follow the rules

    B.   To introduce students to the Asian culture

    C.   To ensure students are getting a variety of genres within the reading curriculum

    D.   To create a culturally responsive classroom

36. Which of the following is an example of implicit instruction?

    A.   The teacher places pictures of short vowel words with the corresponding vowel on the bulletin board.

    B.   The teacher works on the /ch/ sound with a group. Given a picture, students must tell the teacher if the picture begins or ends with the /ch/ sound.

    C.   When teaching the /b/ sound, the teacher has the students put small objects that begin with /b/ in the B bag, as they say the /b/ sound.

    D.   The teacher says the short /a/ sound, shows the letter "a," and has students say the short /a/ sound.

GO ON TO THE NEXT PAGE

37. Which of the following will NOT aid in fostering cultural responsiveness in a teacher's instruction?

    A. Understand that a teacher should communicate high expectations to all students.

    B. Encourage competition between individuals within the classroom.

    C. Encourage students to express themselves and explain cultural expectations when acceptable.

    D. Encourage learners to analyze and discuss the multiple perspectives of various cultures.

38. A teacher is working with her students on a persuasive essay. The teacher displays a model essay on the SMART board and reads each sentence orally to the class. The class then gives an opinion on whether a particular statement is meant to persuade the reader. Which of the following best describes the teacher's purpose in doing this?

    A. To help students understand that audience is important

    B. To show students how this can be done during peer conferencing

    C. To show supporting points in a passage

    D. To help students understand the author's purpose

39. Which of the following examples shows that phonemic awareness is being taught?

    A. The teacher holds up the letter "t," says the /t/ sound, and has students repeat.

    B. The teacher asks students to say the beginning sound of the word *hat* and then to say the word again, but begin it with the same beginning sound as in *soup*.

    C. The teacher gives students the letters "h," "p," "n," "d," "o," and "t" and asks the students to arrange the letters to make the following words: *hot, pot, not, dot.*

    D. The teacher explains the following rule: When two vowels do the walking, the first one does the talking, Then she has the class read the words *read, pail, boat,* and *leak.* As they read each word, the teacher circles the first vowel and reminds students of the rule.

40. Mr. Suma has decided to "shake up" his reading groups a bit by doing an author's study. He has selected four books by the same author. On sign-up sheets, Mr. Suma has written a short blurb about each book and asks students to sign up under the book of their choice. What is Mr. Suma's main purpose in doing this?

    A. Independent reading for all students

    B. To ensure that students read on their instructional level

    C. So that friends can sign up for the same book

    D. Motivation to read

41. Every Monday morning Mrs. Clark brings five or six different books to class. She holds each book up in front of the class and gives students an idea of what the book is about. She then places the books in the class library. What is Mrs. Clark's main reason for doing this?

    A. To promote more independent reading

    B. To build general knowledge

    C. So students will know all the books in the classroom library

    D. To increase the classroom library

42. Which of the following is an effective teaching technique for English Language Learners?

    A. Speak as you normally would so the ELL student doesn't feel different.

    B. Ask questions that make the ELL student answer back with a large number of words.

    C. Use visuals to aid with directions and written explanations.

    D. Start with nouns when teaching vocabulary.

GO ON TO THE NEXT PAGE

43. Mrs. Rogers is having her fifth-grade class read a book on extreme weather and has decided to focus on hurricanes and tornadoes. She hopes this reading will enable her class to understand how hurricanes and tornadoes are alike and how they are different. She has decided to have them fill out a graphic organizer as a post-reading activity. What is the best graphic organizer to use for this purpose?

    A. Venn diagram
    B. Semantic web
    C. T-chart
    D. KWL

44. Mrs. Walker, a fifth-grade teacher, has made up a chart with different types of books: fiction, mystery, fantasy, myth, fable, legend, poetry, biography, nonfiction, and tall tale. She explains to students that over a 3-month period, they have to fill in at least four lines of the chart with a name of the book they read of that type. After reading the books, students will discuss and share in groups. What is Mrs. Walker's main purpose in using this activity?

    A. To encourage more reading in and out of the classroom
    B. To make sure students know the difference between fiction and nonfiction
    C. To ensure her students are reading a variety of genres
    D. To prepare students to write book reports

45. As the third-grade class reads a chapter of *The Whipping Boy,* they have been asked to write down three events that show the prince is a brat. What kind of reading stance will the students take when they read this chapter?

    A. Silent
    B. Efferent
    C. Interactive
    D. Aesthetic

46. Mr. Henry has been reading an Encyclopedia Brown book to his students. These books feature Leroy Brown, a young boy detective who is forever solving mysteries. After finishing the book, Mr. Henry shows the class another seven Encyclopedia Brown books, explaining that they are available for students to read and that there are even more Encyclopedia Brown books in the school library. Which of the following best describes this type of book?

    A. Series
    B. Text sets
    C. Cumulative
    D. Pattern

47. Liam's standardized test results show that he scored in the 37th percentile in comprehension. The teacher is surprised, as she has not noticed any problems with Liam's comprehension in the classroom and he is reading at grade level. What might the teacher do next to ensure that Liam is getting the instruction he needs?

    A. Work with Liam on vocabulary prior to reading.
    B. Use some intervention comprehension techniques to help Liam in his comprehension.
    C. Listen to Liam read orally to make sure he is correctly pronouncing words that he is reading.
    D. Give Liam an informal reading inventory (IRI) to compare results in comprehension.

GO ON TO THE NEXT PAGE

48. A fourth-grade class is going to read a biography of George Washington Carver, the botanist and inventor. Which of the following pre-reading activities would best promote students' comprehension when reading this book?

    A. Have students predict what they think made George Washington Carver famous.
    B. Have students write a short biography of one of their parent's lives.
    C. Have students discuss what they already know about George Washington Carver, botanists, and inventors.
    D. Explain what a biography is and what it usually contains.

Use the passage below to answer the next three questions.

Erica's little sister, an accident waiting to happen, ran toward Erica. As she ran, Bella tripped over the rug binding, hit her head on the hassock, and fell down. Erica was thankful the hassock was cushioned and not a hard footstool. Bella gave a little smile and jumped up into Erica's arms for a kindhearted hug.

49. The teacher has decided that one vocabulary word from this passage needs to be taught prior to the students' reading. Which of the following words should be taught during pre-reading?

    A. *hassock*
    B. *binding*
    C. *accident*
    D. *kindhearted*

50. Which of the following best describes how the author uses the phrase "an accident waiting to happen"?

    A. As an ellipsis
    B. As imagery
    C. To show mood
    D. As a metaphor

51. When the students finished reading the passage, the teacher had them answer the following question: "Tell me how you think Bella felt after the fall; support your answer." Which of the following best describes this type of question?

    A. Inferential
    B. Literal
    C. Factual
    D. Evaluative

52. Standardized tests must have reliability. Which of the following best describes reliability?

    A. The test measures the skill or content it says it will measure.
    B. It has a nine-point scale.
    C. Its measure varies depending on the population being tested.
    D. The test would produce the same results with a different set of people in a different setting.

53. Mr. Jacob's class is doing research projects on different animals. Each student is allowed to pick their animal. Students must use two online sites and two books, all cited in their project. As students begin to look through the books they have gathered, Mr. Jacob notices that many students are skimming through the whole book. Some students say they can't find information on their animal. Which answer below best describes what research technique the students need at this time?

    A. To slow down and reread information
    B. How to locate information in a book by using the table of contents or the index
    C. To organize the procedures so they can take notes
    D. To look for pictures that show what they are researching

GO ON TO THE NEXT PAGE

54. Ms. Smith wants her fourth-grade students to have stronger inference skills. In order to teach them to draw inferences from an informational text, which of the following sentence starters should she ask them to complete?

   A.   The passage suggests…
   B.   One interesting point is…
   C.   The main idea is…
   D.   It is my opinion that…

55. One reading group in Ms. Barr's second-grade class is using a text set on animal habitats. As students are reading their selected text, Ms. Barr has them fill in a chart that requires the name of the animal and a description of the habitat. What is likely the main reason Ms. Barr has assigned this activity?

   A.   To have the information organized
   B.   So students will be accountable for a certain number of animals
   C.   To ensure students are interacting with the text as they read
   D.   To ensure students are actually reading the books

56. A sixth-grade class is reading a novel about a young man, Josh, who is making good decisions and choices as he grows up. The teacher has the class respond to the writing prompt: *Choose one of the life decisions Josh has made and compare it with a decision you've made in your own life.* Which of the following best supports the teacher's choice of prompt?

   A.   When writing this response, the reader makes a personal connection, which helps him gain insight into the character.
   B.   The teacher is using this as a life lesson, to show the importance of making good decisions.
   C.   It is important to the teacher to increase the amount of writing in the classroom.
   D.   The teacher wants students to analyze how the author ordered the events.

57. Fifth-grade students have just finished reading a work of historical fiction and will be writing a journal response. Which of the following journal prompts could be most successful in developing students' literary response skills?

   A.   Select four events from the book and describe the events.
   B.   Outline the main plot of the novel.
   C.   Discuss the theme of the book and offer evidence from the text that supports this theme.
   D.   Describe the two main characters and describe two of their interactions.

58. Which of the following word sets would best introduce students to the concept of structural analysis?

   A.   *beat, meet, crepe, great*
   B.   *repack, unpack, packing, packed*
   C.   *run, ran, running, runs*
   D.   *glue, through, two, flew*

59. Ms. Mackin noticed that Zoe does not read fluently when reading aloud. What should Ms. Mackin assess first as she examines Zoe's difficulties with reading orally?

   A.   Comprehension
   B.   Inferencing
   C.   Decoding
   D.   Vocabulary

GO ON TO THE NEXT PAGE

60. Read the following sentence in which selected words are missing. Which blank would best be filled by a word with the suffix *-able*?

_____1_____ wondered if it was ____2____ to ____3____ in the ____4____ .

- **A.** Blank 1
- **B.** Blank 2
- **C.** Blank 3
- **D.** Blank 4

Use the scenario below to answer the next <u>two</u> questions.

A second-grade teacher was listening to a student read orally. The first sentence below is from the text; the second sentence is what the child read orally.

Text:	The dog barked and jumped up, making the boy fall.
Student:	The dog bark and jump up and made the boy fall.

After the child finished reading, he reread the sentence correctly.

61. How might the teacher adjust her instruction to meet the needs of this student?

- **A.** Develop comprehension strategies for word recognition.
- **B.** Promote auditory discrimination skills.
- **C.** Demonstrate strategies that will encourage the student to read through the word.
- **D.** Support use of decoding skills to segment words while reading orally.

62. What does the child's rereading of the sentence signify?

- **A.** He has difficulty in decoding.
- **B.** He is self-monitoring his comprehension.
- **C.** He needs problem solving skills so that he can self-monitor his reading.
- **D.** He is not properly tracking print.

63. A first-grade teacher has been given the opportunity to select books for her incoming class of beginning readers for instruction and practice in reading. Which of the following offers the correct criterion or criteria for selecting books for these students?

- **A.** The text should contain complex vocabulary and few pictures that align with the text.
- **B.** The text should contain challenging concepts that require readers to think critically about what is written.
- **C.** The text should use natural language and a variety of punctuation.
- **D.** The text should be decodable and use repeated words or phrases.

64. A principal is concerned about how his school's reading performance compares with that of other students at the same grade level. Which of the following assessments would provide the information the principal is seeking?

- **A.** Norm-referenced test
- **B.** Informal Reading Inventory (IRI)
- **C.** Criterion-referenced test
- **D.** Comprehension checklist

65. A teacher can assess the beginning development of phonemic awareness by having a child

- **A.** use his fingers to show where a word begins and where a word ends.
- **B.** say the word *cap* out loud and tell the teacher the first sound he hears in the word.
- **C.** say the word *cat* and replace the middle sound, /a/, with the /u/ sound.
- **D.** look at the beginning consonant of *cat* and say the letter sound.

GO ON TO THE NEXT PAGE

66. A first-grade teacher is planning to instruct her students on onset and rimes as she begins a word study using word families. Which of the following words would be the best choice to teach her beginning readers the concept of onsets and rimes?

    A. *car*
    B. *edge*
    C. *burn*
    D. *track*

67. Which of the following rationales best explains why it would be important to have spelling instruction in place for first graders?

    A. Effective first-grade spelling can help students learn to recognize the listed words in the texts they are reading.
    B. Effective first-grade spelling can foster new word recognition and aid in understanding words.
    C. Effective first-grade spelling uses common rimes and phonic generalizations, which then support word recognition.
    D. Effective first-grade spelling aids in the segmenting of syllables, and this transfers into the reading arena.

68. Which of the following best explains why having phonemic awareness is important to beginning readers?

    A. Phonemic awareness helps students understand the concept of letters and the concept of words.
    B. Phonemic awareness aids students in understanding that there is a match between the letters and sounds in a word.
    C. Phonemic awareness helps students as they begin to divide words into onsets and rimes.
    D. Phonemic awareness aids students in segmenting words in order to "chunk" pieces of unknown words.

69. Mrs. Frank is looking at assessment results to group her students for word study skills. She reviews students' running records, spelling inventories, writing samples, and standardized test results. Of the following standardized tests, which will most likely give Mrs. Frank information for skills grouping?

    A. Criterion-referenced test
    B. Comparative-referenced test
    C. Norm-referenced test
    D. Inventory-referenced test

70. Which of the following is considered the best instructional technique for teaching primary students traditional spelling?

    A. Teaching a selection of easy to learn words from the books students are reading
    B. Teaching phonics generalizations and irregular verb patterns
    C. Teaching common orthographic patterns
    D. Teaching words with picture cards to ensure understanding

71. Mr. Mendes is having his sixth-grade class read a complex article explaining the controversy over fishing rights among different countries. Through a semantic web, Mr. Mendes has found that his students, who live close to an ocean, are quite knowledgeable about fishing but know little about fishing rights. Which of the following best describes how Mr. Mendes should proceed so his students will understand the difficult concepts in the article?

    A. Build background on fishing and the countries involved.
    B. Have students partner read, stopping every four paragraphs to discuss what has been read.
    C. Have students read the article and have them write down five questions as they read.
    D. Use close reading techniques such as teacher modeling, rereading, and discussion to clarify concepts.

GO ON TO THE NEXT PAGE

72. Standardized tests should be evaluated for validity. Which of the following best describes validity?

    A. The test results will be similar no matter what population is taking the test.

    B. The test measures what it says it will measure.

    C. The test has been given a number of times and has been normed though various populations.

    D. The test is criterion-referenced and therefore is valid.

73. Mrs. Saunders was looking for an informal reading inventory (IRI) as an indicator of reading level when she placed her students in leveled reading groups. As she looked through samples, she was happy to find an inventory that used literal, inferential, and evaluative questions; this way she could also analyze which type of questions her students needed more guidance in. She read a passage that included the following two sentences: "Fido got home and rolled in the dirt. He was happy again." One of the questions, labeled as an inferential question, asked, "What did Fido do when he got home?" Which of the following best describes Mrs. Saunders' opinion of this assessment?

    A. The test has reliability.

    B. The test has validity.

    C. The test is not reliable.

    D. The test is not valid.

74. A third-grade teacher has decided that her students need some guidance in writing fables. She has decided to use mentor texts. Which of the following best describes what the teacher should do?

    A. Give students a paper that begins the fable and tells what the moral of the fable will be.

    B. Have students read a variety of fables and, as a class, analyze the fables' components.

    C. Give students a fable template that allows them to write in it and gives specific directions for writing a fable.

    D. Provide guided questions to help the students write.

75. Which of the following is NOT the best approach for increasing vocabulary?

    A. Prior to reading a text, have students look up the new words in the dictionary and write down their meaning.

    B. Instruct new vocabulary through discussion and actions.

    C. Read aloud using books one or two years above students' reading levels.

    D. Use open-ended follow-up questions to foster the use of new vocabulary.

76. Which of the following best exemplifies cultural responsiveness to parents?

    A. Send notices home with picture cues and lots of information.

    B. Don't ask parents questions about their child, as it will frustrate them.

    C. If parents seem frustrated, try to figure out what is happening to cause their frustration.

    D. Don't send notices home, as they will confuse parents.

77. A student's score on a norm-referenced standardized test placed the student in the 87th percentile for reading comprehension. What does this mean?

    A. The student's raw score was below 87% of the other students taking this test.

    B. The student's raw score was above 87% of the other students taking this test.

    C. The student answered 87 correct out of 100.

    D. The student answered 87% of the given questions correctly.

GO ON TO THE NEXT PAGE

78. A student scored in the 4th stanine on a standardized test. What does this indicate?

    A. The student scored in the 40th percentile.

    B. The student scored in the 4th quartile, which means between the 75th and 100th percentile.

    C. The student scored in the average range.

    D. The student scored in the below average range.

Use the following passage to answer the next <u>two</u> questions.

The area was arid, hot, and blistering. Mike's lips were parched. Vigilant about his water, he took a small drink. As he looked around him, he was astounded by the august view of the dried out, cracked land of brown, gold, and orange hues.

79. After reading the above passage, which of the words below would be most confusing to the students and, therefore, would be best taught prior to reading?

    A. *arid*

    B. *parched*

    C. *vigilant*

    D. *august*

80. After reading this short selection, the teacher is planning to ask a text-dependent evaluative question. Which of the questions below can be identified as evaluative?

    A. How would you feel if you were in an arid area with dried out, cracked land?

    B. Should Mike have been in this area with what seems to be limited water?

    C. Explain why Mike would be vigilant about his water.

    D. What did the land look like?

81. A first-grade teacher is having a small group of students play a matching game in which they must match the uppercase letter with the lowercase letter, so they would match "B" with "b." Which of the following best describes what the teacher is trying to reinforce?

    A. Concepts of print

    B. Phonemic awareness

    C. Phonics

    D. Word usage

82. Fifth-grade students are researching endangered species. They must use two print sources and two credible online sources. Which of the following best describes what the teacher should do to ensure students learn how to use online sources that contain accurate and appropriate information?

    A. Students should be given a list of appropriate websites to use in their research.

    B. The teacher should bookmark approximately eight credible online sources to help manage student work time.

    C. Students should be taught how to identify credible online sources.

    D. The teacher should show students how particular words can help someone using a search engine.

83. Ms. Parker is working with Amelia as she reads this sentence, "The monkey used its tail to jump from tree to tree." Amelia reads "mmm" for *monkey*. Ms. Parker asks Amelia what kind of animal could jump from tree to tree using its tail. Amelia smiles and says, "A monkey!" Amelia then reads the sentence again, this time correctly. Which of the following best describes the word identification strategy that Ms. Parker is trying to teach Amelia?

    A. To chunk words by separating them into parts such as *mon-key*

    B. To ask herself questions as she reads

    C. To analyze each sentence as it is read

    D. To use information from context to identify unknown words

GO ON TO THE NEXT PAGE

84. A kindergarten teacher shows students pictures of a house, a hat, a hot dog, and a hand. Under each picture is the letter "h." The teacher shows the picture of the house, says the word *house,* points to the letter "h," and says the sound /h/. She then asks the students to repeat the sound with her, followed by the word. How would you characterize this activity that contributes to children's developmental reading skills?

  A.   Working with students on onset and rimes
  B.   Focusing on articulation with specific sounds in speech
  C.   Demonstrating that a letter corresponds with a sound
  D.   Illustrating that words symbolize objects

85. Asking students to say the word *bus* and identify the sounds in the word is an activity that should be conducted with students who

  A.   are considered to have high-end phonemic awareness skills.
  B.   have had explicit phonics instruction.
  C.   are considered to have low-end phonemic awareness skills.
  D.   can separate onsets from rimes.

86. A teacher shows students the following chart that has one word covered up in each sentence. She uncovers the first letter of the hidden word and asks students to guess the word. In the chart below, students have read sentence one and are working on sentence two.

  1. The ⬜beach⬜ ball floated into the lake.

  2. I laid on the c⬜⬜ to read a book.

This experience supports students in word identification skills by teaching them to

  A.   read through the word.
  B.   employ semantic and syntactic cues to identify an unknown word.
  C.   use segmentation to identify unknown words.
  D.   use onsets and rimes to identify unknown words.

Use the following information to answer the next <u>three</u> questions.

The following Informal Reading Inventory (IRI) was used with a third-grade class. The selection was at the third-grade level. In Part I, the Word List, the student read aloud to the teacher and errors were coded. In Part II, the Passage was read aloud and the teacher coded errors. The passage section is followed by comprehension questions, which students answered and the teacher scored as frustration, instructional, or independent level. If a student is scored at frustration level on the word list or the comprehension questions, then further assessments are needed, as this indicates that the child is not reading at the third-grade level.

Part I: Word List
fortunate
explore
clever
excellent
mountain
travel

Part II: The Passage
Emily was so happy and she felt so fortunate that she was able to travel. Her family was camping in the mountains, and Emily was about to explore the trail, near the campsite. Her mother warned her to stay close and not get lost. Emily had an excellent plan. As Emily walked on the trail, she made an arrow from sticks when she took a turn on the trail and the arrow pointed to the way back. Emily's clever plan worked. She followed her arrows back and made it to the camp in time for supper!

GO ON TO THE NEXT PAGE

87. Jeremy read the word list and made errors on the words *fortunate, explore,* and *travel.* But when he read the passage, he missed only the word *fortunate.* Which of the following best describes what this tells us about Jeremy as a reader?

    A. The student can use context to identify unknown words.

    B. The student is strong in using phonics to identify unknown words.

    C. The student struggles with words at his grade level.

    D. The student has difficulties with multisyllabic words.

88. Jojo read the word list and is scored at the instructional level. When she read the passage, her word recognition was strong, with only two errors. When answering the comprehension questions, she scored at the frustration level, missing the instructional level by one question. Using this one indicator, which of the following might be a future instructional goal for Jojo?

    A. Place Jojo in a lower level group and work intensively on increasing vocabulary.

    B. Keep Jojo where she is and have her partner read more frequently to increase her fluency.

    C. Place Jojo in a higher level group and check her progress more frequently.

    D. Keep Jojo in the grade level 3 group and work with her intensively via comprehension strategies.

89. Another student read the word list and scored at the instructional level, as he missed the words *excellent* and *explore.* The student reached the independent level for the passage, but read very slowly and had to self-correct a number of times. What might be a future instructional goal for this student?

    A. Work with the student on phonemic awareness skills.

    B. Engage the student in a number of fluency activities to increase reading speed.

    C. Focus on inferential comprehension techniques and practice sheets.

    D. Use close reading to analyze the text at the sentence level.

90. Mr. Welter is going to have his fourth-grade class read a book about survival in the wilderness. He has a number of English Language Learners (ELLs) in his class. Which of the following choices would be the most effective teaching strategy to aid the ELL students in comprehending this text?

    A. Have the ELL students partner read and discuss with a native English speaker in the class.

    B. Select words from the text that may be confusing and have the ELL students look them up in the dictionary.

    C. Activate the students' prior knowledge and teach background information using visuals to explain new vocabulary.

    D. Have the students view a video on techniques needed to survive in the wilderness.

GO ON TO THE NEXT PAGE

Constructed-Response Questions

3 questions

Constructed-Response Question #1

Tanya read the following text to her teacher. The plain text shows the original verbiage. The bold type shows the teacher's marking as she coded the reading. Look carefully at the following and answer the questions below.

---

couldn't

Josh was upset. He had been looking everywhere and <u>could not</u> find his mother's cell phone.

shouldn't

He knew he <u>should not</u> have taken the phone off the kitchen counter without asking his mom first.

neeber's SC   **re-ached**

But she had to go the <u>neighbor's</u> so Josh had <u>reached</u> for the phone. Josh retraced his steps, but still

couldn't

<u>could not</u> find it. He was going to be in big trouble because Mom wasn't going to be happy. He

re-ally

would be <u>really</u> sorry when his mom found out. Suddenly, he heard a familiar sound, it was that

re-ached SC

stupid song his mom used for a ringtone. Following the sound, Josh <u>reached</u> between the couch

reet-ted

cushions as his heart <u>reacted</u> with joy. "Hi, Mom," said Josh. "Oh, I'm fine, I was just reaching for

rem-ote SC

the <u>remote</u> to watch television for a while."

Analyze the above miscues. Using evidence from the teacher's coding, state one strength that Tanya has as a reader, and one weakness. State a learning goal for Tanya and how you might instruct her to attain that goal.

Constructed-Response Question #2

A third-grade teacher is concerned about Matthew's comprehension. She has Matthew read a short story and then has him retell the story in his own words. The following is the result:

Short Story: "Ben's Fishing Trip"

Ben couldn't sleep because he was going fishing in the morning and he had never been before. He had been given a brand-new fishing rod for his birthday, and he could cast with it. His dad had shown him how, and he had been practicing in his backyard. That next morning, Ben's father woke him up very early, before the sun was up, because he said that is when the fish bite the most. They drove down to the river, and Ben's dad helped Ben bait the hook. Ben was ready to catch the big one! Ben brought the fishing pole back and flung his arm forward, but something pulled and the hook and line didn't cast out! Ben couldn't bring his pole forward, so he looked behind him and couldn't believe what he saw! His line had wrapped itself around a huge branch. "You caught a big one all right," his dad said as he helped him get the line loose.

Matthew's Retelling

"Ben went fishing with his dad. They got up early. He had a casting pole and they went to the river to fish. Ben got his hook caught in a tree and they had to get it out."

Reading over Matthew's retelling, state one strength and one weakness in Matthew's comprehension of the story.

GO ON TO THE NEXT PAGE

Constructed-Response Question #3

Read the following scenario:

Working with a group of English Language Learners, Ms. Henson is introducing new vocabulary words to her students prior to their reading a text. Showing pictures of various objects and incidents, Ms. Henson carefully says the word, has the students repeat the word, then explains what it means. She rapidly goes on to the next word, as she is concerned about interfering with the students' reading time.

Answer the following question:

Knowing what you know about effective teaching, if you were observing this teacher, what would you state as one strength in her lesson, and what might you suggest that she change?

Answer Key

1. C	**19.** A	**37.** B	**55.** C	**73.** D
2. D	**20.** C	**38.** D	**56.** A	**74.** B
3. B	**21.** B	**39.** B	**57.** C	**75.** A
4. C	**22.** A	**40.** D	**58.** B	**76.** C
5. B	**23.** D	**41.** A	**59.** C	**77.** B
6. B	**24.** D	**42.** C	**60.** B	**78.** C
7. A	**25.** B	**43.** A	**61.** C	**79.** D
8. A	**26.** D	**44.** C	**62.** B	**80.** B
9. C	**27.** D	**45.** B	**63.** D	**81.** A
10. B	**28.** C	**46.** A	**64.** A	**82.** C
11. B	**29.** D	**47.** D	**65.** B	**83.** D
12. B	**30.** B	**48.** C	**66.** D	**84.** C
13. D	**31.** D	**49.** B	**67.** C	**85.** C
14. D	**32.** C	**50.** D	**68.** B	**86.** B
15. B	**33.** A	**51.** A	**69.** A	**87.** A
16. C	**34.** C	**52.** D	**70.** C	**88.** D
17. A	**35.** D	**53.** B	**71.** D	**89.** B
18. C	**36.** A	**54.** A	**72.** B	**90.** C

Answer Explanations

Selected-Response Questions

1. **C.** The teacher is engaging her students in the reading and, therefore, having them actively participate in the learning of unfamiliar words and new concepts. Students need to understand what they are reading. Although the teacher is modeling new words (choice A) and book handling skills (choice B), these are not the main focus; the question asks for the *main* reason, so you need to consider everything going on in the scenario. The teacher is not selecting letters and saying the sound, making choice D incorrect.

2. **D.** *Hopeful.* A morpheme is the smallest unit of a word with meaning. In the word *hopeful,* both parts of the word (*hope* and *ful*) have meaning; together, they mean "full of hope." The word *mountain* (choice A) has only one meaning. *Playfully* (choice B) has three morphemes, not two—*play, ful,* and *ly.* The suffix *-ly* means "in a way that is [like the adjective in the word]," so *playfully* means "in a way that is full of play." *Notice* (choice C) has only one meaning and, therefore, only one morpheme.

3. **B.** Sarah shows some inferencing skills, as she was able to glean that the baby had become quiet. However, Joey's response shows greater inference; most likely from prior knowledge, he associated the baby's crying with hunger and understood that the baby becoming quiet meant the bottle had satisfied this hunger. Sarah's response demonstrates that she does infer at a surface level, whereas Joey is able to use background knowledge—that a baby cries when it is hungry—to show deeper understanding. Choice A is incorrect, as Sarah's answer is not literal (quiet is not explicitly stated), and there is no evaluative comment from Joey. Choice C is incorrect because Sarah's response does not demonstrate a deep understanding, and Joey is most likely accurate. Choice D is incorrect because there is no evidence that Sarah misunderstood.

4. **C.** The teacher works with Tricia on one of the letters she needs to learn. She has Tricia trace the letter and say its name. Since Tricia does not know her letters at this point, she needs intensive work on letter recognition. Choice A involves letter sounds, not letter recognition. Choice B does not involve working with letters; Tricia may actually have these sight words memorized. Choice D involves working with all of the letters, which could be good reinforcement once Tricia can identify all of them.

5. **B.** Show students a series of statements and questions containing no end marks. Go through each sentence and explain why you are adding a period, question mark, or exclamation point. Choice A focuses on just the exclamation point and does not include periods and question marks; end marks include all three types. Choice C does not entail explicit teaching. Choice D does not involve any teaching.

6. **B.** *Gnat.* A phoneme is a single unit of sound. *Gnat* has three phonemes (*n, a, t*), as the "g" is silent. Choice A has three syllables and choice C has two phonemes. Even though choice D has three letters, it has only two phonemes, as the double "e" makes the long /e/ sound.

7. **A.** Phonemic awareness. This exercise assesses the students' ability to hear individual letter sounds in a word. Choice B is incorrect, as the teacher is not mentioning letter names. Hearing ability, choice C, is not the best choice, as it cannot be accurately evaluated in this activity. Choice D is incorrect, as a morpheme is the smallest unit of sound that has meaning; a letter sound doesn't have meaning.

8. **A.** Organization. The student is stating facts at random and not in any coherent order. Sentences about food should be grouped together, as should the sentences about the table being crowded. The other three traits, ideas (choice B), voice (choice C), and word choice (choice D), should be worked on eventually, but at this time, organization should be the student's initial writing goal.

9. **C.** Fluency. The question states that Tasha often pauses to figure out words; since it does not appear to interfere with her comprehension, she needs quicker word recognition. Decoding (choice A) is not a serious problem because Tasha is able to figure out the words. Look-back strategies (choice B) do not appear to be needed at this time. Vocabulary (choice D) is an unknown, as once Tasha figures out the word, she may immediately incorporate it into her oral vocabulary.

10. **B.** Words contain vowels. Choice A is not correct, as not all of the sentences begin with a capital letter. Choice C is incorrect, as *is* is a sight word but both instances of it are misspelled. Choice D is a bit close, as some vowel sounds are wrong, but there is evidence that the child uses, although incorrectly, some phonics generalizations.

11. **B. Digraphs.** A digraph is when two letters make one sound. The child could use help in this area, as evidenced in the word *mene* instead of *mean* and *grate* instead of *great*. Choice A is incorrect, as the child does use end marks correctly. Choice C is incorrect, as the sentences, although extremely simple, are properly organized. Choice D is incorrect; the child didn't use diphthongs, so we have no basis for judgment. A diphthong is two vowels that make a glided sound like the /oi/ in *oil*.

12. **B.** *Too, you,* and *blue* all have the long "double o" sound, but the sound is spelled differently in each word ("oo," "ou," and "ue"). The words in the other answer choices do not demonstrate different letters making the same speech sound. In choice A, all three words start with "f" to make the /f/ sound. In choice C, all of the words end with *-er,* making the same sound at the end (note that if *mentor* had been in this group, choice C could have been the answer, as "er" and "or" sound the same). In choice D, all of the words begin with "c" to make the /k/ sound.

13. **D. To hold students accountable for listening.** Choice A is incorrect, as the scenario says nothing about a follow-up quiz. Choice B is incorrect, as the scientific vocabulary will most likely not be in the book and while discussion introduces students to vocabulary, it doesn't give students enough exposure to learn the words. Although the discussion on hurricanes could bring deeper understanding of the events in the story and may help students understand the actions of the characters, learning about the formation of hurricanes will not provide insight into character traits (choice C).

14. **D. Pre-teach vocabulary with the students and build background on elections.** This gives the students time to ask questions about difficult concepts and gain understanding of infrequently used election terminology. Choice A is incorrect because, while pre-teaching selected vocabulary may help, reading orally does not necessarily improve comprehension. Choice B is incorrect; the scenario states that Alicia is a fluent reader, so working on blending and letter sounds would be remedial in her case! Having Alicia reread the article (choice C) may be beneficial if there were close reading tasks to go along with the rereading, but that is not what is happening in this scenario.

15. **B.** Learning language and learning to write both have developmental stages that follow a linear progression. Choice A is incorrect; children learn to identify letters before they begin to write them. Choices C and D are incorrect, as developmental writing begins with scribbling, just as oral language begins with babbling.

16. **C.** Having a strong oral language vocabulary aids students in comprehension, as they read known words within the text. Choice A is not a good connection; although oral language would help children understand phonics, it does not ensure learning phonics. Choice B is incorrect because strong oral language may not help with word identification. Having a strong oral vocabulary (choice D) does not guarantee a reader will read with expression.

17. **A. Concepts of print.** The teacher is teaching children how to identify what a word is. Children will often pretend read by pointing to a place in the book and saying the sentence they have memorized, but they do not know where the words are in print. Alphabetic principle (choice B) is incorrect because letter sounds are not being discussed. Choice C is incorrect, as encoding is writing the letter that makes a particular sound. Choice D is incorrect, as structural analysis is analyzing word parts, such as root words and affixes.

18. **C. Cause and effect.** The man's work on the boat's engine has caused the film of gas to appear on the surface of the water. This is not stated explicitly, but the author wants the reader to figure out the cause of the film. Choice A is incorrect, as no solution is given. Choices B and D could be argued as somewhat correct, as the author does describe the scene and it is written in chronological order, but the main focus of the paragraph is cause and effect.

19. **A. Teaching homophones.** Words that sound alike but are spelled differently are called homophones, such as *there/they're, pale/pail,* and *right/write*. Homographs (choice B) are words that are spelled alike but sound different, such as the two pronunciations of *minute*. Contractions (choice C) are two words combined into a shorter word, such as *they're* for *they are*. Idioms (choice D) are sayings that mean something other than what they appear to, such as "Go fly a kite."

20. **C. Directionality of print.** All the answer choices are aspects of the concepts of print. However, choice A is incorrect because the teacher is not focusing on each word or explaining this to the children. Choice B is incorrect, as the scenario does not include him stopping at the end of sentences, but does include him continuing to point in the direction he is reading. Choice D is incorrect, as meaning is not being discussed in this scenario.

21. **B.** Voice. Voice is the strongest trait in the passage. Choice A is incorrect, as the words are simple and not unusual. Choice C is not the best choice because this short passage includes few distinct ideas. Choice D is not the best choice, as some sentences are short and choppy. It is voice that makes this passage appealing.

22. **A.** Readers' Theater. If students are reading slowly and without expression, they need to be given a reason to reread, using expression. Readers' Theater forces students to practice with each other and dramatize what they are reading. Increasing silent reading time (choice B) will not necessarily help students with expression. Focusing on visualization skills (choice C) is a comprehension strategy, not a fluency strategy. Using word cards to increase vocabulary skills (choice D) won't help; to increase speed and expression, the students need to read sentences and words in context, not individual words.

23. **D.** Give students a self-evaluation checklist. Mrs. Gomez can structure this checklist to include all areas the students do not seem to be addressing; this will hold them more accountable for their own work. Choice A is incorrect; more hours for writing workshop sounds like a good idea, but a teacher should not take time designated for another subject, and more time might not help without the proper tools in place. Using a variety of texts (choice B) allows good exposure to writing, but it is not going to help the students with editing. Using spell-check (choice C) helps with only one area of conventions, but it won't help with end marks or grammar or making the piece better.

24. **D.** Use close reading techniques such as selecting complex lines of the poem to discuss. Choice A would be correct if the activity focused on the proper war (Paul Revere was involved in the Revolutionary War, not the Civil War). Showing students where the towns are located (choice B) will give some insight, but not enough for complete understanding. Partner reading the poem (choice C) may help some students, but this activity does not include teacher modeling and explanations, students analyzing the poem, and rereading of the poem, which are all close reading techniques.

25. **B.** Listening, speaking, reading, and writing. Choice A is incorrect; although receptive language is reading and listening, and expressive language is talking and writing, thinking is not a type of language. Choice C is incorrect; pragmatics involves expression, and telegraphic refers to a baby's short talk, such as "me, bottle." Choice D is incorrect, as these are not types of language.

26. **D.** Learning that "y" says the sound of long /e/ at the ends of words and digraphs. This is shown in the corrections of putting a "y" at the end of *kandy* and *eesy*. Choices A and C are incorrect, as there are no diphthongs in this assessment (a diphthong is a blended vowel sound such as /oi/ in *oil* and /oy/ in *boy*). Choice B is incorrect, as we are not sure if the child knows the letter "c" makes the /k/ sound or if he is aware of the existence of the suffix *-er*.

27. **D.** Working with the hard and soft sounds of the letter "c." The hard sound of "c" is the /k/ sound, and the soft sound of "c" is the /s/ sound. Both *candy* and *cane* were spelled with the letter "k" at the beginning. Choice A is incorrect because in *candy* and *easy*, the "y" is not a suffix, but part of the word; therefore, "y" as a suffix is not part of this spelling inventory. Choice B, working with diphthongs, is incorrect because diphthongs are not in this spelling inventory. Choice C is also incorrect, as the VCe rule was also not assessed in this spelling inventory.

28. **C.** Product. The product is what the students do as a reader response as a follow-up to a lesson. Choice A is incorrect, as the teacher would have the students reading different leveled books. Choices B and D are incorrect, as the process is the instruction and nothing was said about the teaching being changed to match students' differences.

29. **D.** Encoding. When a person connects the oral sound to the written letter we call that encoding. Sarah is not blending letters together (choice A), but segmenting. Decoding (choice B) is what is done when we read words; we decode the letters into sounds. Separating onsets from rimes (choice C) is incorrect, as Sarah would have had to say "*l/ike*" to show onset and rime.

30. **B.** To help students bridge from what they know to what they will learn. Using a semantic web activates prior knowledge. Choice A is incorrect, as this is part of the fourth-grade curriculum and therefore must be covered in some way. Choice C is incorrect, as close reading techniques do not necessarily include activating prior knowledge. Choice D is incorrect, as a conversation using a semantic web will share knowledge, but all students will not necessarily have the same depth of knowledge.

31. D. She uses flexible grouping in her classroom. The question asks for the best description. Since the scenario shows Mrs. Clive moving two children up into another group, we can see that she uses flexible grouping. This scenario demonstrates her grouping by levels and interest. Choice A is also true, but it is not the best choice; although the scenario implies the groups are leveled, as Jerome and Katelyn are going into the next highest group, that is not the best summation of her techniques. What is important here is that Jerome and Katelyn are not kept in the same group simply because they started there. Also, the teacher used interest groups as well as leveled groups. There is no information to support choice B, skills groups. Choice C is incorrect, as a reading workshop implies that children are reading books individually, often on level, and not in leveled reading groups.

32. C. Tier 2. The RTI model does not contain a Tier 0 (choice A). In the three-tiered model, Tier 1 involves working with the teacher through various differentiation techniques, so choice B is also incorrect. If a child cannot keep up with intervention by the teacher alone, the child is placed in Tier 2, which gives the child some help from a specialist. Choice D is incorrect, as Tier 3 refers to intense, often one-on-one sessions with a specialist.

33. A. *Pail, mail, fail.* A digraph is two letters (consonants or vowels) that make one sound like the "ai" in *pail* or the "ph" in *graph*. Choice B has the same vowel combinations in each of the words, but three different sounds. Choice C has the same vowel sound spelled three different ways. In choice D, *tight* does not contain a vowel digraph, although "gh" is a consonant digraph and the "gh" is silent in the cluster "igh."

34. C. Morphemic analysis. Morphemic analysis (sometimes called structural analysis) is the examination of the smallest chunk of a word with meaning. The suffix -*ate* is present in all of the words in this web; it means "state or quality of." Choice A is incorrect, as sixth grade is considered extremely late for teaching phonemic awareness, or the understanding that words have different sounds in them. Choice B is incorrect, as the web doesn't show the words divided into syllables. Choice D is incorrect because -*ate* is a suffix, not a prefix.

35. D. To create a culturally responsive classroom. Choice A is incorrect as the teacher is not creating more rules. Choice B is incorrect, as the students are learning about Hispanic culture, not Asian culture. Regarding choice C, we have no way of knowing the genres the teacher will be using for her read alouds, so this choice is incorrect.

36. A. The teacher places pictures of short vowel words with the corresponding vowel on the bulletin board. In this scenario, there is no direct instruction, so the teaching is considered implicit; students will look at the pictures and the letters and learn the short vowel sounds. Choices B, C, and D all contain direct instruction; the teacher is working with the students as they learn.

37. B. Encourage competition between individuals within the classroom. In a culturally responsive classroom, a teacher should build collaborative activities into classroom instruction. Setting up a competitive classroom culture will not foster responsiveness to all cultures. The other three choices are considered aspects of culturally responsive teaching.

38. D. To help students understand the author's purpose. In this case, the class is identifying sentences that persuade, which is the author's purpose. This scenario does not include the concept of audience (choice A). Choice B is incorrect, as this activity would not occur during peer conferencing. Choice C is incorrect, as this lesson is not focusing on supporting points or evidence.

39. B. The teacher asks students to say the beginning sound of the word *hat* and then to say the word again, but begin it with the same beginning sound as in *soup*. Phonemic awareness is the realization that there are different sounds in a word; it is auditory. Choice B correctly refers only to sounds. The other three choices all include sounds and letters; these options refer to letter-sound correspondence, which is the teaching of phonics, not phonemic awareness.

40. D. Motivation to read. When children have choice in their reading, they are motivated. The students are signing up for groups, not independent reading (choice A). Choice B is incorrect because students are not required to pick a book on their instructional level. Although some students may sign up just to be with a friend (choice C), most will sign up due to their interest.

41. A. To promote more independent reading. Research shows that when book talks are done in the classroom, students will gravitate toward those books. Choice B is incorrect, as we have no way of knowing what the books contain and this would not be an effective way to build general knowledge. Choices C and D can't be proven.

42. **C. Use visuals to aid with directions and written explanations.** This will help ease the ELL into traditional reading. When working with ELLs, the teacher should not speak normally (choice A); instead, the teacher should slow down her speech just a bit and clearly enunciate. It is advisable to ask questions that can be answered with one or two words or by pointing, not questions that require a large number of words to answer (choice B). Starting with nouns (choice D) is not necessary.

43. **A. Venn diagram.** A Venn diagram is composed of two (or more) overlapping circles. Students would put hurricane information in one circle and tornado information in the other. In the overlapping section, they would write how hurricanes and tornadoes are alike. A semantic web (choice B) is good for brainstorming, collecting facts, or activating prior knowledge. A T-chart (choice C) is a two-column chart that can help students compare facts, but doesn't necessarily help them organize how two things are alike. A KWL (choice D) is used in pre-reading and post-reading to collect information on what students already <u>k</u>now, <u>w</u>hat they want to learn, and what they have <u>l</u>earned; it does not help with comparisons.

44. **C. To ensure her students are reading a variety of genres.** Encouraging reading in and out of the classroom (choice A) doesn't take into consideration that the teacher is asking the students to read at least four different genres of books. The difference between fiction and nonfiction (choice B) needs to be explicitly explained to students. Choice D is also incorrect; the scenario does not mention book reports, but discussions.

45. **B. Efferent.** There are two types of reading stances: efferent and aesthetic. The efferent stance is used when a person is reading for information—in this case three ways in which the prince shows he is a brat. Silent (choice A) is a mode of reading. Interactive (choice C) is a tempting answer choice, as the students are interacting with the text, but interactive is not a stance of reading. Aesthetic (choice D) means that the reader is reading for pleasure and there is no outside pressure to perform—not the case in this scenario.

46. **A. Series.** Series books have the same characters and usually the same setting, but vary their problem and solution. Students like series books because they can become very familiar with the characters, many of whom appear throughout the whole series. Text sets (choice B) are books on the same topic or by the same author, but do not necessarily contain the same characters or setting. There is no such thing as a cumulative book (choice C). A pattern book (choice D) repeats scenes, events, and so forth in the same book; pattern books are usually written for beginning readers.

47. **D. Give Liam an informal reading inventory (IRI) to compare results in comprehension.** One test result should not be used to define a child's reading level or problem. Liam may have skipped a number of questions or not felt well the day he took the standardized test; the teacher needs another measure. We don't know if vocabulary (choice A) is a problem, as no results show this. We need to make sure Liam has a problem with comprehension before beginning intervention (choice B). Mispronouncing words while reading silently (choice C) may not necessarily interfere with comprehension.

48. **C. Have students discuss what they already know about George Washington Carver, botanists, and inventors.** This allows students to begin thinking about the information and concepts that will most likely appear in the book they are about to read. Choice A is incorrect because at this point students would simply be guessing. Writing a short biography of a parent (choice B) will not necessarily help students comprehend the George Washington Carver biography. Choice D is good information for students to know, but it will not help them comprehend this biography.

49. **B. *Binding*.** There is not much in the context that helps students understand that the rug's binding is the edge of the rug; they could see it as a corner or the pile (top) of the rug. *Hassock* (choice A) and *accident* (choice C) should not be pre-taught because students can glean the meaning of these words from the context. The definition of *hassock* is alluded to as a cushioned footstool, and when Bella falls down students will reread and figure out the word *accident*. Students should be able to figure out what *kindhearted* (choice D) means through structural analysis by separating the compound word into *kind* and *hearted*.

50. **D. As a metaphor.** A metaphor states that one thing is another; in this case Bella is an accident waiting to happen. An ellipsis (choice A) is when the author omits information for the reader to fill in. Imagery (choice B) is incorrect as the fall itself provides more imagery than the phrase "an accident waiting to happen." Choice C is incorrect, as mood is an emotional attitude portrayed in the story, and that is not strong here.

51. A. Inferential. Inferences entail readers taking what they know and what they learn from the author and read beyond the text. In this case, since Bella smiled after she fell, she must not be badly hurt or upset about falling. Choice B is incorrect, as literal would mean that the author directly stated how Bella felt. The same reasoning applies to choice C. Choice D is incorrect, as there is no evaluation or judgment required in answering this question.

52. D. The test would produce the same results with a different set of people in a different setting. Choice A defines validity, not reliability. Choice B defines stanines. Choice C involves an unreliable test, as the test wouldn't have a standardized measure.

53. B. How to locate information in a book by using the table of contents or the index. Students are searching for information, so this is not the time to slow down and reread (choice A). Choice C is incorrect, as the students are having a hard time finding what they need to read to take notes. Choice D is incorrect, as pictures of the topic may not include the needed information.

54. A. The passage suggests… The word *suggests* signals an inference, as it is not saying exactly what the author states. Choices B and C involve asking students for facts from the text rather than their inferences. An opinion (choice D) is what the reader thinks, not what the author is implying.

55. C. To ensure students are interacting with the text as they read. Choices A, B, and D may involve results of this activity, but these are not the main reason Ms. Barr has chosen it.

56. A. When writing this response, the reader makes a personal connection, which helps him gain insight into the character. Choice B, while a nice thought, is incorrect; we are looking at reading goals in this scenario. There is no basis in the question for choice C. Choice D is incorrect, as the prompt says to compare events, not to order them.

57. C. Discuss the theme of the book and offer evidence from the text that supports this theme. When literary response is discussed on the Praxis (5203), the answer will be in the deeper thinking mode. A literary response will require thinking beyond what appears in the text. Choices A, B, and D refer to recall questions; the students just need to report what happened in the book and not infer or analyze in any way.

58. B. *Repack, unpack, packing, packed.* In structural analysis, which is word work that starts after phonics is learned, students analyze word parts for meaning and pronunciation. These four words have added morphemes that change the meaning of the root word. Choice A is a random list of words with "ea" and "e" vowels—not even the same pronunciation. Choice C contains derivatives of the word *run,* an irregular verb. Choice D shows different ways of spelling the long double /o/ sound.

59. C. Decoding. Since Zoe is not fluent, the teacher needs to analyze if she is having word attack difficulties. If not, then further assessments are needed. Choices A and B both focus on comprehension, and the scenario doesn't show that Ms. Mackin notices a problem with comprehension at this point. Choice D, vocabulary, could help, but it is not the first area of concern.

60. B. Blank 2. The sentence relies on your knowing grammar and being able to infer. The first blank would need to be a person or character of some sort. The second blank would need to be an adjective, describing what *it* was. The third blank would need to be a verb, as *it* is to take action or do something. The fourth blank must be a noun. So the sentence could be "She wondered if it was manageable to study in the cafeteria." Or, it could be "Phil wondered if it was inevitable to lose in the tiebreaker."

61. C. Demonstrate strategies that will encourage the student to read through the word. The three words that had errors, *barked, jumped,* and *making,* were initially read without their suffixes. This means the child is not reading through the whole word, but just the beginning, sometimes guessing at the ending sound. Choice A is incorrect because the child is monitoring his understanding. Choice B is incorrect, as there is no basis here for promoting auditory discrimination skills. Choice D is incorrect, as the student knows phonics; also, *barked* and *jumped* are one-syllable words, so segmenting would not necessarily help.

62. B. He is self-monitoring his comprehension. A child's rereading and self-correcting his errors is an excellent indication that he is reading for meaning and, with self-monitoring, noticing when something does not sound right. There is no indication that the child has difficulty in decoding (choice A), as he self-corrected. Choice C is incorrect, as the child is already monitoring his reading. Choice D is incorrect, as the child's directionality is fine.

63. D. The text should be decodable and use repeated words or phrases. Having decodable words aids beginning readers in the use of phonics, and repetition of words aids in developing the reader's personal sight word vocabulary. Choice A is incorrect, as beginning readers should not be faced with complex vocabulary when they are trying to read, although pictures aligned with the text are helpful. Choice B is incorrect; the students are beginning readers, and challenging concepts could deter their understanding at this beginning stage. Choice C is incorrect, as a variety of punctuation could get confusing for beginning readers (although using natural language is a plus).

64. A. Norm-referenced test. In a norm-referenced test, students are compared to other populations, and the results "rank" students in a percentile against other students. An Informal Reading Inventory (IRI) (choice B) can provide one indicator of a student's reading level, but it is not comparative against other students'. A criterion-referenced test (choice C) is set up to test certain criteria and does not provide a comparative result. A comprehension checklist (choice D) might exist, but that would not provide any indication of a student's performance compared with that of his peers'.

65. B. Say the word *cap* out loud and tell the teacher the first sound he hears in the word. Being able to replace the initial sound in a word is considered the first stage in phonemic awareness development. Choice A is incorrect, as indicating where a word begins and ends is a concept of print, and a child can have phonemic awareness without knowing letters exist. Choice C is incorrect, as being able to substitute the medial phoneme is considered the highest level of phonemic awareness, not the beginning level. Choice D is incorrect because phonemic awareness does not involve letters, just letter sounds.

66. D. *Track.* Choices A (*car*) and C (*burn*) have onsets and rimes, but the "r"-controlled vowels make this harder for the beginning reader. Choice B (*edge*) does not have an onset, which is defined as the consonant before the first vowel.

67. C. Effective first-grade spelling uses common rimes and phonic generalizations, which then support word recognition. Choices A and B might be possible, but these are not the best reasons, as phonics generalizations can aid students in reading unknown words. Choice D is incorrect; spelling may aid students in segmenting syllables, but first-grade spelling instruction is very simple and most likely covers simple onsets and rimes such as *cat, hat, pat,* and *bat.*

68. B. Phonemic awareness aids students in understanding that there is a match between the letters and sounds in a word. Choices A, C, and D are initially too complicated, as students first need to learn that a sound corresponds to a letter.

69. A. Criterion-referenced test. A criterion-referenced test shows results by area, such as letter identification, short vowels sounds, grammar usage, comprehension, and so forth. Choices B and D are incorrect names for standardized tests; tests with these names most likely don't exist. A norm-referenced test (choice C) gives the percentile in which a student scored; it is used for comparison.

70. C. Teaching common orthographic patterns. Teaching children basic patterns of how words are spelled (how they look) allows them to master the spelling of many words beyond the ones they are taught. Choice A is incorrect, as a list of random words, although memorized by some, is not effective. Choice B is incorrect; while learning phonetic generalizations could be helpful, teachers should not target irregular verb patterns for beginning spellers. Using picture cards (choice D) would be useful for ELLs and other students, but only if the words corresponding to the pictures have a common orthographic pattern.

71. D. Use close reading techniques such as teacher modeling, rereading, and discussion to clarify concepts. In this way, the teacher can show students how to approach complex texts and help the students understand the article. Choices A, B, and C all have pieces that can be used, but they are not the best for this particular reading. Building background on the controversy (choice A) could be helpful, but knowing the background on particular countries will not help in understanding the fishing rights controversy. Partner reading and discussion (choice B) and writing questions (choice C) are good techniques for comprehension monitoring, but not the best for this complex article.

72. B. The test measures what it says it will measure. If a test says it is measuring letter identification and it asks students to say the sound of the letter, then that is not letter identification; it is letter-sound correspondence, which relates to phonics. Such a test would not be valid. Choices A and C refer to the reliability of a test. Criterion-referenced tests (choice D) must also be checked for reliability.

73. D. The test is not valid. A test that has validity measures what it says it measures. The question asks what Fido did when he got home, and it is labeled an inferential question. But the text states explicitly, "Fido got home and rolled in the dirt." The question is literal, not inferential; so the IRI says it is measuring inference when it is not (in this question, anyway). Choice B is, therefore, incorrect, as this test does not have validity. Choices A and C are incorrect, as there is no proof of test reliability in this question. A test is reliable if it would produce the same results with a different set of people in a different setting.

74. B. Have students read a variety of fables and, as a class, analyze the fables' components. Mentor texts are used by teachers as a model of what the students will be writing. Choice A is incorrect as that is not a model. Choices C and D are incorrect as these approaches entail scaffold writing, but do not use mentor text.

75. A. Prior to reading a text, have students look up the new words in the dictionary and write down their meaning. Although this is not harmful, children need much more exposure to new words; they need to use the vocabulary and see or hear it in context. Choices B, C, and D all include effective means of helping children increase their vocabulary.

76. C. If parents seem frustrated, try to figure out what is happening to cause their frustration. Choices A and D are incorrect. When possible, send notices home in the parent's language, although picture cues would be better than plain English. Choice B is incorrect, as you should ask parents questions that will aid in their child's learning.

77. B. The student's raw score was above 87% of the other students taking this test. A norm-referenced test compares students with other populations, and gives a percentile that ranks the student as being above and below corresponding percentages of other students. If a student receives a score in the 75th percentile, this means that the child scored above 75% of the students who took the test, and below 25% of them. Choice A is incorrect, as it is the opposite of this statement. Choices C and D are incorrect, as the percentile score is not determined by the number of questions.

78. C. The student scored in the average range. A stanine is a method of scaling test scores on a 9-point scale that is used for normalized test scores: 1–3 is below average, 4–6 is average, and 7–9 is above average. Choice A is incorrect, as although the 4th stanine may correspond to a range of percentiles, it not necessarily the 40th. Choice B is incorrect, as it isn't logical. Choice D is incorrect, as stanine 4 is in the average range, not below average.

79. D. *August.* The meanings of the words in choices A, B, and C (*arid, parched,* and *vigilant*) can be determined to some extent from the context of the reading. Although students may not guess the absolute definitions, the surrounding information will give them an idea of meaning. On the other hand, the word *august* is a positive, serious word, placed in a context that symbolizes respect and grandeur. It would be more difficult to understand in this context that the author is saying the land looks beautiful.

80. B. Should Mike have been in this area with what seems to be limited water? This question is evaluative because to answer it, a judgment must be made. It is text-dependent because a student would need to read the text in order to answer the question. The question in choice A is not text-dependent, and can be answered without reading the passage; it is also not evaluative. Choice C is an inferential text-dependent question. Choice D is a literal text-dependent question.

81. A. Concepts of print. One of the concepts of print for beginning readers is to match upper- and lowercase letters, so they know that these letters are the same and will eventually know that these letters, whether uppercase or lowercase, make the same sound. Choice B is incorrect, as a child who has phonemic awareness does not need to know that letters exist. Choice C is incorrect, as there is no matching of sounds to the letters indicated here. Choice D is incorrect, as there is no word-work in this activity.

82. C. Students should be taught how to identify credible online sources. Identifying credible online sources will become a life research skill. Choices A and B solve the immediate problem, but these approaches don't teach the children how to find credible online sources on their own. Choice D is useful information for researching, but knowing good search terms doesn't mean the students will be able to identify a credible site.

83. **D.** To use information from context to identify unknown words. By asking Amelia what kind of animal could jump from tree to tree using its tail, the teacher is teaching her to identify unknown words from context. Chunking words (choice A) could have been a strategy to use, as the word *monkey* is easily chunked, but it is not what the teacher is doing. Asking herself questions as she reads (choice B) is a good way for Amelia to improve her comprehension, but this question is about word identification, not comprehension. Analyzing each sentence as it is read (choice C) is a close reading technique used to comprehend a confusing passage.

84. **C.** Demonstrating that a letter corresponds with a sound. This is the explicit teaching of phonics; the teacher introduces the letter and then the sound it makes. The pictures aid students in gaining the concept that the word begins with the corresponding letter. Choice A is incorrect, as the beginning letter sound is the onset, but rimes are not addressed. Choice B is incorrect, as the teacher is working with sounds and letters, not just sounds. Choice D is incorrect, as symbolism is not being worked on in this scenario.

85. **C.** Are considered to have low-end phonemic awareness skills. Segmenting sounds is considered a beginning level of phonemic awareness. Choice A is incorrect because substituting sounds is at the higher end of phonemic awareness; the medial sound is considered the most difficult. Choice B is incorrect as there are no visual letters in the activity. Choice D is incorrect as letter sounds are being segmented, not word parts.

86. **B.** Employ semantic and syntactic cues to identify an unknown word. Covering up the word forces students to guess the meaning of the word through context, which employs semantics (meaning) and syntax (structure, knowing what type of word would fit in the blank). When the first letter is shown, the phonics cuing system comes into play. Choice A is incorrect, as the entire word is not visible. Choices C and D are incorrect, as the teacher is not segmenting letter or word parts, but simply showing the first letter as a hint.

87. **A.** The student can use context to identify unknown words. Choice B is incorrect because if Jeremy were strong in phonics, he would have been able to read the word list correctly. Choices C and D are incorrect as Jeremy was able to read all but one of these words correctly in context by using semantics, syntax, and phonics to identify the unknown words.

88. **D.** Keep Jojo in the grade level 3 group and work with her intensively via comprehension strategies. She has shown she can read the words, but scored at frustration level on comprehension, missing instructional level by one question. Choice A would be the next best answer, as increasing vocabulary can aid in comprehension, but since Jojo was so strong in her reading, lowering her group level is not the best goal. Choice B is incorrect, as there was never an indication that fluency is a problem. Choice C is incorrect, as the higher level group could yield a frustration level score in both word recognition and comprehension.

89. **B.** Engage the student in a number of fluency activities to increase reading speed. The slowness of the reading and high number of self-corrections indicate a problem with fluency. Choice A refers to phonemic awareness, which this student has mastered as he is using phonics. Choice C, focus on inferential comprehension techniques and practice sheets, is incorrect; we have no basis for this goal, as the student did receive an independent level score, which incorporated comprehension questions. The same applies to choice D and close reading techniques.

90. **C.** Activate the students' prior knowledge and teach background information using visuals to explain new vocabulary. ELLs need visuals, and they need to have explanations at a level they can understand. Choice A is incorrect, as pairing ELLs with a native English speaker may not help them understand the concepts. Choice B is incorrect because sometimes dictionary definitions at the fourth-grade level can be as confusing as the new word. While viewing a video on wilderness survival techniques (choice D) does give ELLs visuals, we cannot be sure that the ELLs will understand the narration that goes with the video.

Model Answers to Constructed-Response Questions

Before you begin writing an answer, you should remember what is expected to obtain a score of 3. To paraphrase expectations:

- Clearly and directly answer *all parts* of the question.
- Show reading content and your understanding. Be accurate in that content.
- Write a strong explanation—support what you say!

Then analyze the question that the test asks you to answer. Two strong responses are given for each constructed-response question.

Constructed-Response Question #1

Model Answer 1

The coding on Tanya's running record clearly shows a strength and a weakness. Tanya's strength is that she uses semantic cues to identify words. Tanya's weakness pertains to her inaccuracy with prefixes, showing she needs to be more morphologically aware.

Tanya's strength, using semantics, is evidenced in the coding of her reading. Although she made the same type of error twice, reading *couldn't* for *could not* and reading *shouldn't* for *should not,* there is no meaning change. In addition, Tanya made three self-corrections in which semantics were used. She corrected *neeber's* to *neighbor's,* the second instance of *re-ached* to *reached,* and *rem-ote* to *remote* when the words did not make sense.

Tanya's weakness is her overuse of morphemes, most specifically, the prefix *re-,* which means "again" or "back or backwards." In this text, it appears that Tanya overused the prefix *re-* as she read *re-ached* and *re-ally.* Furthermore, Tanya self-corrected when reading *reached between the couch cushions,* as she was able to read *reach* correctly in this context. As she read on, she didn't read *reacted* and *remote* using the morpheme *re,* and finally, she used her strength, the use of semantics, to self-correct *remote.*

An immediate instructional goal for Tanya is in the area of morphological analysis using various affixes, beginning with the prefix *re-.* Through explicit instruction, Tanya would learn that although a word may begin with "re" it may actually be part of the word and not a prefix; a discussion of the words *read* and *reread* would provide examples. She also must always check to make sure the word she reads makes sense and sounds right in the sentence. Other examples will be used. Using a word sort format, Tanya will sort words that begin with *re-* into two categories: one with prefixes and one without.

Model Answer 2

The coding on Tanya's running record indicates a strength and a weakness. Tanya's strength is in her knowledge of sight words. Tanya's weakness is her confusion with contractions.

Tanya's reading shows that she has a large bank of sight words and was able to read this passage with fluency. Small words like *was, and, have, the, but,* and *it* were read easily. Fairly common words such as *taken, phone, counter, sound,* and *cushions* were also read with ease, showing that when she encounters common words, Tanya has strong word identification skills.

In Tanya's reading of this passage, she made nine errors, three of them with contractions. Tanya twice read *could not* as *couldn't* and read *should not* as *shouldn't.* Since these substitutions are semantically correct, and contractions and their matching words are used interchangeably, there are no meaning errors, but the oral reading is still not correct. It is best that Tanya read without errors. It seems that she may have been relying on her sight word bank and automatically reading what she thought she was seeing.

A learning goal for Tanya is to recognize contractions as shortened words that represent two words, and that in formal writing, often the two words are used instead of the contraction. Tanya should be given some direct instruction on contractions in context. Then her progress should be watched as she reads orally.

Constructed-Response Question #2

Model Answer 1

When reading over Matthew's retelling, there is both a noticeable strength and a noticeable weakness in his comprehension. Matthew's strength is his ability to restate the story in chronological order. Matthew's weakness is that his retelling lacks a great amount of detail, which leads to an inadequate recall of information.

Matthew's strength, retelling in chronological order, shows that he has been able to recall the story in the correct sequence. He begins with the main idea of the story: Ben going fishing. Then, he states that Ben and his dad got up early, that Ben got his line caught in a tree, and they were getting the line loose. Although lacking in a number of details, the storyline is in the correct order.

Matthew's weakness is the lack of detail. He does not mention that Ben had never been fishing before. Matthew does not state that Ben got a new casting pole for his birthday, that he had to get up before the sun was up, or that

Ben's dad helped him bait the hook. Matthew also doesn't mention that Ben looked behind him or that the line was actually wrapped around a huge branch. The story states, "His line had wrapped itself around a huge branch." Matthew stated, "Ben got his hook caught in a tree." Matthew assumes the hook was caught, although it might not have been, and he doesn't mention the details about the line being wrapped around a huge branch.

Model Answer 2

Matthew's retelling of the short story "Ben's Fishing Trip" has both a strength and a weakness. Matthew's strength lies in his literal comprehension. Matthew's weakness is his lack of inferences from the story.

Matthew's retelling shows a strength in literal comprehension. Although the retelling shows a lack of detail, what Matthew states in his retelling are literal events that do happen in the story. Matthew and his dad do go fishing, as stated in the retelling. They did get up early and went to the river. Matthew stated, "Ben got his hook caught in a tree and they had to get it out." Although the story read "His line had wrapped itself around a huge branch," the idea is similar and the meaning is literal.

Matthew's retelling shows a weakness in inferential comprehension. The story says Ben couldn't sleep because he was going fishing, and Matthew makes no mention of Ben's excitement about going. Matthew does not mention that Ben had been practicing in his backyard, which implies that it was important to Ben to be good at casting when he went fishing. After the line was caught on the branch, the story states, "...he looked behind him and couldn't believe what he saw." Matthew does not infer that this would be upsetting to Ben. Finally, when Ben's father says, "You caught a big one all right," Matthew seems oblivious to the implied humor of the situation.

Constructed-Response Question #3

Model Answer 1

One of Ms. Henson's strengths is that she is pre-teaching vocabulary prior to reading. It is an effective practice to explicitly pre-teach vocabulary when word definitions cannot be figured out in the context of the text. In this case, Ms. Henson is working with a group of English Language Learners; therefore, meeting new words in the text for the first time would hinder their reading and decrease their comprehension of the text. By pre-teaching the words, the teacher exposes students to their meaning; the students, therefore, will be better able to comprehend what they are reading.

In the scenario, Ms. Henson "rapidly goes on to the next word, as she is concerned about interfering with the students' reading time." Not interfering with reading time is important, as children need time to read in the classroom; in this case, however, protecting that time becomes a weakness, as ELLs need teachers to enunciate slowly and clearly and need time to process what is being said. Trying to speed up this instruction so students can read may prevent them from internalizing the new vocabulary and hinder their comprehension of the material read.

Model Answer 2

Ms. Henson shows a strength in her lesson by using visuals to help her teach new vocabulary words to English Language Learners. Seeing words in context helps all students understand the words more thoroughly and learn each word's meaning at a deeper level. Since Ms. Henson is working with ELLs, the visuals are especially important, as using visuals is a best practice with ELLs helping them connect the meaning of the word to the word itself.

However, there is a concern about Ms. Henson's approach to teaching ELLs new vocabulary. The scenario shows that Ms. Henson says the word and then has the students repeat it. The modeling and practice and saying the word aloud are all important. After the students say the word, Ms. Henson explains what it means as she shows the visuals. This too is good, but the concern centers on the fact that the ELLs are not discussing the new words themselves. Building in discussion and activities that allow ELLs to speak is an effective practice for teaching them. In this case, Ms. Henson is doing most of the talking and not allowing the students to converse, preventing them from using the new word. When students apply new words in discussion, they are more apt to remember them. More opportunities for the ELLs to engage in speaking with the vocabulary during this lesson would be helpful.

CPSIA information can be obtained
at www.ICGtesting.com
Printed in the USA
LVHW061059240619
622139LV00010B/1139/P